A powerful, unflinching and deep look from multiple vertices into our contemporary collective descent, epitomized by the COVID-19 pandemic and systemic racism in societies makes *Shame, Temporality and Social Change* a strong, psychoactive read. The editors have brought forward the wisdom of an impressive coterie of authors who can address the tenuousness of hope for a better future together with reflective awareness of the spur of shame in the service of social justice. This volume can serve as a much needed guide for the troubled times we are traversing in this archetypal moment in global history.
— **Joseph Cambray**, *President/CEO, Pacifica Graduate Institute*

Both timely and timeless, *Shame, Temporality and Social Change* probes the darker aspects of the passageways from one fraught state of being to the next. Widely varying phenomena are addressed, from an everyday psychoanalytic session in turbulent times, to random, uncanny personal encounters on the street, to societal malaise and breakdown, to genocide. The essays offer clarifying and insightful explications of these experiences, drawing from such luminaries as Derrida, Lacan, Bion, Winnicott, Levinas, and Stiegler. Editors Hinton and Willemsen have given us an invaluable aid in understanding and withstanding the massive upheavals of the present day.
— **Margaret Crastnopol (Peggy), PhD**, *is a Seattle-based psychoanalyst and the author of* Micro-trauma: A Psychoanalytic Understanding of Cumulative Psychic Injury, *who writes and speaks on micro-trauma as well as on character and selfhood, the analyst's Achilles's heels, and grappling with obstacles to psychic growth*

Hinton and Willemsen's welcome follow-up to their award-winning *Shame and Temporality* is another collection of essays put together by these two expert editors whose latest volume brings to mind Schopenhauer's insight that the world could be regarded as a giant penitentiary. *Shame, Temporality and Social Change* is a book for those who crave something more than utopian resolutions. Instead, the pages of this extraordinarily thought-provoking book are emblazoned with foundational ideas from original thinkers such as Derrida's différance, Heidegger's thrownness, Giegerich's (and others') noetics, Lacan's hontologie, Nietzsche's simplified nihilism, and Stiegler's neganthropocene. It is an exciting read and is highly recommended.
— **Ann Casement, LP, FRAI, FRSM**, *Professor, Oriental Academy of Analytical Psychology*

Shame, Temporality and Social Change

There is a broad consensus that we are in a time of profound transition. There is worldwide political and social turbulence, with an underlying loss of hope and confidence about the future. Technological change and the stresses of late-stage capitalism, along with climate change, undermine social trust and hope for a future worth living. Shameless behaviour is rampant, undermining respect for habits and institutions that hold societies together. *Shame, Temporality and Social Change* offers multi-disciplinary insight into these concerns.

Hinton and Willemsen's collection covers themes including racism, cultural norms, memory and vulnerability, with examinations of shame at its core. It explores the meaning and significance of shame in a world of social media, autocratic leaders and algorithms and what we can learn from myth as we progress. Increased awareness of the inter-connection of shame and temporality with the ominous transitions of our times provides thought-provoking insights for theory and practice and the ethical decisions of everyday life.

Psychoanalysts, psychotherapists, philosophers, anthropologists and academics and students engaged in cultural studies and critical theory will gain valuable insights from this book's rich and engaging variety of perspectives on our times.

Ladson Hinton, MA, MD, is a psychoanalyst who lives, practices and teaches in Seattle. He is a founding member of the New School for Analytical Psychology. The volume *Temporality and Shame: Perspectives from Psychoanalysis and Philosophy*, co-edited with Hessel Willemsen, won the prize of the American Board & Academy of Psychology and Psychoanalysis for books published in 2018.

Hessel Willemsen, DClinPsych, is a training and supervising analyst with the Society of Analytical Psychology in London and a member of the New School for Analytical Psychology. He lives, practices and teaches in central London.

Philosophy & Psychoanalysis Book Series
Jon Mills
Series Editor

Philosophy & Psychoanalysis is dedicated to current developments and cutting-edge research in the philosophical sciences, phenomenology, hermeneutics, existentialism, logic, semiotics, cultural studies, social criticism, and the humanities that engage and enrich psychoanalytic thought through philosophical rigor. With the philosophical turn in psychoanalysis comes a new era of theoretical research that revisits past paradigms while invigorating new approaches to theoretical, historical, contemporary, and applied psychoanalysis. No subject or discipline is immune from psychoanalytic reflection within a philosophical context including psychology, sociology, anthropology, politics, the arts, religion, science, culture, physics, and the nature of morality. Philosophical approaches to psychoanalysis may stimulate new areas of knowledge that have conceptual and applied value beyond the consulting room reflective of greater society at large. In the spirit of pluralism, *Philosophy & Psychoanalysis* is open to any theoretical school in philosophy and psychoanalysis that offers novel, scholarly, and important insights in the way we come to understand our world.

Romantic Metasubjectivity Through Schelling and Jung: Rethinking the Romantic Subject
Gord Barentsen

Jung, Deleuze, and the Problematic Whole
Edited by Roderick Main, Christian McMillan, and David Henderson

Psychology as Ethics: Reading Jung with Kant, Nietzsche and Aristotle
Giovanni Colacicchi

Shame, Temporality and Social Change: Ominous Transitions
Edited by Ladson Hinton and Hessel Willemsen

For a full list of titles in this series, please visit
www.routledge.com/Philosophy-and-Psychoanalysis/book-series/PHILPSY

Shame, Temporality and Social Change

Ominous Transitions

Edited by Ladson Hinton and Hessel Willemsen

To my old friend Pat
with Warmest Regards!

Ladson.

 Routledge
Taylor & Francis Group

LONDON AND NEW YORK

First published 2021
by Routledge
2 Park Square, Milton Park, Abingdon, Oxon OX14 4RN

and by Routledge
52 Vanderbilt Avenue, New York, NY 10017

Routledge is an imprint of the Taylor & Francis Group, an informa business

British Library Cataloguing-in-Publication Data
A catalogue record for this book is available from the British Library

Library of Congress Cataloging-in-Publication Data
A catalog record for this book has been requested

ISBN: 978-0-367-54903-9 (hbk)
ISBN: 978-0-367-54905-3 (pbk)
ISBN: 978-1-003-09112-7 (ebk)

Typeset in Times
by Apex CoVantage, LLC

Love and gratitude to my wonderful sons, Ladson IV, Devon, and Alex

– L.H.

To my parents – Voor mijn ouders

– H.W.

Contents

Acknowledgements

First of all, we would like to thank the faculty of the New School for Analytical Psychology in Seattle for their extensive support. Founded in 2013, the core purpose of the New School is giving voice to a multi-disciplinary analysis and critique of the basic concerns of our times. Since 2016, the theme of the public lectures and seminars has been 'Ominous Transitions'. This context provided the background for the creation of this volume. Many of those who wrote chapters are faculty members of the New School.

We are grateful to our authors, who created outstanding works amidst the turbulent and stressful atmosphere of a viral pandemic and the eruption of the Black Lives Matter movement. The present psychic atmosphere makes it difficult to concentrate, research and write.

The series editor, John Mills, has been a constant support, and Susannah Frearson of Routledge has been invariably kind and helpful in assisting us through the publication process. We very much appreciate their help.

Last but not least, we would like to express our deep appreciation to Pramila Bennett, whose astute editing and wise perspective have been essential to the process.

Ladson Hinton and Hessel Willemsen

Contributors

Maxine Anderson, MD, trained in psychoanalysis in Seattle, Washington, and London, England. She is currently a training and supervising analyst for several psychoanalytic institutes in North America including the Northwestern Psychoanalytic Society and Institute (Seattle), where she is also a founding member of the Seattle Psychoanalytic Society and Institute and the Canadian Psychoanalytic Institute. She is a fellow of the International Psychoanalytical Association and of the British Institute of Psychoanalysis. She has written several papers and chapters as well as two books, *The Wisdom of Lived Experience* (Karnac, 2016) and *From Tribal Division to Welcoming Inclusion: Psychoanalytic Perspectives* (Routledge, 2019). Although she teaches and practices psychoanalysis primarily in Seattle, she also offers courses in Portland, Oregon, Vancouver, BC, and other North American cities. maxinekander@gmail.com.

Robin McCoy Brooks is a Jungian analyst in private practice in Seattle, Washington. She is co-editor-in-chief of the *International Journal of Jungian Studies* and serves on the board of directors of the International Association for Jungian Studies. Brooks is also a founding member of the New School for Analytical Psychology and an active analyst member of the Inter-Regional Society of Jungian Analysts. A nationally certified Trainer, Educator and Practitioner of Group Psychotherapy, Sociometry and Psychodrama, she is the author of numerous articles and chapters and is presently is writing a book titled *Psychoanalysis and Social Transformation: Catastrophe and Trans-subjectivity*. She lives aboard a wooden boat on Salmon Bay with her husband and their two Siamese cats. robin.mccoy@comcast.net.

Jeffrey Eaton, MA, is a graduate and faculty member of the Northwestern Psychoanalytic Society and Institute and a member of the International Psychoanalytical Association. Eaton provides psychotherapy and psychoanalysis to children and adults and consultation to therapists and analysts around the world. An aspiring writer, he received the Frances Tustin Memorial Lecture Prize in 2006 and has been the Beta Rank Memorial lecturer at the Boston Psychoanalytic Society, the Margaret Jarvie Memorial lecturer at the University of Edinburgh and a presenter at the Tavistock, London. He has also been a frequent guest speaker at the International Frances Tustin Trust meetings as well as at International Bion meetings. In 2017 he was the international guest lecturer of the Australian Psychoanalytic Society in Melbourne. A senior consulting child psychotherapist for the Gunawirra Foundation in Sydney, he was a founder of the Alliance Community Psychotherapy Clinic, a project of The Northwest Alliance for Psychoanalytic Study. He is the author of *A Fruitful Harvest: Essays after Bion* and several chapters in edited collections. Information about his writing and practice can be found at www.jleaton.com. He is currently at work on a second book, tentatively titled *An Open Gate: Listening after Bion.*

Sharon R. Green, MSSW, has a private practice of psychoanalysis and clinical consultation in Seattle, Washington. She is a member of the International Association of Analytical Psychology and a founding member of the New School for Analytical Psychology. Her work has appeared in the *Journal of Analytical Psychology*, and she has contributed chapters to a number of books, including *Temporality and Shame: Perspectives from Psychoanalysis and Philosophy*, which was awarded the 2018 best edited book prize by the American Board and Academy of Psychoanalysis. Her most recent chapter appears in *Thresholds and Pathways between Jung and Lacan: On the Blazing Sublime*, an edited volume that was a result of the first international Jung/Lacan conference held in Cambridge, England. srgreen1@gmail.com.

Ladson Hinton is a psychiatrist, psychoanalyst and philosopher. He is a member of the Society of Jungian Analysts of Northern California and the Institute for Contemporary Psychoanalysis in Los Angeles and was a founding member of both Palo Alto University and the New School for Analytical Psychology. He serves on the editorial board of the *Journal of Analytical Psychology* and practices, consults and teaches in Seattle. In 2009 he received an Award for Distinguished Contributions to Psychoanalytic Education from the International Forum for Psychoanalytic Education. His paper, "Temporality and the Torments of Time," was a finalist for the Gradiva Award in 2016. *Temporality and Shame: Psychoanalytic and Philosophical Perspectives*, co-edited with Hessel Willemsen (Routledge, 2018), won the prize of the American Board and Academy of Psychoanalysis for books published in 2018. Some of his core interests are shame and temporality, and a multidimensional understanding of our ongoing cultural crisis. ladsonhinton3@gmail.com.

Kenneth A. Kimmel has been a Jungian analyst, psychotherapist and consultant in private practice since 1983 in Seattle, Washington. He is a co-founding director and faculty member of The New School for Analytical Psychology, and author of the book *Eros and the Shattering Gaze: Transcending Narcissism* (Fisher King Press, 2011). He was chair of the Seattle Inter-Institute Committee whose vision was to create a cross-training programme between candidates and analysts from Seattle's schools of psychoanalysis that would engender an ethos of mutual respect for their common ground and differences. Kimmel continues to embody that ethos in both his writing and inter-disciplinary studies. He has taught and lectured widely throughout his career and been published through the *Journal of Analytical Psychology, Fisher King Press, Jung Journal: Culture & Psyche,* and *Daimon Verlag,* respectively. For the past twenty-five years, he has been a student of *kabbalah,* the mystical interpretation of Jewish tradition. He can be reached at kenkimmel@comcast.net.

Ouyang Man obtained her master's degree in philosophy of Science and Technology from Shanghai University with a thesis discussing the potential for human authentic living in the infosphere, starting from an analysis of the maker phenomenon and drawing on the work of Martin Heidegger and Luciano Floridi. Her current research interest is focused on how Bernard Stiegler's notions of exorganology and neganthropology can be related to Peter Sloterdijk's notions of spherology and immunology and, more specifically, on the implications of connecting the work of these two philosophers for a new understanding of psycho-social pathologies and consequently for the development of a new psycho-social therapeutics, drawing as well on the theoretical and clinical ideas and practices of Donald Winnicott. She has been accepted into the doctoral programme at Durham University, where she is continuing her research on these questions. erehwonrm@foxmail.com.

Daniel Ross obtained his doctorate from Monash University in 2002 with a thesis on "Heidegger and the Question of the Political". His book *Violent Democracy* (Cambridge University Press) was published in 2004, and the same year saw the premier at the Rotterdam International Film Festival of a feature documentary that he co-directed with David Barison. The film, titled *The Ister,* went on to win prizes at film festivals in Marseilles and Montreal and prominently featured interviews with philosophers Philippe Lacoue-Labarthe, Jean-Luc Nancy and Bernard Stiegler and filmmaker Hans-Jürgen Syberberg. Among other universities, he has taught at the University of Melbourne, Yachay Tech and Tongji University. Ross has worked extensively with Stiegler, written numerous articles on his work and related questions, and has published eleven volumes of translation of Stiegler's work, most recently *The Age of Disruption: Technology and Madness in Computational Capitalism* (Polity, 2019) and *Nanjing Lectures 2016–2019* (Open Humanities Press). His book *Psychopolitical Anaphylaxis: Steps Towards a Metacosmics* is forthcoming from Open Humanities Press. djrossmail@gmail.com.

Eric R. Severson is a philosopher specializing in the work of Emmanuel Levinas. He is the author of *Before Ethics* (Kendall-Hunt, 2020), *Levinas's Philosophy of Time* (Duquesne University Press, 2013) and *Scandalous Obligation* (Beacon Hill Press, 2011) and editor of eight books on philosophy, psychology, ethics, theology and the philosophy of religion. He lives in Kenmore, Washington, and teaches philosophy at Seattle University. seversoe@seattleu.edu.

Michael Whan, MA, is a Jungian analyst with the Independent Group of Analytical Psychologists, the International Association for Analytical Psychology, the College of Psychoanalysts-UK, and a member of the International Society for Psychology as a Discipline of Interiority. In 2013, his article "Myth, Disenchantment and Loss of Sacred Place" was cited by Psychology Progress, a Canadian Academic Organization, as notably contributing to the advancement of psychology. He is also a senior associate of the Royal Society of Medicine and patron of the Department of Germanic Studies of the Institute of Modern Languages, University of London. He has published extensively in psychology journals and contributed chapters to a number of books, the last of which, *Temporality and Shame: Perspectives from Psychoanalysis and Philosophy*, was awarded the 2018 best edited book prize by the American Board and Academy of Psychoanalysis.

Hessel Willemsen, DClinPsych (UK), studied chemistry at Delft University and clinical psychology at Leiden University. He is a training and supervising analyst with the Society of Analytical Psychology in London, a member of the New School of Analytical Psychology and of the International Association of Analytical Psychology. He lives, practices and teaches in central London. His recent publication "Primo Levi's Bearing Witness and the Reinterpreted Past: Post-truth and the Authoritarian Other" appeared in the *Journal of Analytical Psychology*. The book *Temporality and Shame: Psychoanalytic and Philosophical Perspectives*, co-edited with Ladson Hinton, won the best edited book prize by the American Board and Academy of Psychoanalysis in 2018. He has published and taught on affect and the body; his interests include violence, post-truth, the authoritarian other and Primo Levi. hw@psychresolution.co.uk.

A note on the cover image

Edvard Munch (b. Norway, 1863–1944)
Evening on Karl Johan, 1892
Oil on canvas, 84.5 x 121 cm
KODE Art Museums and Composer Homes, The Rasmus Meyer Collection

In the latter part of the nineteenth century scenes of the hectic life of big cities were common in European painting. By various formal, stylistic and thematic means, the Realists, Naturalists and Impressionists had conquered the city, that primary subject for the painter of modern life. Munch's urban scene in the painting *Evening on Karl Johan* conjures up a human drama that his contemporaries had difficulty in accepting. Oslo's main street is shown from the Royal Palace looking towards the Starting, the parliament building, in a radically foreshortened perspective. Squarely facing the advancing crowd, the viewer is forced into direct confrontation with the seemingly never-ending procession of ghost-like figures. Like crazed souls from a different, hopeless world, their eyes stare vacantly out at us from sallow, mask-like figures. The sun is about to set, its last rays reflected in the window panes. Under a gloomy, deep-blue evening sky, the back of a lonely figure is seen hurrying down the middle of the empty street. *Evening on Karl Johan* is the first painting in which Munch presents his figures with ghostly, mask-like countenances. The work of the Belgian Symbolist artist James Ensor is generally regarded as the inspiration for these angst-ridden faces. But though some of Munch's drawings can be said to reflect Ensor's masterpiece, *The Entry of Christ into Brussels* (1889), there are few direct indications to support this argument.

Reference

Ydstie I. in Sandvik, F. et al. (2008). *Bergen Art Museum. Highlights*. Bergen: Bergen Art Museum, p. 82.

Introduction

A nation or culture will not thrive, and may not survive, unless its citizens can look forward to a life worth living. Failure to provide a hope for the future, particularly for its youths, foments extreme turbulence and sometimes a sense of mad disruption: a prospect of *Ominous Transitions*. This uncertainty about a hopeful future is the basic condition of our times and is the focus of this volume. From multiple perspectives in psychoanalysis, philosophy, history, social studies and anthropology, the authors discuss the dimensions of our dire situation, how they came to be and how they might develop. The emergence of the COVID-19 pandemic, followed by the profound shock from the killing of an African-American man by a policeman in Minneapolis, Minnesota, United States, were thrown into an already-turbulent mixture.[1] The often-suppressed memories of chattel slavery,[2] along with racism and colonialism, have surged to the fore in collective consciousness, joined by the lurking reality of a silent viral killer that seems to lurk everywhere, dealing out deaths of violent suffocation.

These ongoing shocks are mightily testing governmental capabilities around the world to manage death tolls and injustice. This is true of the United States. Hyldgaard brilliantly describes how "The Cause of the Subject" is "An Ill-Timed Accident" (2000); that is, the 'structure' of the individual subject emerges in a non-linear fashion through major or minor disruptions. 'Ill-timed accident' also describes the dramatic change of social collectives, when a violent, potent flow of cultural and historical events is unleashed. Such traumatic shattering in the present in turn awakens more cascades of repressed, often unacknowledged, historical traumas. Trauma awakens trauma (Caruth, 1996; LaCapra, 2014). Synchronous time gives place to diachronous time.[3] "The centre cannot hold . . . The best lack all conviction, while the worst are full of passionate intensity" (Yeats, 1921). We seem to dwell amidst a kind of cultural madness with an uncertain outcome.

As individuals, we are all 'thrown' into the world to live our lives at a certain time in history, in a certain family and cultural surround. Understanding mostly comes after the fact. We see this dramatically in much of our art and literature, such as *Oedipus Rex*. Study of human events and undertakings, as they have unfolded in time, cannot teach us final truths but can teach us shame and humility, and the wisdom of listening and reflecting. How can we find meaning amidst the often overwhelming streams of turbulence and trauma? In *Oedipus at Colonus*, the third play in the trilogy, a transformation of identity emerges through his accepting and enduring the shameful truths of his past (Stoykova, 2018; Hinton, 2020).

Amidst a vision of dire uncertainty, how do we find the makings of a life worth living, a sense of future, a sense of material security and personal meaning? Samuel Beckett describes the uncertainty of the contemporary person, proceeding cautiously in an ambiguous world: "I know where I am going, it is no longer the ancient night. . . . I am going to play. . . . I shall play a great part of the time, from here on" (Beckett, 1956/1997, pp. 204–205). Reflecting upon our time of 'ominous transitions' in their unique ways, our authors provide hope that with a capacity for both critique and imagination, the possibility of playful and responsible creation still resides in our species.

The perspectives that protected other peoples from madness and destruction, and enabled lives worth living, can contribute useful advice. In the Greek myth of origins, following the initial creation of the human race, and after Epimetheus and Prometheus gave the new race the gifts of creative arts and fire, the new set of human creatures was still in dire straits (Stiegler, 1998, pp. 200–201). Having no capacities enabling them to get along in community, they quarreled endlessly in warlike ways, and they were in danger of destroying the entire species. To save them, Zeus sent Hermes two major gifts or qualities. One was *aido*: shame, respect for others, modesty and a sense of finitude. The other gift was *dikē*: a sense of justice, something that would create bonds of friendship, union and discourse in politics (ibid). Only then did the human species have the tools to develop civilization.

According to the myth, *aido* and dikē became essential characteristics shared by all humans, who were originally without such capacities for survival. They found that these new gifts were not fixed but always in negotiation and process. A sense of time was part of this process, stemming from a new awareness of death, shame and finitude. The human race, lacking qualities necessary for survival, was saved by these *prosthetic* gifts, crucial supplements to allow them to endure and thrive.[4] These were the roots of culture and civilization. Due to their newfound capacities for self-reflection, human lives are always in process and bound by time, seeking more effective means of survival. They also know they will die, in contrast to the immortal gods.

In our present time of 'ominous transitions', the Greek perspective is useful in reflecting upon the plight of our species and can provide a perspective for our survival. Most of our authors focus extensively on shame (*aido*), viewing that emotion as something built into the species and of vital relevance to our troubled times. Shame is perhaps the most crucial and prime emotion in the formation of a sense of being a worthy person or the opposite. In that way, it is a guide or teacher (Hinton, 1998). It is a core reference point in our earliest formation and is basic to the sense of having a meaningful life versus living in a state of "Symbolic Misery" (Stiegler, 2014, pp. 1–14).[5] Shame has a deep role in shaping a sense of honour and respect for self and others; it is the core of justice and is crucial in shaping human life (Nelissen et al., 2013; Sánchez, 2015).

As depicted in the Greek myth of creation, the very survival of the species is dependent upon the workings of shame. Without humility and respect among human creatures, societies cannot function, and life becomes chaotic and meaningless. Shamelessness destroys cultures. In the anarchic strangeness of present times, shame can be a crucial beacon. It shapes us, makes us slow down and take notice of the truth of our situation. Shame has an ontological dimension, is at the core of our being and opens new dimensions and perspectives on self and world (Hultberg, 1986).

When we suffer from a disorienting, excessive turbulence, we would like to escape, but there is no escape from shame (Levinas, 2003). It can be cruel and negative when misused by the powerful, but it normally sets essential limits on emotions and behaviours that are excessive, helping form a unique core of self, a complex gestalt of emotion and cognition that must become organized so that we can function as the unique creatures that we are.

The ongoing process of *nachträglichkeit*, an endless shaping and reshaping of memory, also involves shame.[6] Shame stops us and causes us to look back and reflect again on times past. In that process, our past shifts in large or small ways. The effects can be dramatic when we look back and recall our blindness and narcissism for the first time. Shame is a teacher and often alters our sense of time and memory (Hinton, 1998). By slowing us down, it allows us to 'see' heretofore forgotten areas of personal or collective experience, reorienting our search for meaning and opening new possibilities of a future life that is worth living.

In this time of ominous transitions, we are set topsy-turvy in a state of utter confusion and uncertainty. The invisible COVID-19 thrusts our mortality in our faces. Our extreme vulnerability evokes shame. To wear a protective mask is a sign of accepting our vulnerability, but refusal seems to stem from a denial of death, an escape from the shame of mortality. It can also manifest as a giddy inflation from the illusion of escaping death.

Bernard Stiegler, echoing Adorno and Horkheimer, describes a "new age of barbarism" in the world (Adorno & Horkheimer, 2002; Stiegler, 2019, pp. 35–43). He asserts that our age suffers from an "absence of epoch", a time of extreme disruption (Stiegler, 2019, pp. 46–49, 152–154). Our human capacity for imaginative solutions has become exhausted due to endless consumerism, guided by algorithms that influence and control many of our personal and social decisions. Since the development of tools began some 3 million years ago, human culture has evolved from the effects of imagination on raw matter (Koukouti & Malafouris, 2020; Stiegler, 2013, pp. 59–79). That is, through an act of imagination, a rock can become a tool. The capacity to imagine, and the related memories of our tools and other memory devices, lies at the heart of what we are; that is, we *are* our tools, language and memories. Our inherited organic brains don't have the capacity to remember even a fraction of what we need to know to run our factories, professions, trades and daily lives. We require inorganic, now faster-than-light modalities to get along.

Saturated with algorithmically guided media that detects and influences our tastes and purchases, including our everyday personal habits, we are increasingly controlled and shaped by the machines we have created. Media and algorithms increasingly make our social and personal decisions. We are 'trained' to consume. According to Stiegler, this results in a condition he calls the "Proletarianization of the mind", the diminishment of the human capacity for creative reflection and long-term perspectives (Stiegler, 2017, 2019, pp. 152–154; Vesco, 2015). This affects our public as well as our private lives by making us more susceptible to the scapegoating, falsehoods and seductions of autocratic leaders.

The human being has a pool of narcissistic energy which is undifferentiated and pre-individual and is the heritage of our restless species. We are filled with drive *(trieb)* that is objectless and goalless (Laplanche & Pontalis, 1973, pp. 214–215). To achieve a moral and creative sublimation of this roiling psychic energy requires shaping from elders and culture (Civitarese, 2016). We and our children and grandchildren have become more enmeshed with and dependent upon our 'devices', controlled and directed by algorithms, accessing in a nanosecond their vast expanses of memory. More and more these take the role of adviser, as the authority on cultural norms, rather than family and elders. This distracts from knowing or valuing funds of cultural memory in a way that is situated and real. It bypasses the organic experience of shame and limits, and contributes to a sense of alienation. The sense of organic connection with the past is greatly diminished.

As a result, there has been a lessening of our imaginative capacity for creative engagement with self and world, and our restless drives have fewer creative modes of expression. This has been a negatively reinforcing quality. The result is a kind of *disindividuation*, a forfeiture of differentiated personhood.[7] Sublimation becomes less possible, and the unshaped life energies have nowhere to go. That is why at the extreme we have madness, an infernal spiral of chaos that has little containment (Stiegler, 2019, pp. 132–148).

Stiegler uses the concept of *entropy* as the core of what we are facing now.[8] The present American administration is a prime example of an altogether careless dissipation of energy, actually destroying sublimating structures – the structures created by the collective imagination of our forebears over 3 million years. Stiegler sees the only hope as a movement toward *negentropy*, which means a building up of newly conceived and imagined cultural forms and habits, as opposed to steadily dissipating that which is sustaining and containing.[9] Partly following Heidegger, he calls for a culture of *care* that enables new imaginative and containing structures with more emphasis on the well-being of community.[10] Care is an attitude of fostering negentropy, a building up of structures that modulate and create. Shame can open the perspective of care based on reflection and truth. *Sorge*, the original German word translated as 'care', has broader connotations than 'care' has in English. It seems closely intermeshed with truth, with a 'little t' (Mills, 2014). Without truth and discernment, along with respect for others and for tradition, we will care for the wrong things. Truth is a basic dimension of caring for the world, and care opens the possibility of having a world that is, at the least, less inhuman.

Shame, justice and the basic human tools of truth and care, in various forms and from varying perspectives, are core concerns of our chapter authors. With truth and care we may become "new moral beings", more "deproletarianized", and more capable of creative dreaming (Stiegler, 2019, pp. 286–312). Together, we seek to find a meaningful way through ominous transitions toward a life that is worthwhile in a future that is unknown.

Our authors take different paths toward exploring their common destination. Ladson speaks about witnessing a dramatic incident in early 2019 on Capitol Hill in Seattle. An African-American man was blocking traffic in a street intersection, heartily singing gospel songs. After the man voluntarily left the intersection, Hinton spoke to him, and there was a special moment of meeting between them. Hinton later imagined the scene as a situation of "Man versus Machine", in which the blocked cars of the affluent represented a radical slowing of the speedy race of technology and capitalism, the mad race that fosters neglect of basic human needs.

He discusses Bernard Stiegler's work in light of this meeting, reflecting upon the history of racism in the United States and the coincidental emergence of 'black hole capitalism', slavery, computational technology and automation. Gospel music was a crucial element in the capacity of black culture to survive and thrive amidst gross repression. In an epilogue Hinton discusses COVID-19 and the recent killing of an African American man on May, 25, 2020, by Minneapolis police, a little over a year after the incident he witnessed on Capitol Hill. He ends with a reflection on the tragic myth of Oedipus, with the core thought that only facing painful truth gives hope for an ethical future.

Eaton discusses how 'ominous transitions' occur during the process of everyday life. He speaks to the idea of caesura, first introduced by W.R. Bion to suggest a link between mature emotions and thinking and intra-uterine life and thereby changing the focus from self or object to the link between. Caesura signifies a paradoxical space that contains both similarity and difference and focuses on simultaneity and complexity rather than linear ideas of cause and effect. This chapter explores the relationship to time as well as a destructive form of shame that undermines the capacity for creativity and communication. Eaton's personal experiences are woven into reflections on the work of Bion.

In her chapter, Maxine Anderson considers that complex reality is often more than the mind can register. In response, the mind may seek to simplify reality by reverting to early defences such as denial and projection, which create a polarizing lens upon the world and fundamental myths that go unquestioned. The myth of white supremacy is one entrenched example. Such reversion of reality, however, also introduces violence because reverting to simpler realities collapses the mind's potential capacities for wide-ranging and discerning thoughts about self, other and the wider world. Anderson points out that the individual then dwells amidst inhuman dangers of eruptive impulses, unmodified affects and projections. The ominous transitions encountered in these situations when reality reverts to early defences involve the fragility of our humanity when the mind is traumatized from primarily internal sources.

A return from this simplified reality or the rescue from this traumatized territory ironically requires the humanizing capacities lost to the fractured mind. That is, discerning thought and an openness to receive, via suffering, a transformation of traumatic intensities into potential meaning. Suffering via compassion for the shattered self is often central to the restoration of one's humanity, without which we may be condemned to the more inhumane existence defined by polarized certainties and unquestionable myths.

Robin McCoy Brooks elaborates a notion of trans-subjectivity through a close reading of Lacan's 1945 essay titled "Logical Time and the Assertion of Anticipated Certainty", whereby Lacan delineates three iterative moments of logical time towards a culminating expression of collective truth (Lacan, 1945/2006). Whereas Lacan used the allegory of the prisoner's dilemma to illustrate his theses, Brooks uses a clinical vignette taken from a therapy retreat attended by persons living with AIDS in the early days of the pandemic. She elaborates the symbolic structures underlying the movements among subject, inter-subjective and trans-subjective logic and the culminating expression of a shared solution to a posed dilemma. The events took place during times that were both dark and illuminating. Solidarity existed only in those trans-subjective moments that lifted and informed individuals, and sometimes groups of individuals, toward a kind of concrete action that often furthered its collective purpose.

During times of ominous transitions, Sharon R. Green argues, it is necessary to question the ways in which we have been socialized to the norms of culture. Although shame can strengthen social bonds, it can also enforce conformity and unquestioning obedience to the values of society. Green explains that the concept of 'shame' has been described in multiple ways: theories of shame range from those that understand it as a toxic and pathological affect to be avoided, to those that see shame as the fundamental sentiment of what it means to be human. Although Lacan refers to shame throughout his work, he does not offer a detailed analysis of it. Using a Lacanian psychoanalytic perspective, in dialogue with multiple models of shame – especially that of the American psychologist Sylvan Tomkins – Green explores the relationship between the traumatic structure of subjectivity, shame and culture during times of ominous transitions. The relevance of shame to such key Lacanian concepts as the Real, jouissance, *objet petit a*, the divided subject and the barred Other are explored.

Although 'nihilism' predates Nietzsche's pronouncement that 'God is dead', it was Nietzsche who most notably defined and articulated its meaning, essentially, the end of meaning with a big M. According to Michael Whan, Nietzsche subtly differentiated between its two forms: 'complete nihilism' and 'incomplete nihilism'. The latter is largely prevalent in the world today, especially in the West. Paradoxically, it is actually a form of defence against nihilism.

The forms of incomplete nihilism, while seeming to offer 'meaning', a 'return to religion' and a return of 'depth' to events and experiences, as Nietzsche pointed out, actually deepen nihilism. Such defensive forms often take Nietzsche's words regarding nihilism literally, which of course, is itself an interpretation. Nietzsche, with dialectical insight, perceived that nihilism was itself the product of Christianity. Indeed, as philosophers such as Gianni Vattimo and others have recognized, nihilism is the historical unfolding and *telos* of Christianity. Whan points out how nihilism is the dialectical self-negation by Christianity of itself. His chapter explores the nature of incomplete nihilism, the implications of the loss of meaning, and discusses the functioning of simulation and depth psychology as forms of incomplete nihilism as well as the internal rupture of Christianity as it faithfully followed its own truth.

Daniel Ross and Ouyang Man discuss Derrida and Sloterdijk, who diagnosed forms of social crisis through an immunological paradigm drawing together questions of locality and questions of technological communication. Bernard Stiegler avoided such a paradigm but raised similar questions, framed in terms of a pharmacology that he more recently contextualized in relation to the struggle against entropy. Ross and Man argue that these perspectives can be integrated by conceiving immune processes as retentional, or as having to do with memory. On this basis, the authors propose an account of shame as a fundamental *Stimmung*, a 'mood' that involves an affectivity and attitude. To elaborate their perspective, they draw upon Winnicott's account of the transitional object as well as his distinction between regression and withdrawal and his concept of holding.

By setting an account of the relationship between shame, guilt and shamelessness within what they propose calling a *metacosmic* standpoint, a path to a new critique of contemporary crisis opens up. This expands the insights of Derrida and Sloterdijk concerning the teletechnological basis of present-day troubles of belonging as well as Stiegler's powerful diagnosis of the way in which analogico-digital technologies have led to a collapse of psychic and collective individuation while also adding a perspective capable of seeing how such phenomena are inextricably entwined with regressions from shame that are also inevitably sexual regressions.

The 'germ seed' of Kenneth A. Kimmel's chapter came about in the early morning following the 2016 American presidential election, when Kimmel dreamt of a rampaging grizzly. The dream provoked grave concerns in him about these ominous times ahead and how to respond ethically to them. Responding to this urgency, Kimmel embarks on a broad meditation on the Hebrew phrase *Hineni* – from the 'Abraham and Isaac story' in the book of *Genesis*, which is translated, 'I am here'. Its philosophical meaning has come to be understood as the individual's infinite responsibility for the human being suffering in their midst and the singular individual's recognition of the profound shame he/she bears for their part in *all* suffering. Through inter-textual, inter-disciplinary scholarship that builds upon the meaning of *Hineni*, Kimmel draws on the 'dialogical imagination' within self and society. Giving voice to paradox and multiple perspectives, dialogical thought opens temporal life that is without closure, undermining the single, total-izing narrative that excludes or appropriates human otherness. Hebrew tradition, philosophy, theology, kabbalah, cultural theory, literature, poetry, psychology and genocidal studies inform the ideas comprising this chapter.

Severson provides a philosophical inquiry into the phenomenon of shame as it relates to contemporary racism. Shame, he argues, is tangled up in the concept of time and particularly in the way that powerful people control the temporality of shame's operation. By investigating the relationship between time and shame, Severson presents multiple versions of shame – a beneficial shame and an oppres-sive version – exposing the way racism is enabled and protected by one form and pointing to alternatives available through other ways of conceiving time. The roots of racism, and the powerful force of shame in reinforcing racism, are deep taproots that run down through the history of European civilization. His efforts to reconsider shame and point to a healthy version of shame begin with Plato and Aristotle. After reviewing and critiquing their push for synchrony in their philoso-phies of time and shame, he turns to contemporary manifestations of racism and white supremacy. Drawing on the work of Emmanuel Levinas, Severson suggests that if understood alongside another, more disruptive modality of time, which he calls 'diachronic', shame opens up dimensions of responsibility, solidarity and justice. The psychological professions, Severson argues, would be wise to attend to the cultivation of diachronic shame.

Notes

1 On May 25, 2020, George Floyd, a 46-year-old black man, was killed in Minneapolis, Minnesota, during an arrest for allegedly using a counterfeit bill. A white police officer knelt on Floyd's neck for more than eight minutes while Floyd was handcuffed, lying facedown, begging for his life, and repeatedly saying, "I can't breathe". Other police officers further restrained Floyd, while another prevented bystanders from interven-ing. During the final three minutes, Floyd was motionless and had no pulse while the officer ignored onlookers' pleas to remove his knee. He did not remove it until medics told him to.

2 A chattel slave is an enslaved person who is owned forever and whose children and children's children are automatically enslaved. Chattel slaves are individuals treated as personal property to be bought and sold as commodities. Chattel slavery was supported and made legal by European governments and monarchs.

3 Synchronous time is the smooth-running side of life, relatively unchanging and stable. It can be stifling and lacking a sense of meaning and future. Diachronous time is dis-ruption, which can open the way to new horizons or, conversely, to disorientation or cultural madness.

4 In Stiegler's view, *Homo sapiens* is a 'prosthetic' being because of co-evolution with *technos*: tools of every sort, from stone tools, to language, to modern technology and memory devices. 'Prosthetic' refers to a state of deficiency or default that was/is intrin-sic to the human condition. From his point of view, following Leroi-Gourhan, Stiegler asserts that the brain and "external memory" developed together. The human species co-evolved with its "add-ons" (Stiegler, 1998, pp. 11–12, 50).

5 By "Symbolic Misery", Stiegler seems to mean the loss of a place for basic human imagination: the production of symbols. It is a loss of a sense of creativity in everyday

work, intellectual creativity, and the arts of everyday life – a capacity that has been at the core of the life of the human species since the invention of tools. The spirit of calculation, the idea that all human activities can be quantified and marketed, slowly eliminates the space of creation. Life becomes more like the "spirit of the anthill" (Stiegler, 2014, pp. 45–80). Since the emergence of automation and late-stage capitalism, the need for input from workers has slowly been eliminated. With the emergence of light-speed technology, most of the managerial class is largely in the same position: decisions are ruled by calculation rather than human values that require reflection and invention. With the predominance of consumer capitalism and advertising, guided by algorithms, existence for most people has become that of 'the consumer'. The objectless energies of the psyche have fewer and fewer areas for creative sublimation. The result is a kind of restless, ill-defined sense of misery, a deeply unconscious shame at feeling aimless and useless. This can lead towards violence in both the personal and social worlds.

6 *Nachträglichkeit* refers to the endless revisions of memory with time. The details of memory are rearranged due to the impact of new experience. This lends a relative groundlessness to existence but also an element of freedom. With age, wisdom may come: the capacity to consciously reflect, using the process of memory as a tool for wondering, imagination, and the future. Gerald Edelman has described how this view accords with the findings of neuroscience, using the analogy of an iceberg that melts seasonally, but how each season the streams and rivulets take a somewhat different form (Edelman, 2004, pp. 52–53). However, we cannot invent a wholly other reality, and change always appears in a context. The point is that our memories are never final. This lack of certainty can create shame but over time may lead to a humble wisdom that acknowledges our incompletion, making us more open to new and unexpected elements of experience.

7 Stiegler sees technology from the standpoint of the *Pharmakon*, a view that things have different proportions of poison and cure. In the case of our present relation to technology, the 'poison' side of technology has become more predominant. Stiegler is not a Luddite. He feels that the human species is intrinsically technological. Brain and tool developed together. Human development could not be imagined without tools, including the complex technological devices we see today (Stiegler, 2013, pp. 18–19).

8 The idea of entropy comes from a principle of thermodynamics dealing with energy. It usually refers to the idea that everything in the universe eventually moves from order to disorder, and entropy is the measurement of that change. Stiegler considers the process of climate change as a process of entropy, and care and 'negentropy' have to do with conserving and building up.

9 Negentropy involves new ways of being together in the world that build up or conserve energy. Care is intimately facilitative of this approach to life.

10 Heidegger explains the radical role of care by pointing to the tendency of the human self to turn away from its own authentic being to seek security in the crowd. It accommodates itself to what people think and forms its conduct in accordance with the expectations of public opinion. Care is a turning back toward the being of the world (Stiegler, 2019, pp. 259–260).

References

Adorno, T. W. & Horkheimer, M. (2002). "The Culture Industry: Enlightenment as Mass Deception." In *Dialectic of Enlightenment: Philosophical Fragments*. Trans. Edmund Jephcott, pp. 94–136. Stanford: Stanford University Press.

Beckett, S. (1956/1997). *Molloy, Malone Dies, The Unnamable*. New York: Everyman's Library.

Caruth, C. (1996). *Unclaimed Experience: Trauma, Narrative and History*. Baltimore: The Johns Hopkins University Press.

Civitarese, G. (2016). "On Sublimation." *The International Journal of Psychoanalysis*, 97, 1369–1392.

Edelman, G. (2004). *Wider Than the Sky: The Phenomenal Gift of Consciousness*. New Haven: Yale University Press.

Hinton, W. L. (1998). "Shame as a Teacher: 'Lowly Wisdom' at the Millenium." In *Florence 98: Destruction and Creation: Personal and Cultural Transformations*. Ed. Mary Ann Mattoon. Zürich: Daimon Press.

———. (2020). "The Unsilencing of Oedipus: Time, Monstrousness, Truth and Shame." In *Other/Wise, International Forum of Psychoanalytic Education*, 1 (online publication).

Hultberg, P. (1986). "Shame: An Overlooked Emotion." In *Berlin 1986: The Archetype of Shadow in a Split World*. Ed. Mary Ann Mattoon. Zürich: Daimon Press.

Hyldgaard, K. (2000). "The Cause of the Subject as an Ill-Timed Accident." *Umbr(a), A Journal of the Unconscious*, 67–80.

Koukouti, M. D. & Malafouris, L. (2020). "Material Imagination: An Anthropological Perspective." In *The Cambridge Handbook of the Imagination*. Ed. Anna Abraham, pp. 30–46. Cambridge: Cambridge University Press.

Lacan, J. (1945/2006). *Écrits: The First Complete Edition in English*. Trans. B. Fink. New York & London: W. W. Norton.

LaCapra, D. (2014). *Writing History, Writing Trauma*. Baltimore: Johns Hopkins University Press.

Laplanche, J. & Pontalis, J.-B. (1973). *The Language of Psychoanalysis*. Trans. Donald Nicholson-Smith. New York: W. W. Norton.

Levinas, E. (2003). *On Escape: De l'évasion (Cultural Memory in the Present)*. Stanford: Stanford University Press.

Mills, J. (2014). "Truth." *Journal of the American Psychoanalytic Association*, 62, 2, 267–293. DOI:10.1177/0003065114529458.

Nelissen, M. A., Breugelmans, S. M. & Zeelenberg, M. (2013). "Reappraising the Moral Nature of Emotions in Decision Making: The Case of Shame and Guilt." *Social and Personality Psychology Compass*, 7/6, 355–365. DOI:10.1111/spc3.12030.

Sánchez, A. M. (2015). "Shame and the Internalized Other." *Etica & Politica / Ethics & Politics*, XVII, 2, 180–199.

Stiegler, B. (1998). *Technics and Time, 1: The Fault of Epimetheus*. Trans. Richard Beardsworth & George Collins. Stanford: Stanford University Press.

———. (2004/2014). *Symbolic Misery*, vol. 1. Malden, MA: Polity Press.

———. (2013). *What Makes Life Worth Living*. Trans. Daniel Ross. Malden, MA: Polity Press.

———. (2016/2019). *The Age of Disruption: Technology and Madness in Computational Capitalism*. Malden, MA: Polity Press.

———. (2017). "The Proletarianization of Sensibility." *Boundary*, 2, 44, 1, 6–18. Durham, NC: Duke University Press. DOI:10.1215/01903659-3725833.

Stoykova, D. (2018). "Oedipus – Myth, Reality and the Distribution of Guilt: With Special Consideration of *Oedipus at Colonus*." In *Other/Wise, International Forum of Psychoanalytic Education*, 1 (online publication).

Vesco, S. (2015). "Collective Disindividuation and/or Barbarism: Technics and Proletarianization." *Boundary*, 2, 83–104. Durham, NC: Duke University Press. DOI:10.1215/01903659-2866576.

Yeats, W. B. (1921/2018). "The Second Coming." In *The Collected Poetry of W. B. Yeats*, pp. 145–146. Digireads.com Publishing (online publication).

Chapter 1

Man and machine
Dilemmas of the human[1]

Ladson Hinton

Prelude

This chapter is composed as a reflection that unfolds, its dimensions revealed in the process of reading. Layers of thought and memory, of present, past and future, unfold as life experience, as a texture, not in a linear and machine-like fashion.

The central focus is a random happening on the streets of Seattle that disrupted the flow of the everyday, the familiar, and opened multiple dimensions of thought and imagination, leading from immediate impacts and impressions to a reflection on the nature of the human, the vicissitudes of capitalism, and the sad history of chattel slavery and its haunting aura.

The epilogue is a brief reflection on the appearance of the coronavirus.

The encounter[2]

One afternoon I went to the pharmacy to pick up a prescription, and when I emerged from the store, there was tension in the air. Cars were lined up in all directions. There was an African American man at the center of the nearby inter- section, loudly and energetically singing gospel songs. His performance was stop- ping the traffic. His voice was loud and clear, and he threw his head back to give full-throated expression to his songs.

The drivers were confused, some clearly angry and impatient, honking at times, and others looked puzzled or curious. Clumps of people along the sidewalks were attentively watching the scene, and it quickly engaged my full attention. What was going on?

My Capitol Hill neighborhood in Seattle is at the edge of the urban core of Seattle, and 15th Street is filled with shops, restaurants, and coffee houses. To the south is a region of apartment houses and small dwellings, as well as half- way houses, whereas to the north is an upscale area of larger family dwellings. It is a varied neighborhood of the modestly affluent and the affluent, and many residents are connected with technology industries. The area is mainly white but with a broad smattering of people from varied racial and ethnic backgrounds. The atmosphere is moderately avant-garde.

The presence of psychotic or 'disturbed' people on the street is not at all rare in the neighborhood, but this man did not have an air of fragmenting anxiety or explosiveness. He felt present to me and connected to the *surround*.[3] There wasn't a hostile edge in his voice or manner, and his presence felt almost welcoming. I intended to cross the street to have a cup of coffee, and as I approached the intersection, I could see that he was nicely dressed, as if prepared for a performance. He was average height and build and was well-trimmed.

The man suddenly stopped singing, left the middle of the street, and walked to the street corner that I was approaching. His demeanor had become quiet and contained, and it felt as if he were leaving a stage, like a performer who had done his job. The traffic quickly began to move normally, settling back into its constant, *synchronous* pace.[4]

People faded back on the street corner as the man approached. I hesitated for a moment, unsure of what might then emerge, but shrugged it off and proceeded to the crossing to wait for the light alongside him. The now-contained world of stoplights, pedestrians, traffic, and crosswalks was reassembling itself. In a moment I was there beside him.

The man was half a head shorter than me, and as I came closer, I could see that he now looked depleted, emptied of energy and slightly anxious, his posture a bit slumped as he gazed downward. He glanced at me out of the corner of his eye, with a quick look of appraisal and a glimmer of fearful uncertainty, subtly cringing, probably feeling the gaze of an affluent white man.[5]

His songs and his proud, expressive voice were still alive in my mind, and I felt an urge to respond to him, something beyond good manners or protocol, perhaps like the call-and-response mode of gospel (Williams-Jones, 1975, p. 375). Feeling friendly, I looked at him directly and said, "You have a pretty good voice!" His visage changed abruptly, and his face suddenly looked almost joyful. Our eyes met, and I felt a momentary mutuality, a respect, a reciprocity. He shed the hint of cringe, the trace of shame at his visible performance (Jay, 1994, p. 311). The crossing light changed, and he gave me a quick nod, straightened his posture with a renewed air of pride, looked me in the eye, and said in a clear voice, "Thank you, brother! Thank you, brother!"

I was subtly but profoundly moved by this special moment of meeting. He and I crossed the street together, then he turned and proceeded quietly down the sidewalk, returning to his own workaday world, apparently satisfied that his more special work was completed for now. I went into the corner coffee shop and reflected on this incident that had disrupted my intimate territory. The experience has lingered in my mind ever since, provoking many dimensions of reflection.

On my immediate level of thought, I was struck how the event highlighted the presence of affluence, technology, and race in my intimate space, a space that I, for the most part, took for granted. However, in such territory, the boundary of 'interior' and 'exterior' can always shift, in ways that are not clear, fostering an undercurrent of the *uncanny*.[6] Disruptive and yet exciting, such openings can lend a sense of uncertainty as well as possibility to life.

At yet another level, one could also see the implicit presence of race and slavery as the shadow of capital accumulation, along with technology and the temporal landscapes and enclaves associated with it. The man, with his song, was disruptive, even haunting, to the comfortable surroundings on the 15th. There was also a hint of something different, an openness to new life. The presence of the man and his song, as well as the contrasting levels of experience that he invoked, provoked my mind into a whirl of reflection.

My perspective

This experience has percolated in my mind for several months now. It was dreamlike in a way, but to call it dreamlike would diminish it, not quite honoring its stark realness. My memories are probably different, perhaps quite different, from the experiences of others on the scene. I mused to myself, "Were those really gospel songs the man was singing? How exactly was he dressed?" The memory has its shifting shades of real and less real, but the core remains absolutely clear and influences my sense of those surroundings and my strong take on events. In 2020, a black man stood in that intersection near my house, singing gospel songs in an engaging fashion, not apparently angry or psychotic, and for a short period of time totally *stopped the flow of traffic* in my familiar world.

We tend to take our intimate surroundings for granted, but it is the everyday 'grammar' of our lives.[7] The unspoken surround of past history is always with us (Slaby, 2020, p. 174). When we are surprised by disruptions of the synchronous, customary flow of everyday life, we often slow down or stop and become more aware how much we are woven, unconsciously entwined in a deep-woven network of history and culture. Disruptions of the everyday and customary can open up diachronic time, revealing hints of imaginative, creative threads that we usually overlook because they are inauspicious, unapparent, hidden in the flow of everyday consciousness (Alvis, 2018, pp. 211–238).

My experience on 15th Street was a prime example. What had caught my eye most immediately at that time, when I first left the pharmacy and engaged the outside world, was the locked parade of automobiles stretching in four directions. The machines seemed to exude a pent-up energy and growling impatience, and their drivers peered out, some honking impatiently, others looking puzzled or angry.[8] When I spotted the man singing gospel was the fulcrum of the action, performing loudly in the middle of the intersection, it indeed felt like a fundamental encounter of man and machine – 'machine' with all its implications – in the midst of my everyday world (see note 1).

The everyday world has interconnections with the whole of human history, if you can let them surface in your mind. It is always there. 'Details' are not isolated facts but rest upon pulsating human life over millions of years. Without such a vast temporal perspective, human beings become creatures of the moment, lacking any anchor in the vast flow of time and lacking the sense of debt to the endless generations of ancestors who enable us to be (Bloch, 2008, pp. 2055–2061). To broaden that perspective, and its connection to the basic scene in the street, I will explore some deep background perspectives in myth, paleoanthropology, philosophy, and psychoanalysis. These perspectives will highlight my experience on 15th Street, illustrating the ongoing, everyday presence of multiple dimensions of human history, from evolution to slavery and racism, capitalism, and technology.

A story about origins

Such a moving encounter evokes profound questions about the nature of the human, including the origin of our species. We seek insight about what is always already there in our human world. Using a genealogical[9] approach, Bernard Stiegler often refers to the myth of Epimetheus and Prometheus to lend perspective for understanding human evolution and especially the meaning and use of tools (Stiegler, 1998, pp. 187–188).

This is a creation story that begins with the making of creatures to populate the new world. Before that there were only gods and no mortal creatures. The gods delegated an important task to two brothers, Epimetheus and Prometheus, who were also gods. They were to allocate special powers of survival to each new species to compensate for any deficiencies in their makeup. For instance, rabbits would be given speed to compensate for their lack of strength to fight. Epimetheus persuaded his brother to allow him to carry out the distribution of the special attributes. However, he was not a good planner and had a poor memory. By the time he got to the human race, he had used up all the compensatory powers. On the day they were to emerge into the new world, Prometheus came to inspect the results, and he found humankind naked, barefooted, and defenseless. Fearing for the survival of the human race, he stole the gifts of art and invention, along with fire, from Hephaestus and Athena, and gave them to the human species to compensate for their weakness.

From that time, therefore, humankind had a share of the powers of the gods and erected altars and created images to honor them. Soon, using their gifts, humans discovered words and speech, invented houses and clothes, and shoes and bedding, and grew food from the earth. They had some powers like the gods, but they were still human in other respects, such as mortality. Due to their unique origins, they were caught between worlds.[10]

Humankind was born of a double fault, an act of forgetfulness by Epimetheus and an act of theft, the crime of Prometheus (ibid., p. 188). Due to the original theft and its sequelae, the human race was also born into a conflict between the gods. This view of human genealogy is not a fall from an earlier state, a Paradise Lost, as depicted in the Biblical story of Adam and Eve. In the Greek myth, the species required rescue from a fatal vulnerability; there was not *loss* at their origin but a *fault*. There is a *de-fault of origin* or *origin as default*. This lends an important, humbler perspective to human existence. There is no lost Paradise to regain but only the flow of existence.

The stolen gift of the arts became technology in all its dimensions, of all our large and small 'machines' driven by their fire. This conveys the distinctive tone of human existence, according to Stiegler (ibid). *Man is a prosthetic being* who must depend on special, acquired qualities to survive, haunted by a sense of being 'in default' at the core.

From that perspective, one can re-imagine the gospel singer confronting mechanical fire chariots on 15th Street, Seattle, his presence highlighting the fragile, prosthetic defensiveness of the daily processions of machines and affluence. Through arts stolen from the gods, human beings developed their fire chariots as an ultimate prosthesis of speed and power. Despite this dramatic creation of speed and seeming invulnerability, an ancient sense of default and shame persists, along with a haunting awareness of mortality. Human beings try to evade the shame of their underlying sense of default and fear of death. However, nothing can erase the primal default of origin. We earthly creatures remain mortal and prosthetic unlike the gods!

The tool as brainmaker

This genealogical story sets the stage for reflection upon some empirical findings regarding human evolution. There was a slowly emerging bifurcation in human development around 1.75 million years ago, a simultaneous step forward in both stonecutting and cortical development.[11] The freeing of the human hand and bipedal locomotion (erect posture) had set the stage for this possibility (Leroi-Gourhans, 1993, p. 70; McHenry, 2009, p. 263).

It is not possible to say which developed first, the brain or the tool.

> *A tool is, before anything else, memory"* (my italics) . . . the transformations provoked by the technical. . . [evolved] . . . on a timescale that spans countless millennia. . . . One can hardly imagine the human as its . . . inventor; rather, one more readily imagines the human as what is invented.
>
> (Leroi-Gourhans, 1993, pp. 134, 254)

Henceforth it became difficult, if not impossible, to separate the 'who' of the human and the 'what' of *technos* (see note 1).

Tools involved *speed* in accomplishment, of environmental mastery, of the increasing possibilities for finding food. Tools also involved *anticipation* – an emergence of a sense of the 'what might happen' by means of a tool, the emergence of a sense of *time* (Suddendorf et al., 2009, pp. 1317–1324). In Simondon's words, "Every technical gesture implicates the future" (Simondon, 1965, pp. 17–23; Nielsen, 2017, p. 66). This is the same speed and temporality that we now experience with our *light-speed* technology. Evolution has become no longer genetic but *the pursuit of living by means of other than life,* that is, by means of *technos*: tools and language. Henceforth, *epiphylogenesis* supersedes *phylogenesis*, supersedes that which stems from the genetic makeup of the individual human being (Stiegler, 1996, pp. 135, 140).[12]

Social groups were of course present from the 'beginning,' but memory in its *external* forms adds vastly to the complexities and dimensions of communal existence. Stiegler describes a form of memory, "tertiary retention," or tertiary memory that is essential in this crucial shift. This involves cultural memories and structures, history both written and 'forgotten,' language forms, music, as well as, regrettably, advertising that manipulates and endlessly influences our patterns of consumption on all levels (Stiegler, 2014, pp. 34–35, 52–56, 88–89).

It is difficult or impossible to discern what is 'inside' and what is 'outside.' This quality is similar to what Lacan called the "extimate" (*extimité*), "something strange to me although it is at the heart of me" (Zwart, 2017). Our memories, our language – *technos* in general – are both 'inside' and 'outside.' This makes subjectivity possible and yet can feel 'Other,' alien, uncanny. We live at that fulcrum. The happening on 15th Street was certainly an example of that.

There was no singular creative act or set of acts at the core of human emergence. We must live as the prosthetic creatures we are, as beings who are always incomplete, origins ambiguous, dependent on our prosthetic devices, especially those we drive down the street.

Capitalism and desire

As creatures 'in default,' human history often seems like an enactment of the Prometheus/Epimetheus story. Capitalism is the form of default and desire that dominates our own era. Since the development of the Jacquard Loom in the early 19th century, the savoir faire of the worker has been more assumed by the machine.[13] Machine memory is far superior to human memory, and the machine is also more capable of repetitious tasks. As we sit before our computers, we have access to a seeming infinity of memories on the World Wide Web. It never forgets.

Increasing human dependence on memory technologies and automation, as well as endless, complex incitements of desire through algorithms and advertising, has resulted in a diminished capacity to form dreams of a meaningful future. Stiegler terms this process "The Proletarianization of the Mind" (Vesco, 2015). According to McGowan (2016), we live lives substantially controlled by the wedding of desire and capitalism: a kind of black hole capitalism that never creates final satisfaction (Wilson & Bayón, 2016). Capitalism sustains subjects in a state of desire that keeps the system in motion. We are constantly on the edge of having our desires realized, *but we never reach the point of realization* (McGowan, 2016, p. 11). This is an inherently unstable structure because no object is ultimately fulfilling (ibid, p. 24). There is no perfect commodity. The power of advertising in all its overt and covert forms keeps us consuming the plethora of objects our smart machines present to us, but we are never satisfied because we are mortal creatures always 'in default.' Black hole capitalism depends on the impossibility of final satisfaction to sustain the chain of production and consumption. If consumption were to stop, the system would likely collapse. This machine-like pattern seems independent of the formal qualities of government, capitalist or communist (ibid, p. 19).

The people on 15th Street that were brought to a halt by the singing man were behind the wheel of their computerized, metal-skinned fire chariots, mostly on unthinking quests for satisfaction to buy or sell. His songs stopped the inexorable parade for a brief time. It was in many ways an act of courage. He brought the surroundings into a brief awareness of addiction to speed, consumption, and the pursuit of some unnamable thing of the future (Stiegler, 2013, pp. 38–39). To be halted is to realize at some level, for a few moments, that addiction and the void or default that lies underneath. Awareness of our finitude can evoke a deeper sense of shame and guilt for our plight and a sense of responsibility to our ancestors and future generations. This is the vision of a moral future. The appearance of the man singing gospel had somehow, for a brief time, placed the speed world of commerce and consumption into question. There was a joy in his tones, like a proud African American preacher, "forged in the fiery furnace" of slavery (Chandler, 2017, p. 159). That memory still inspires and intrigues me.

Reflections: the singularity of being

Who was this man who sang gospel in the middle of the street? Was his act an act of madness? The mind wants to capture and then dismiss what disrupts experience, have it 'wriggling on a pin,' captured in a cliché. Was he on a drug high, perhaps someone with an addiction who had been in a local halfway house, rebelling against the constraints of a drug program, imbibing some of the cannabis products readily available on 15th Street? Did he have a 'mood disorder' and was out of medicated control? It was clear that he had a religious background. Might he be a frustrated preacher, looking for a place to express his calling? Was his behavior merely a manifestation of the politics and the confrontational dynamic of race?

'Madness' resists definition (Hinton, 2007, 2009). To quote Derrida (Stiegler, 2019, p. 145; Derrida, 1978, p. 60), "From its very first breath, speech, submitted to the temporal rhythm and reawakening, is able to open the space for speech only by enclosing madness." That is, *madness calls forth speech*; "it creates a caesura and a wound that *open up* life as *historicity in general*" (Derrida, 1978, p. 54). Without 'madness,' things stay the same.

In his 'madness,' I strongly believe that this man expressed the best aspect of the human race. His appearance on the street of machines was a singular act of 'mad' imagination, and, "singularity expresses the individual's nonnegotiable distinctiveness, eccentricity, or idiosyncrasy. . . . It opens to layers of rebelliousness that indicate that there are components of human life that exceed the realm of normative sociality" (Ruti, 2010, p. 1113, 2014, pp. 297–314).

Our situational reactions are heavily influenced by the past, but some people are able to visualize, to enact, something that shines forth as unique, a thread of emergence of a new dimension of being. "It is precisely human creative activity that makes the human being a creature oriented toward the future, creating the future and thus altering his own present" (Vygotsky, 2004, p. 9; Zittoun et al., 2020, p. 5). I am indebted to this courageous man whom I briefly encountered on the streets of my city. His imaginative act evoked an interlude in the course of time that was free of the sway of the 'machinic unconscious' (Stiegler, 2016, p. 127). He helped me glimpse a future to come.

Historical unconscious/chattel slavery

My experiences with the man in the street evoke layers of what one might call the 'historical unconscious' (Zeddies, 2002; Frie, 2020, p. 5). Intertwined with these levels is the obvious fact that the gospel-singing man was an African American with all the sad, complex, and heroic history that entails. His performance provoked not only an awareness of the prosthetic creatures we are, compensating with our speedy omnipotence, but also the shameful heritage of chattel slavery in North America. This primal shame was certainly a major reason why his presence was disruptive. His presence evoked many levels of historical truth as well as our tendency to flee from it. To write history is to write trauma and to begin to own unclaimed experience (Caruth, 1996; Hinton, 2006; LaCapra, 2014). That is a difficult, gut-wrenching task. I am a white man, and although I have been involved in racial equality activities since my teenage years, the shame of that history still jolts me.

The evolution of chattel slavery – the commodification of human beings – began in North America in the 17th century. It is important to remember that this perverse institution coincided in time with the evolution of modern capitalism and the invention of computer-like machines and automated technology (Autor, 2001, pp. 3–4; Kolchin, 2016). The slave was a cog in the machine.

"Joy Songs, Trumpet Blasts, and Hallelujah Shouts" have been essential elements of the African American preaching tradition (Stewart, 1997). That inspiration kept hope alive and nurtured a sense of self and future amidst the chronic terrors of racism. When a person is reduced to nothing, a mere thing of a master, it forces them to face the raw reality of the human condition (George, 2018, p. 281, 2016, p. 70). It is that proud tradition that the man on 15th conveyed.

Gospel music epitomizes the enduring depth and creativity of a pertinent African American culture. Its African roots, combined with Christian themes, represent a continuity with a past before slavery as well as something new and unique. It is a social music that calls for responses from the listeners so that they feel actively engaged. That responsiveness, with its play with discourse and language, is also very much a part of the spirit of jazz and blues. It is a democratic wellspring, a togetherness of audience and preacher or performer, incarnating a vision of hope both in the present and into the future. In a broader sense, it is a community of joy and a celebration of the creative vitality of the human race.

The man who sang gospel in the street brought the mad rush of things to a stop for a moment, proudly yet humbly offering his own perspective, drawing attention to another possibility, a slowing down, and a hint of the joy that could emerge if given a chance. He shared a gift of possibility and joy, created amidst the catastrophic losses and cruelties of enslavement. The event will stay in my mind the rest of my life, especially in light of what later ensued with COVID-19.

Epilogue: COVID-19 and miasma

As I was writing this chapter, life in Seattle and in the world radically shifted. The parade of cars on 15th Street vanished. A few scattered pedestrians scurry about the sidewalk, mostly wearing masks, alert and fearful that anyone might come close. The lively shops are closed except for grocery stores and pharmacies. A mood of miasma, a sense of deadly pollution, has come upon the land in the form of a deadly viral pandemic: COVID-19.

Twenty-five hundred years ago, during a plague in Athens, Thucydides observed (Thucydides, 2019, p. 51; Manoussakis, 2020, p. 2):

> It was appalling how rapidly men caught the infection, dying like sheep if they attended on one another; and this was the principal cause of mortality.

At the present time we are living this reality, much like the ancient Greeks.

The virus is one of huge phylum of entities, a thing so tiny that it can barely be imagined (Huerta-Cepas et al., 2019). There are more viruses than stars in the universe (Wu, 2020). Philosophers debate whether viruses are actually forms of life because they cannot replicate on their own but must use biological life for reproduction (Koonin & Starokadomsky, 2016). We give each one a number and create virtual depictions of its structure to provide a reassuring sense of a manageable reality. However, it persists in its aura of an unassimilable real. This unknown thing pervades and disrupts our land and like our ruler has great resistance to the science and truth.

In *Oedipus Rex*, Thebes was also in the grips of miasma because their King Oedipus avoided the truth, taking attempts to speak the truth as a personal insult. The citizens encouraged his denial, and he became extremely angry when the wise men spoke of truth. He believed only in his personal will. When Oedipus finally learnt the terrible truth, it resulted in a profound personal and collective anguish.

This mythic story is a striking parallel with the present times. In the United States we have a president who has a violent and visceral disdain for the truth. The free press is denigrated or eliminated and scapegoats are blamed for any problem. Immigrants are violently mistreated, sometimes kept in cages as if they were the disease causing the problems in the land. They are treated like 'vermin' and are scapegoated and denigrated. Another disturbing truth of the pandemic is its disproportionate effects on the poor around the world, including many African Americans (Eligon et al., 2020). It often feels like a continuation of the heritage of slavery.

Our land is polluted, and we are in a crisis of truth. The pandemic has struck us and the whole world. Scientific knowledge, an aspect of truth that might save the land, is disparaged like an enemy. Truth nourishes the soul but can also be painful and shattering; it is our only real hope in times when endless lies pollute the land (Grotstein, 2004).

Like the age of Oedipus, our age is in a crisis of truth, and the disruption of a man singing gospel in the street was a small, disruptive harbinger of such truth, the truth of the pollution and madness of our world, the truth of our blind pursuit of money and power, and the terrible truth of slavery.

A black man singing gospel brought conventional traffic to a halt for a time on 15th Street and also brought a new possibility. It is uncertain whether our leaders and our populace have the capacity to endure the suffering that the future might entail. Truth itself is not a peaceful companion and often evokes deep disturbances and violent perturbations (Grotstein, 2004).

In the future we may see glorification of a 'lost' group unity that never was, with continued persecution of minorities accused of bringing 'impurity' to the land, and perhaps flight to a parental regime that will maintain a facade of unity by algorithmic government and suppression of dissent. The dire unknown of COVID-19, with its economic and psychosocial impacts, will likely foment an exaggeration of these tendencies (Sly, 2020).

The challenge will be to maintain the stance of critical thought and reflection amidst these illusions, that is, to hold fast to a respect for truth. It possible that the capacity for critical thought has so deteriorated that the center cannot hold (Sly, 2020). It may swing widely and over an extended period of time. However, the man on 15th provided a fragment of hopeful counsel that a future with care, joy, and meaning can emerge from the worst of ominous transitions. He was also a living reminder of neglected truth.

Notes

1 I am using 'machine' to describe an imaginal entity that conveys an embodied sense of technology (Krakauer, 2020). For instance, we get angry at our computer when it crashes. In a much broader way, when we think of the World Wide Web, we think of a concrete web of energy or light encircling the Earth. In these times, it conveys more and more a computational capitalism in which everything is calculable; we are all cogs in an economic machine, the opposite of care. Such an invisible algorithmic governability gives rise to images of a 'deep state' running things. This eventuates in a sense of victimhood and a proneness to totalitarian rule by 'saviors' (Stiegler, 2016, p. 23). *A dream that thinks can* provide hints and shreds of new realizations for a future worth living (ibid, p. 72). That is the core topic of this chapter.

I will use *technos* to imply all the uses that the human species has developed to be involved creatively with the environment, endogenous and genetic, or the exogenous givens of existence. This contrasts with pure nature that comes into presence on its own (Doucet, 2017, p. 3). I reserve *technology* to signify the mushrooming developments in memory and calculation since the coming forth of the Jacquard Loom in the early 19th century.

2 This encounter took place a year before a Minneapolis policeman murdered George Floyd, an African American, during an arrest on May 25, 2020. There were extensive national and international Black Lives Matter protests and demonstrations, including many in Seattle, and often centered on Capitol Hill. The present chapter was written two months before the death of George Floyd.

3 I had extensive experience with psychotic patients during my residency at Stanford and in my early years of practice. R. D. Laing was a visiting professor. What is 'psychotic' and what is 'normal' is a difficult question. My own take on it is based on a gut-level feeling of how much a person is prone to go so far off the rails as to be unable to minimally adapt to everyday life. I do not romanticize madness. We all have mad parts, and these can be generative of creative works (Kristeva, 1987, p. 87; Hinton, 2007). Someone who cannot sublimate significant dimensions of their madness into creative, eccentric adaptation is usually in a chronically unhappy state – not a romantic exponent of underground 'truth.'

4 Levinas described 'synchronous' time as the time of sameness, of just going on, of everyday being. The disruption of the 'in-synch' traffic on 15th Street was 'diachronic.' In diachronicity, "the self [is] pierced . . . by time's transcendent dimensions, the irrecuperable past and the unforeseeable future" (Gant & Williams, 2002, p. 44; Severson, 2013).

5 Eric Santner mentions the 'cringe' as a posture of the human being as a *creature* who is regarded as outside the law (2006, p. 86). I take this as feeling 'caught' in a sort of anonymous, collective gaze and that brings into doubt any hope of recourse to ordinary authority or justice. It is akin to the 'downcast eyes' of shame but with an extra twist of exposure without recourse (Jay, 1994). It is related to the experience of those who are seen as 'outside the law,' such as racial minorities, scapegoated groups, and others who are seen as outside the normal structures of the state.

6 I am referring here to Lacan's term *extimité*. It implies that what is 'exterior' is also, potentially, the most intimate. That is, 'inside' and 'outside' are not so distinct. The enigmatic otherness of the 'inside' is equally the enigmatic otherness of the 'outside' (Miller, 1994). The lack of unity or certainty regarding the boundary between 'inside' and 'outside' is also related to Freud's concept of the *uncanny* (Barnaby, 2014). In the setting of my neighborhood, my emotional response transcended the 'inner' or 'outer.' The unusual event was indeed a bit uncanny.

7

> For Stiegler [this] refers to the broader analytical process by which temporal and perceptual flows of all kinds are rendered discrete and reproducible through being spatialized, to the grammatization of the manual gestures of the worker or the craftsman that are spatialized [by] being programmed into the machinery of the industrial revolution, and finally to what is unfolding right now: the grammatization of 'everything' made possible by the inscription of binary code into central processing units composed of silicon.
>
> (Ross, 2018, pp. 20–21)

8 The automobile is a useful tool that has gotten out of control. We don't have to recreate its fire on our own; it does that for us and translates that released energy to the wheels. It always 'remembers' and incarnates the human history with fire and tools in many ways (how upset we get when it won't start!). We merge with our mighty tools and feel safe and powerful behind the wheel and within its metal armor. It becomes a question of how much we control our technologies or they control us.

The automobile is also a symbol of unthinking mass production, consumerism, and the specter of climate change. Our complex technological tools often seem to function as a kind of 'grammar of our minds' (Stiegler, 2013, p. 19ff).

In the everyday sense, most of us enjoy our cars and find them extremely useful! Stiegler often uses the *Pharmakon*, which refers to the idea that things are both poison and cure. This is the best way to view the automobile. Now the 'poison' side has become a threat to our survival as a species. It is a good metaphor for our ambivalent relation to *technos* or *technology* in the present era (see note 1). The question is, how much have we become subservient to the remarkable tools we have created? Has the tool become the master? Do we drive it, or does it drive us? (ibid, p. 37)

9 "Genealogy is a form of historical critique, designed to overturn our norms by revealing their origins" (Hill, R. K., 1998). It was pioneered by Nietzsche and Foucault.

"To produce the shock and confusion that are needed to help subjects to disengage from [their customary contexts and presuppositions] techniques of estrangement and confrontation with the unfamiliar . . . have to be used" (Saar, 2008).

10 Later on, the behavior of the human race was so destructive and turbulent that Zeus feared the species would destroy itself. Hoping to preserve them, he sent Hermes to impart to humans the qualities of respect for others (*aidōs*: shame, modesty, respect; a sense of finitude; and *dikē*, a sense of justice; Stiegler, 1996, p. 200).

11 The Zinjanthropian was discovered in 1959: it is an Austrolanthropian, dating back 1.75 million years, whose oldest biped ascendants go back 3.6 million years. It weighs about 30 kilos. It is a true biped: it has an occipital hole exactly perpendicular to the top of its cranial box. It has by then freed its rear legs for motricity: they are henceforth essentially destined to make tools and to expression, that is, to *exteriorization*. Its skeleton was found with its tools in the Olduvai ravine. Based on these facts, Leroi-Gourhan showed that what constitutes the humanity of the human, and which is a break in the history of life, is *the process of the exteriorization of the living*. That which up to then was a part of the living, namely, conditions of predation and defence, passes outside the domain of the living: the struggle for life – or rather for existence – can no longer be limited to the Darwinian scene. The human conducts this struggle that we could say is spiritual in nature, by nonbiological organs, that is, by *artificial organs that are techniques* (http://arsindustrialis.org/anamnesis-and-hypomnesis).

12 George Hogenson has discussed a somewhat similar idea that influenced Jung's ideas on evolution (2001, pp. 591–611).

13

The substitution of machinery for repetitive human labor has of course been a central thrust of technological change since (at least) the industrial revolution. . . . What computer capital uniquely contributes to this process is the capability to perform symbolic processing, that is, to calculate, store, retrieve, sort and act upon information. Although symbolic processing depends on little more than Boolean algebra, the remarkable generality of this tool allows computers to supplant or augment human cognition in a vast range of information processing tasks that had historically been the mind's exclusive dominion. In economic terms, advances in information technology have sharply lowered the price of accomplishing procedural-cognitive tasks (i.e., rules-based reasoning). Accordingly, computers increasingly substitute for the routine information processing, communications and coordinating functions performed by clerks, cashiers, telephone operators, bank tellers, bookkeepers, and other handlers of repetitive information-processing tasks.

References

Alvis, J. W. (2018). "Making Sense of Heidegger's 'Phenomenology of the Inconspicuous' or Napparent." (*Phänomenologie des Unscheinbaren*). *Continental Philosophy Review*, 42, 211–238.

Autor, D. H., Levy, F. & Murnane, R. (2001). "The Skill Content of Recent Technological Change: An Empirical Exploration." Massachusetts Institute of Technology, Department of Economics, Working Paper Series.

Bloch, M. (2008). "Why Religion Is Nothing Special but Is Central." *Philosophical Transactions of The Royal Society B.*, 363, 2055–2061. DOI:10.1098/rstb.2008.0007.

Caruth, C. (1996). *Unclaimed Experience*. Baltimore: Johns Hopkins University Press.

Chandler, D. J. (2017). "African American Spirituality: Through Another Lens." *Journal of Spiritual Formation & Soul Care*, 10, 2, 159–181.

Derrida, J. (1967/1978). "Cogito and the History of Madness." In *Writing and Difference*. Trans. Alan Bass, pp. 31–63. Chicago: University of Chicago Press.

Doucet, T. A. (2017). "Heidegger, Foucault & Taylor: A Phenomenology of Technology and Being." Field Exam Question #3, The University of Texas at Dallas.

Eligon, J., Burch, A. D. S., Searcey, D. & Oppel Jr., R. A. (2020). "Black Americans Face Alarming Rates of Coronavirus Infections in Some States." *New York Times*, April 7. www.nytimes.com/2020/04/07/us/coronavirus-race.html?smid=em-share

Frie, R. (2020). "Facing the Nazi Past: Silence, Memory, and Inhabiting Responsibility." *Psychoanalysis, Self and Context*, 15, 1, 5–9. DOI:10.1080/24720038.2019.1688331.

Gant, E. E. & Williams, R. N. (2002). *Psychology for the Other*. Pittsburgh: Duquesne University Press.

George, S. (2016). *Trauma and Race: A Lacanian Study of African-American Racial Identity*. Waco: Baylor University Press.

———. (2018). "*Jouissance* and Discontent: A meeting of psychoanalysis, race and American slavery." *Psychoanalysis, Culture & Society*, 23, 3, 267–289.

Grotstein, J. S. (2004). "The Seventh Servant: The Implications of a Truth Drive in Bion's Theory of 'O'." *International Journal of Psychoanalysis*, 85, 5, 1081–1101.

Hill, R. K. (1998). "Genealogy." In *Routledge Encyclopedia of Philosophy*. New York: Taylor and Francis. DOI:10.4324/9780415249126-DE024-1.

Hinton, L. (2006). "The Sheltering Sky." In *The San Francisco Jung Institute Library Journal*, vol. 25, 4, pp. 61–67. Berkeley: University of California Press.

———. (2007). "Black Holes, Uncanny Spaces, and Radical Shifts in Awareness." *Journal of Analytical Psychology*, 52, 433–447.

———. (2009). "The Enigmatic Signifier and the Decentred Subject." *Journal of Analytical Psychology*, 54, 637–657.

Hogenson, G. (2001). "The Baldwin Effect: A Neglected Influence on C. G. Jung's Evolutionary Theory." *Journal of Analytical Psychology*, 46, 591–611.

Huerta-Cepas, J., Szklarczk, D., Heller, D., Hernández-Plaza, A., Fborkorslund, S. K., Cook. Mende, D. R., Letunic, I., Rattel, T., Jensen, L. J., von Mering, C. & Bork, P. (2019). "eggNOG 5.0: A Hierarchical, Functionally and Phylogenetically Annotated Orthology Resource Based on 5090 Organisms and 2502 Viruses." *Nucleic Acids Research*, 27, Database Issue D309–D314. DOI:10.1093/nar/gky1085.

Jay, M. (1994). *Downcast Eyes: The Denigration of Vision in Twentieth Century French Thought*. Berkeley: University of California Press.

Kolchin, P. (2016). "Slavery, Commodification, and Capitalism." *American History*, 44, 217–226. Baltimore: Johns Hopkins University Press.

Koonin, E. V. & Starokadomsky. (2016). "Are Viruses Alive? The Replicator Paradigm Sheds Decisive Light on an Old but Misguided Question." *Studies in the History and Philosophy of Science Part C.*, 59, 125–134.

Krakauer, D. C. (2020). "At the Limits of Thought." *Aeon*, April 20.

LaCapra, D. (2014). *Writing History, Writing Trauma*. Baltimore: Johns Hopkins University Press.

Leroi-Gourhans, A. (1993*). Gesture and Speech*. Trans. Anna Bostock Berger. Cambridge, MA: MIT Press.

Manoussakis, J. P. (2020). "The City is Sick." *Church Life Journal* (University of Notre Dame), 1–8.

Maybank, A. (2020). "The Pandemic's Missing Data." *New York Times*, April 7. www.nytimes.com/2020/04/07/opinion/coronavirus-blacks.html?smid=em-share

McGowan, T. (2016). *Capitalism and Desire: The Psychic Cost of Free Markets*. New York: Columbia University Press.

McHenry, H. M. (2009). "Human Evolution." In *Evolution: The First Four Billion Years*. Eds. Michael Ruse & Joseph Travis, p. 263. Cambridge, MA: The Belknap Press of Harvard University Press.

Miller, J.-A. (1994). "Extimité." In *Lacanian Theory of Discourse*. Eds. Mark Bracher, Marshall Alcorn, Ronald Corthell & Françoise Massardier-Kenney, pp. 74–87. New York: New York University Press.

Nielsen, M. A. (2017). *What Makes Us Who We Are: On the Relationship Between Human Existence and Technics, Thinking and Technology, and the Philosopher and the Technician*. Unpublished Master's Thesis, University of Oslo, Oslo.

Ross, D. (2018). "Introduction." In *The Neganthropocene*. Ed. B. Stiegler, pp. 5–32. London: Open Humanities Press.

Ruti, M. (2010). "The Singularity of Being: Lacan and the Immortal Within." *Journal of the American Psychoanalytic Association*, 58, 1113. DOI:10.1177/0003065110396083.

———. (2014). "In Search of Defiant Subjects: Resistance, Rebellion, and Political Agency." In Lacan and Marcuse, *Psychoanalysis, Culture & Society*, 19, 297–314.

Saar, M. (2008). "Understanding Genealogy: History, Power, and the Self." *Journal of the Philosophy of History*, 2, 295–314. Leiden: Brill NV.

Santner, E. L. (2006). *On Creaturely Life*. Chicago and London: The University of Chicago Press.

Severson, E. (2013). *Levinas's Philosophy of Time: Gift, Responsibility, Diachrony, Hope*. Pittsburgh: Duquesne University Press.

Simondon, G. (1965). "Culture and Technics" translated by Olivia Lucca Fraser: revised by Giovanni Menegalle, in *Radical Philosophy*, 189, January–February 2015, 17–23.

Slaby, J. (2020). "The Weight of History: From Heidegger to Afro-Pessimism." In *Phenomenology as Performative Exercise*. Eds. L. Guidi & T. Rentsch. Leiden/Boston: Brill NV.

Sly, L. (2020). "Stirrings of Unrest Around the World Could Portend Turmoil as Economies Collapse." *Washington Post*, April 19. www.washingtonpost.com/world/coronavirus-protests-lebanon-india-iraq/2020/04/19/1581dde4–7e5f-11ea-84c2–0792d8591911_story.html.

Stewart, C. F. (1997). *Joy Songs, Trumpet Blasts, and Hallelujah Shouts*. Lima, OH: CS Publishing Company.

Stiegler, B. (1996/1998). *Technics and Time, 1: The Fault of Epimetheus*. Stanford: Stanford University Press.

———. (2013). *What Makes Life Worth Living: On Pharmacology*. Malden, MA: Polity Press.

———. (2014). *Symbolic Misery (Book 1); The Hyperindustrial Epoch*. Trans. Barnaby Norman. Malden, MA: Polity Press.

———. (2016). *Automatic Society, Volume 1: The Future of Work*. Trans. Dan Ross. Malden, MA: Polity Press.

———. (2019). *The Age of Disruption: Technology and Madness in Computational Capitalism*. Malden, MA: Polity Press.

Suddendorf, T., Addis, D. R. & Corballis, M. C. (2009). "Mental Time Travel and the Shaping of the Human Mind." *Philosophical Transactions of the Royal Society B.*, 364, 1317–1324. DOI:10.1098/rstb.2008.0301.

Thucydides. (2019/431 BC). *The History of the Peloponnesian War*. Transl. Richard Craw-
ley. Compass Circle.

Vesco, S. (2015). "Collective Disindividuation and/or Barbarism: Technics and Proletarianization." *Boundary*, 2, 42, 2. Duke University Press.

Vygotsky, L. S. (2004). "Imagination and Creativity in Childhood." *Journal of Russian &
East European Psychology*, 42, 1, 7–97. DOI:10.1080/10610405.2004.11059210.

Williams-Jones, P. (1975). "A Crystallization of the Black Aesthetic." *Ethnomusicology*,
19, 3, 373–385.

Wilson, J. & Bayón, M. (2016). "Black Hole Capitalism." *City*, 20, 3, 350–367. London:
Routledge.

Wu, K. J. (2020). "There Are More Viruses Than Stars in the Universe. Why Do Only
Some Infect Us?" *National Geographic*, April 15. www.nationalgeographic.com/sci
ence/2020/04/factors-allow-viruses-infect-humans-coronavirus.html.

Zeddies, T. J. (2002). "Behind, Beneath, Above, and Beyond: The Historical Unconscious."
Journal of the American Academy of Psychoanalysis, 30, 2, 211–229.

Zittoun, T., Glăveanu, V. & Hawlina, H. (2020). "A Sociocultural Perspective on Imagination." In *Cambridge Handbook of the Imagination*. Ed. Anna Abraham. Cambridge:
Cambridge University Press.

Zwart, H. (2017). "'Extimate' Technologies and Techno-Cultural Discontent: A Lacanian
Analysis of Pervasive Gadgets." *Techné: Research in Philosophy and Technology*, 21,
1, 24–55.

Chapter 2

On caesura, temporality and ego-destructive shame

Ominous transitions in everyday life

Jeffrey Eaton

How often do you feel now-here, rooted in your body, attuned to your environment and open to the present moment as it unfolds? The capacity to be present to what any moment might call forth is often obscured by habits of attention that repeat familiar expected patterns. In fact, every day contains the possibility of ominous transitions.

At some moments, transitions may be large like a life-threatening illness, the loss of a job, the birth of a child or the death of a loved one. These kinds of events are turning points. They can evoke anxiety and uncertainty. Turning points, however, are not always large, dramatic events. Some transitions may seem tiny, like awareness of a surprising new thought, a shift from one mood to another or the experience of a novel, perhaps disturbing sensation.

The English psychoanalyst W. R. Bion described what he called a "caesura", a moment that can both separate and connect (Bion, 1989). His focus shifted from attention to the self and the object to the link between. Investigating the complexity of changing qualities of emotional links enhances awareness of uncertainty as well as possibility.

In what follows I draw on moments in the life and work of W. R. Bion. I do not offer a systematic presentation of his ideas. Instead, I share impressionistic glimpses to explore the notion of caesura. I include personal reflections to investigate links among the recognition of a caesura, temporality and a specific and devastating affect called ego-destructive shame. The combination of these factors can illuminate moments of ominous transition in everyday life.

A caesura creates a crossroads. Imagine a young man asking his girlfriend to marry him. The story could be told from the point of view of the man or from the point of view of the woman. Perhaps the man is unsure of what the woman will say, whereas the woman wonders why the man has waited so long to ask. We usually think about the meaning of an experience from the point of view of the patient in the session or, in this example, from the point of view of the characters in a vignette. Emphasis on a caesura shifts attention to the action happening *between* self and other. In this example, asking a question, "Will you marry me?" is a moment of caesura, of an ominous transition. The question creates a space of uncertainty where many possible futures hang in the balance. Whether the answer is yes or no, there is now a time before the question and a time after the answer. The familiar is not always the best guide in choosing what the next step will be. What is at stake is not what the right answer is but what kind of life can or will unfold. Shifting focus to the caesura highlights the direction of an experience, its movement and momentum.

Bion fought in many major battles in World War I. His war experience haunted him to the end of his life. His autobiography, *The Long Weekend* (1985), written late in life, is filled with harrowing recollections of combat. He describes nearly dying, dissociative states that follow terror, and emotional numbness after witnessing fellow soldiers violently die, sometimes literally in his arms. Likewise, his three-part novel, *A Memoir of the Future* (1991), contains searing moments of the personal experience of combat.

In *The Bhagavad Gita* (Miller, 1986), a text that Bion admired, Arjuna pauses on the battlefield before initiating attack. In this caesura an extended dialogue takes place with Lord Krishna. Arjuna seeks Krishna's guidance. He expresses many reservations and questions. It is a dramatic dialogue, and Arjuna wrestles with conflicting values, loyalties, emotions and anxieties. It dramatizes the struggle over how and when to act.

As a soldier there is a time before the war and a time after. There are the days before the battles of Ypres, Cambrai and Amiens and their aftermaths. There are poignant moments like waking on a quiet morning and hours later being immersed in the chaos of battle. Caesura must have been an impressive reality for Bion when he did not know if he would live another minute, much less to the end of the day.

Bion was awarded one of the highest honours in the British Army, the Distinguished Service Order for courageous action in combat. In *The Long Weekend* Bion repeatedly castigates himself for what he regards as his cowardice, even though others considered him a hero. His subjective experience was that he had no control over his actions while in combat. This was a source of profound, disorienting shame. Unlike Arjuna, Bion had no Krishna to turn to when seeking perspective and meaning.

After battle, Bion felt confusion, horror, guilt and shame at surviving when so many others did not. He felt a sense of meaninglessness threaten to engulf him. As Lord Krishna explains, some men of "dark inertia, sacrifice to corpses and to ghosts" (Miller, 1987, p. 137). The revelations of the Nazi death camps after World War II and the explosions of atomic bombs over Hiroshima and Nagasaki only deepened Bion's wariness about human beings and the cruelty they are capable of. His emphasis on the differentiation of a psychotic from a non-psychotic part of the personality perhaps represents an early intuition of the importance of caesura.

The trauma of his combat experience could not be put in the past. I believe there was a part of Bion's personality that was always trapped at war in the timeless aftermath of the battles he improbably survived. This traumatized aspect of Bion's personality may be linked to his feeling of psychic death and to the challenge of going on living afterwards (Bion, 1985). I think Bion was keenly sensitive to a caesura between meaning ←→ meaninglessness. The threat of meaninglessness can sponsor a reification of meaning that is equally destructive to the search for truth. Bion's career as a psychoanalyst records the construction of a narrow path between the twin dangers of fundamentalism and nihilism he called "thinking".

Before the internet, I wrote letters to my friend Paul, who lived in Germany. Long-distance calls were expensive, so we talked only two or three times a year. Letters sustained our connection. I used a typewriter, folded the finished sheets of paper, and placed them in a blue airmail envelope. I walked to the post office to buy special airmail stamps. I knew it would take a week for my letter to reach Munich; a week for Paul to receive, read and reply to it; and at least another week before his letter would arrive. We could usually expect about one letter a month from each other.

The experience of time can be measured objectively, like the time it takes to receive a letter from Germany. It can also be experienced subjectively. The subjective experience of time (temporality) is often outside of awareness. It is not necessarily repressed or split off but simply unattended to. Bringing attention to the subjective experience of time opens new avenues of self-experience.

One of the things that awareness of a span of time might make possible is a space for the work of memory. I am not a visual person, so it is hard for me to call up a vivid image of an absent object. To the extent that I can, it requires concentrated effort and is not instantaneous. The concrete sensuous details of Paul's image, voice and movement cannot be easily rendered in memory. However, the emotional significance of our relationship is a vivid continuing link sustained by our correspondence.

The gap between letters was a kind of caesura; it both separated and connected us. I was sometimes frustrated when waiting for Paul's letters. However, I also felt a keen sense of anticipation. Our friendship never got lost across the gap of time or space. Writing each letter created a new opportunity for reflection, imagination, and memory. It involved trying to keep him in mind. He gradually became a kind of welcoming internal presence.

Looking back, I think that writing was part of an unconscious process of creating *an internal workspace*. In the act of writing, I could explore my experience, elaborate it, and express it. I got to know my own mind better because I had a trusted audience.

Whether writing or speaking, you must risk finding out what you think. Without a welcoming internal object to sponsor your exploration, you may encounter a caesura that can stop you in your tracks. Some people report suffering under the weight of a demand that they should always already know what they think. They feel forbidden to take the time necessary to find out. For some people there even seems to be a terror of punishment, perhaps for the hubris of trying to think your own thoughts. In such circumstances, the act of thinking is somehow entangled with a deep sense of shame.

The house where I lived as a little boy had a long driveway. There was a split rail cedar fence near the end of the driveway that separated our property from a busy road. I could play in the front yard, but I was told not to go past the rose garden and outside the fence.

One day, when I was still quite young, I was playing on the wrong side of the fence. My mother, who was gardening, looked for me and did not see me. Suddenly I heard her stern and fearful voice call out. I ran back to her, and she scolded me harshly. She sent me back into the house. I felt a terrible sense of shame, although I could not name the feeling at that time.

A few minutes later, she came inside and found me. She explained that I was not to go near the street because it was dangerous. Cars coming down the road might not see me. She wanted me to understand why she had been so harsh. I was not "bad". She was trying to protect me. Even as a young child, I could sense the impact of fear on her.

Shame has an important role in healthy emotional development. Under certain conditions, it can help modulate a child's excitement and impulsiveness. If a parent has a trusting relationship with a child, then shame can be a way of getting the child's attention. Shame acts as a necessary brake before a child has the ego strength to be self-reflective.

When shame can act as a signal, it can be one ingredient in the complex relational process of helping a child begin to learn self-regulation. A shameless child is a child at risk. A shameless child will have trouble not only with teachers and authority figures but also with sharing, co-operating, playing, and fitting in with peers. Accepting limits is necessary to adapt to social life. Shameless children have trouble tolerating limits. They tend to feel that limits are a personal insult or attack.

I remember a high-spirited friend who hated limits. He was told it was dangerous to climb too high in trees. But he was a dare devil and had the attitude "I can do anything". Once he climbed too high in an old Madrona tree. The branch cracked, and he fell and broke his arm. After that he had a new respect for the concepts: "danger" and "pain" – which before had just been words.

Ego-destructive shame is different from ordinary shame. It does not function as a signal. Instead, it is an unbearably painful affect. It feels like an attack that will destroy the self.

Sean is good looking, polite and shy. He was diagnosed with autism as a child. He attends college but is socially isolated. He is reticent to speak even with the people whom he trusts. Face-to-face contact feels intimidating.

He comes to his sessions in a hurry. He apologizes if he is a minute or two late. He takes off his shoes and arranges the pillows on the couch. He always seems to be trying to make everything "just right". He lies still except when he twirls his long hair with his fingers.

A long time passes before Sean begins to speak. His silence feels like an ominous transition. I wonder to myself if he is gathering his thoughts or escaping to some faraway place in his imagination. Before I am about to speak, Sean yells, "Please, just let me think!"

In this moment it is as if Sean is Oedipus facing a Sphinx-like figure in me. He seems to feel that by being present to each other, I am demanding that he answer a riddle and that he is in danger of a violent confrontation. I describe this, and Sean says politely, "No, I'm not afraid of *you*, Jeff". Suddenly, it is as if we are in another session. The shift took place almost instantly. Sean does not withdraw; he goes "elsewhere".

His feelings are complex. He yearns to return to a childhood that never was. Sean says that time is his enemy. He would step out of his body if he could. Existing in time shames him. It robs him of a sense of uninterrupted comfort. What he calls memory, I think, is idealized in his imagination. His childhood was not the paradise he claims to remember. He contends that his imagination *is* more real than the external world. For Sean, shame does not function as a signal. Instead, ego-destructive shame feels like an attack that comes from out of nowhere, at any time and from any direction.

The first intimations of intimacy probably occur before birth through the capacity of a foetus to bond with the presence of a mother's voice. The song and dance tones and rhythms of mother's voice probably transmit her emotions and even fantasies about her unborn child. Foetal registration of the presence and absence of a mother's voice may play a role in preparation for the discovery of her as a separate object after birth.

During infancy, the interactions between a mother and her baby slowly develop a floor for emotional experience (Eaton, 2014). Infants are unable to regulate emotion and anxiety all on their own and so depend upon the care provided by others to establish a reliable transformation from distress to comfort. The realization of a reliable transformation from distress to comfort, sponsored by a mother's sensitive attention and care, allows an infant to shift attention gradually outward to explore and learn about the world.

Bion emphasized that an infant's primitive communications of distress require registration, reflection and reply from another. Infants who can be soothed after expressing distress develop an unconscious faith in the efficacy of communication. Slowly a floor for emotional experience develops through the myriad contingent communications shared and embedded in daily interactions.

There are many ways, however, that a floor for emotional experience can be interrupted during its construction. Trauma overwhelms a nascent ego, but it also interrupts the facilitating link *between* mother and infant. It creates a disturbing caesura. Trauma jeopardizes the impulse to seek and connect with another. It problematizes how to connect and separate, to approach and withdraw. In the most difficult scenarios, it can create a frozen paralysis around connection.

I think that one of the deepest forms of anxiety involves a link between two people in pain. In this scenario, what it means to be emotionally connected is to experience an amplification of distress. A patient feels that their pain cannot be tolerated or soothed by another, and in addition, the very act of communicating can evoke retaliation from the other.

Where a floor for emotional experience should be, instead there is a mysterious echoing darkness, an unconscious background of catastrophe. In this scenario, approaching connecting emotionally with another separate person evokes with greater intensity the uncanny threat of disaster.

Bion explored this painful and disturbing form of transference and described what he called an obstructive object relationship (Bion, 1984). An obstructive object is a projective identification rejecting object that has become internalized and now is ego destructive (Eaton, 2011). An obstructive object configuration has dire consequences for communication, both interpersonally and within the self.

Perhaps the most important thing to appreciate about an obstructive object relationship is that in the transference any sense of emotional contact with the analyst evokes anticipation of immediate catastrophe. That is because the link between self and other is an actual or anticipated experience of unmodified pain. It is not just that the patient suffers. Distress is evoked in the analyst, and distress suffuses the atmosphere of the analytic field.

An obstructive object scenario can be pictured as the encounter of Oedipus with the Sphinx. Recall that Thebes had been plagued by the persecution of the Sphinx, who poses a riddle to people seeking entrance to the city. When the riddle cannot be solved, a citizen of Thebes is sacrificed (Edmonds, 1985). The meeting of Oedipus and the Sphinx is a caesura that results in the Sphinx killing herself by leaping to her death, while Oedipus becomes king of Thebes and marries Jocasta, who he will later shamefully learn is his mother. When Oedipus approaches the Sphinx to face the challenge of her riddle, what interests me is not the content of the riddle but the atmosphere of the encounter.

There are several famous paintings that imagine the encounter between Oedipus and the Sphinx. The Sphinx is a female monster, part bird, part lion and part woman. In Gustav Moreau's famous version, Oedipus and the Sphinx gaze directly into each other's eyes. The Sphinx clings to Oedipus almost like a lover. The painting suggests a mixture of erotic and violent energies in the link between them.

An equally important image comes from Jean Auguste Dominique Ingres. In this version Oedipus stands slightly bent beneath the Sphinx, who is perched higher at the entrance to a cave. Oedipus leans toward the monster with one finger pointing at her. As in the Moreau portrait, Oedipus is nearly naked, draped only by a tunic over his shoulder. At his foot is a dead body, one of the victims of the Sphinx, and in the background a frantic man calls out for Oedipus to flee. The atmosphere in this painting is of catastrophe as a background, while Oedipus and the Sphinx are matched in a battle of will and wits. They each have an expression of intense concentration which seems to shut out awareness of everything else. A variation on this image by the same artist shows Oedipus pointing down at skeletal remains, while the Sphinx turns her head away, eyes wide with surprise, perhaps in the moment after Oedipus has solved the riddle.

Finally, in a painting by François-Emile Ehrmann, Oedipus is shown with a look of shock, confusion, and perhaps even disgust, whereas the Sphinx is given a human face but one suffused with unmistakable predatory aggression. The atmosphere of this painting seems to emphasize a caesura between the beast and the human and to portray an experience at the edge of what can be tolerable or thinkable.

Some aspects of the Oedipus myth imply the importance of a feeling of profound ego-destructive shame. Fonagy and his co-authors (2003, p. 444) describe ego-destructive shame as an experience "tantamount to the destruction of self". Wille (2014) identifies an extreme form of shame he calls "the shame of existing". He writes (Wille, p. 710), "the shame of existing stems in my view from a disturbance of holding and handling right from birth, due to rejection and hatred of the baby by the mother and other primary objects". This dire feeling of ego-destructive shame, in my experience, accompanies an obstructive object scenario. It is symbolized in many aspects of the Oedipus story.

The Oedipus myth shows the conditions of an infantile catastrophe. Laius and Jocasta were forbidden to have a child, but they ignored the sanction against procreation imposed on Laius because of his shameful actions. After the birth of his son Oedipus, Laius became fearful of the consequences of ignoring the prohibition. He determined to have his infant son destroyed by giving him to a shepherd who was told to stake Oedipus to a hillside and leave him to die of exposure.

There are many variations of the story (Edmunds, 1996). In one version, Oedipus was rescued by a compassionate shepherd from an adjoining kingdom. He was taken to be raised by King Polybus and his queen, Merope, who Oedipus came to believe were his actual parents. Oedipus, ignorant of his origins, including his near death as an infant, has the trauma nonetheless inscribed in his very name, which means "swollen foot".

An obstructive object is an ego-destructive internal object that threatens the vulnerable infantile aspect of the self. It can be pictured as having three different levels of ego-destructive influence. There are probably unrepresented dimensions, as suggested by the plague that troubles Thebes. The three levels I draw attention to can be thought of as forms of unconscious phantasy saturated with ego-destructive shame and dramatized by three moments from the Oedipus story.

The first moment involves Jocasta agreeing to allow her son to be murdered. I call this a *maternal dimension* of ego-destructive shame. It takes the unconscious form of a conviction in a patient: "I have no right to exist". Wille (2014, p. 714) described it:

> The shame of existing concerns not only who or what I am or do, but the fact that I am. It concerns existence in itself and is therefore situated at one extreme of the continuum represented by the emotion of shame.

Patients with this form of unconscious phantasy cannot relax. They feel alien, unchosen, even inhuman, as if they have been exiled from the human tribe. They do not rest or sleep or feel a sense of "going on being". They are often constantly on the move, searching for a viable space to exist, or they have given up and collapsed into a kind of living psychic death. They avoid emotional contact with anyone. Emotional contact generates panic and fear of destruction, both toward self and of other.

The second moment involves Oedipus encountering the Sphinx. The Sphinx poses a riddle that must be solved. The riddle is the link between Oedipus and the Sphinx. In other words, connection or relationship is a kind of riddle that ends in the destruction of one of the participants. This shows what I call the *paternal dimension* of ego-destructive shame. It takes the unconscious form of a conviction in the patient: "I have no right to be in relationship". Patients with this form of unconscious ego-destructive shame always feel already intruded upon. They are hypersensitive and hypervigilant. They are always looking over their shoulders or around the next corner. They preemptively blow up connections because they cannot stand the "riddle" of communication. There is an ominous sense of a predator-prey link when emotional contact is made. Such patients generate fight-flight dynamics in the transference and are prone to action to evacuate their dread. They try to control others who they anticipate have violent intentions towards them. Their intrusive attempts to control the object constellate violent acting out or confrontation. They are never able to find a reliable space for thinking because of the intrusion of an internal shaming object that constantly undermines connection with self and other.

The third moment involves the recognition by Oedipus that he has married his mother and fathered children with her. The origin of his infantile catastrophe becomes clear to him. When he learns this, he blinds himself. This shows what I call the *parental dimension* of ego-destructive shame. It takes the unconscious form of a conviction in the patient that "I have no right to create anything". Patients with this form of unconscious ego-destructive shame undo whatever creative acts they attempt. They anticipate a rendezvous with a catastrophic discovery, so they withdraw, or they are flooded with grievances. No movement toward mourning is possible because grievance becomes a kind of carapace. They live on the edge of meaninglessness.

The impact of these forms of unconscious phantasy leads a person to withdraw from exploring or getting to know experience. There is a hatred of experience because of the pain it might inevitably reveal. Sharing and cooperating are impossible. Sometimes an illusion of omnipotence carries a person to many conventional achievements, but unspeakable loneliness dominates emotional life. The possibility of play never develops. Intimacy is equated with catastrophe. Such a person turns away from real separate others and turns inward, often becoming lost in imagination, creating a widening retreat from body and time.

Some years ago, on a summer trip with my wife, we were hiking a scenic mountain trail in Maine. We walked for some time inside a dense forest canopy. We came to a path that led up a natural stone staircase next to a waterfall. It took some time to go up, and when we emerged at the top of the steep path, the plateau was completely socked in with fog. We could barely see an outstretched hand.

Agreeing it was unsafe to try to finish the hike, we decided to turn back. As we started down the path along the waterfall, it began to rain, making the descent along the uneven stones dangerously slippery. As the rain came down harder, we had to slow to a crawl. Each footstep became an exercise in anxious mindfulness.

While concerned for my own safety, I was more concerned for my wife. I had little control over how she would negotiate the rocky path. I felt a terrible sense of helplessness realizing that if either of us fell, it could be fatal. For a moment I paused and wished we could be anywhere else. It was a childlike feeling, a strong wish to deny the intimidating circumstances. This was a moment of caesura. I felt a sense of shame at my fear. And I felt I was trapped in a timeless moment of dread. Then, thankfully, something shifted. The direction of my thinking changed. I realized that I had a choice to be here now. Nothing I thought or wished would change the situation. Reality imposed itself. Careful, deliberate action was called for. We had to pay attention to every single step. Every step mattered. Every moment counted.

I learned from that experience that what matters is the fate of your attention. Making a shift from shame to acceptance allowed me to harness my attention. Then, by placing my attention on each footstep, I became incrementally safer. Letting my attention wander to fears of the future put me in jeopardy. I knew there was no guarantee that we would make it down the trail safely. I accepted that reality. Take things one day at a time is good advice. Sometimes, taking things one step at a time is called for.

How often do we acknowledge an ominous transition between the necessity of accepting the reality of danger and the impulse to deny it? In our speedy world, full of myriad distractions, we need to hone the capacity to vary our pace, speeding up sometimes and learning how to slow down at other times.

According to Buddhist psychology, we are alienated from our experience and from a deeper perception of reality. This alienation is said to be the consequence of a form of perception that radically separates the world into the categories of subject and object. These categories are then unconsciously reified. The reification causes us to form judgements about the objects we perceive. As we fall into a trap of concreteness, we seek some objects and are averse to others. We cling to what we enjoy and fight what we despise. We try to possess and prolong positive experiences and we try to avoid or deny negative ones. Through our desire and fear, we populate the world with phantoms born of our anxieties.

Every instant is an opportunity to notice another form of perceptual transformation. Every moment is a moment of choice. This has been made vivid now by the experience of living in a pandemic. What do I think is real? Shall I go out in public today? Shall I wear a mask? Shall I stay six feet away from others? Shall I respect the advice of authorities? Can I open to and tolerate the intimidating uncertainty? What happens when you can no longer take refuge in the familiar?

I have started noticing the beauty of the sky at dawn, and the beauty of bird song in the morning. I listen happily to the caw of the crows, to the haunting honks of geese and to the cry of gulls as they fly overhead. I marvel at the actual melodies of the smaller birds that are gathering material and building nests. I notice the colour coming into the sky and the smell and feel of the freshness of early-morning air.

Death is certain, but its time unknown. I have had trouble sleeping during the pandemic. I learned three of my mentors died in a span of three months. Every day I felt some of the sadness of those facts. My sleeplessness worsened after viewing, many times, the horrible video of George Floyd and the eight minutes and forty-six seconds that Derek Chauvin had his knee on Mr. Floyd's neck while three other police officers stood by and watched.

Cruelty and beauty co-exist. The spiritual teacher Stephen Levine used to say that there is room for it all if we learn to listen with our hearts. If I open my heart, what do I feel? Shock? Anger? Disbelief? Disgust? Sadness? Fear? How do we make room for all the emotions that arise moment to moment, day to day? Ominous transitions test the possibility of making room for what is really happening. Ominous transitions ask for greater awareness, greater questioning, greater capacity to take in experience, not from one point of view but from as many angles as possible.

Long before the riots and protests over George Floyd's death, one of the white teenagers I worked with was telling me about how angry he gets. He talked about his anger like it was a fire. "I'm afraid," he said, "of how out of control it might get". "I'm afraid", he said. "I want to watch it burn. I want everything to burn down".

"Who is it who gets so angry?" I asked.
He was silent. The question intrigued him.

Who is it who gets so angry? One possible answer is the person who feels they have no one to talk to, no one who will listen and share their experience – no one who takes his pain seriously.

Going to sleep can be an ominous transition. When you go to sleep, you do not know what you will dream. Trauma stops the dreaming process, but conversely, some people feel traumatized by the contents of their dreams. For some people, this uncertainty is intolerable, and they would rather not sleep than risk dreaming.

When you wake, what fragments from dream life remain? Sometimes only an atmosphere or an emotional trace appears in memory. Other times, whole adventures are recollected. How you relate to your dream life upon waking is significant. Important experiences can be lost if you leap too quickly back into the rhythms of the day.

If you wake to an alarm, roll over and check your phone or allow your first thoughts to be dispersed, you suffer an alienation that you may not even be aware of. What if you take a moment or two to be still and notice the quiet of the morning? What you register can be an intimate contact with your own evolving consciousness. Sometimes, what comes in dream life links you to the day or restores something that helps you face the day even when the day intimidates you.

Sometimes when a patient brings a dream to a session, they feel a sense of shame. "I don't know what it means" they anxiously admit. Sometimes they expect me to tell them what the dream means. Then I must admit that I do not know either. The difference is that I am not ashamed of not knowing. Instead, I am curious. I want to explore the details of the dream together. I want to find out what kind of surprising wisdom might emerge from the space that exploring the dream opens between us.

A patient asks me what I can promise if they start therapy with me. I tell them that I am committed to three things. First, I am committed to listening to everything they say with curiosity. Second, I am committed to having an honest conversation about what they say. And, third, I am committed to speaking sincerely.

OK, they say, that is good enough for me.

In his condensed paper "A Theory of Thinking" (1960) Bion described the experience of frustration tolerance as a crucial variable in the development of the capacity to think. According to Bion, if there is adequate capacity to tolerate frustration, a person may discover a space within which a thought might arise. This space for thinking implies tolerance of the passage of time as well as tolerance for the awareness of the absence of an object. When a space for absence can be tolerated, thoughts may arise, and the capacity to welcome thoughts creates the raw material for thinking.

Bion investigated factors that obstruct thinking. If there is insufficient capacity to tolerate frustration, the place where a thought might be discovered becomes *quickly* saturated with a hallucination generated from the memory traces of a past pleasure. A wish fulfilment is not a thought in that it moves away from the challenge of investigating reality into the dominance of a pleasure principle. Finally, if frustration is intolerable, the absence of a good experience becomes *instantly* the presence of a persecutory one.

Tolerance of frustration makes possible a space for thinking which eventually creates the conditions to learn from emotional experience. Intolerance of frustration creates a momentum for hallucination to saturate the space for thinking with a memory of a familiar or past pleasure. Finally, intense intolerance of frustration can instantly generate the presence of a persecutory experience.

Three forms of time are implied in this model. For thinking to develop, tolerance of time must be part of the process. Intolerance of frustration implies intolerance of time. Vividly recalling a past pleasure in the present creates a confusion of the "there and then" with the "here and now". When there is extreme intolerance of frustration, the intensity of mental pain and anxiety generates a terror of being trapped in a timeless catastrophe. This leads to an attack on the awareness of time as a way of trying to get rid of the awareness of pain.

It is painful to acknowledge the feeling "I can't think". It is also painful to admit "I need help to think". Over the years I have observed children begin to express and elaborate their experience through play. Play is a form of feel-thinking. In the early stages of therapy, I see my task as "becoming an audience" to create the conditions to witness a child "making a scene". It has been important with many children to be willing to be an observer before becoming a participant in play. You can feel a moment of caesura when a child risks a spontaneous expression. You can feel a movement across a gap, and a new form of playful connection begins.

Living is filled with moments of caesura and ominous transition. I think one of the most important caesuras can be described as the challenge of weaning. It starts early in life but really lasts a whole life long. The ability to let go of an object makes it possible to discover it again, now as separate, and later still as free. These emotional realizations make different kinds of perceptions and interactions possible.

   Bion's emphasis on a space for absence implies relinquishing the need to possess the object, whether that object is a material thing (like the nipple) or an immaterial thing (like a thought). When there is a space for observing, thinking, and feeling, you can start to sense and experience the importance of many energetic movements. Here are a few caesuras noted from therapy:

   Approach ←→ Avoid
   Too little ←→ Too much
   Clinging ←→ Letting go
   Hiding ←→ Exploring
   Alone ←→ Together
   Control ←→ Play
   Distress ←→ Comfort
   Selfishness ←→ Sharing
   Cruelty ←→ Compassion
   Grievance ←→ Gratitude
   Revenge ←→ Reparation
   Nowhere ←→ Now-here
   Narcissism ←→ Necessity

   There can be increasingly complex and richly textured dynamic movements back and forth among these possibilities. The energetic and emotional movements help map an emotional field of experience. Experience grows in the space between. Sincere expression of experience is a gift, moments of grace. The capacity to receive communication is equally precious.

When you can recognize another person as separate and different from yourself, a virtuous communication cycle can develop. This good-enough communication cycle has three caesuras embedded within it. The first is a tension between registering ←→ refusing. Sometimes separateness, presence, or difference can feel intimidating or threatening. This happens when a person is fixed in their mindset.

If you cling to a fixed picture of the world, refusal feels easier than registering the impact of difference. But when it is possible to register the unique communication of another person, it opens a second caesura between reflecting ←→ reacting.

Reflecting brings into play a tension between self and other, between the familiar and the different, between habit and novelty, between possibility and foreclosure. Only if you can reflect upon the impact of what you register can you move to the third caesura of reply and avoid the trap of reaction, which is driven by the conscious or unconscious commitment to a fixed, unchanging mindset.

In the third phase, reply has a caesura embedded within it between conventional ←→ creative. Both kinds of reply can be meaningful because they build on registering and reflecting. But the conventional reply stays within the boundaries of what is always already known, whereas the creative reply opens a space for evolution and discovery.

Listening psychoanalytically, as well as in course of everyday life, requires an ethics of welcoming (Eaton, 2015), a commitment to register, reflect, and reply to another. When this is possible, time becomes a play space, and shame is transformed into belonging or togetherness. A welcoming function can be observed between mothers and babies, children and parents, lovers, teachers and students, co-workers, and even strangers under favourable conditions. The welcoming function is an antidote to the undermining dynamics of obstructive object relations. Its realization represents a source of hope and even ordinary joy because it unfolds against a background of toleration for both mystery and complexity.

References

Bion, W. R. (1984a). "A Theory of Thinking." In *Second Thoughts*. London: Karnac Books.

———. (1984b). *Second Thoughts*. London: Karnac Books.

———. (1985). *The Long Weekend: Part of a Life*. Perthshire: Clunie Press.

———. (1989). *Two Papers: The Grid and Caesura*. London: Karnac Books.

———. (1991). *A Memoir of the Future*. London: Karnac Books.

Eaton, J. L. (2011). *A Fruitful Harvest: Essays After Bion*. Seattle: Alliance Press.

———. (2014). "Building a Floor for Experience: A Model for Thinking About Children's Experience." In *Transgenerational Trauma and the Aboriginal Preschool Child: Healing Through Intervention*. Ed. N. Tracey. Lanham: Rowan and Littlefield.

———. (2015). "Becoming a Welcoming Object: Personal Notes on Michael Eigen's Impact." In *Living Moments: On the Work of Michael Eigen*. Eds. S. Bloch & L. Daws. London: Karnac Books.

Edmunds, L. (1996). *Oedipus: The Ancient Legend and Its Later Analogues*. Baltimore: Johns Hopkins University Press.

Fonagy, P. et al. (2003). "The Developmental Roots of Borderline Personality Disorder." In *Early Attachment Relationships: A Theory and Some Evidence. Psychoanalytic Inquiry*, 23, 3, 412–459.

Miller, B. (Ed.). (1986). *The Bhagavad-Gita: Krishna's Counsel in Time of War*. New York: Bantam Books.

Wille, R. (2014). "The Shame of Existing: An Extreme Form of Shame." *International Journal of Psycho-Analysis*, 95, 4, 695–717.

Chapter 3

Protecting our humanity in the midst of tribal warfare
Thoughts for our time

Maxine Anderson

Developmental considerations

Human growth and development seem to go counter to the laws of physics, which hold that all matter trends toward disorganization and decay. As thriving beings, we move in the direction of animation instead of de-animation. That is, we 'swim upstream' toward differentiation and organization, going against the sweep of entropic forces.

Contemporary neuroscience (Solms, 2013) reveals that the stirrings that wake us up to life originate in an ancient neural structure, the upper brainstem. Likely present in all vertebrates, these arousals, felt initially as disturbances of quiescence, are considered as the fuel for all neural and motor activity. Solms mentions two sources of sensory input. Stimuli external to the body, conveyed by the peripheral senses, such as touch, vision and audition, are registered in the cerebral cortex and form the bases of memory-based cognition which ultimately gives rise to language and thought. The other major source of neural input occurs deep within the body, the autonomic nervous system serving homeostatic functions to maintain bodily functions within a narrow range. Deviations from a set point are registered as bodily disturbance, examples being hunger, lust and disgust. Solms suggests that these inner arousals comprise the raw affects which run the risk of overwhelming the young self unless they are mediated by attentive, modulating care.

Modern views of *psychic* development suggest that each of us learns to bear the swirl of unmediated reality via the presence of an attentive other, someone who soothes the tensions and distresses from internal (hunger, pain, fear) as well as external (startling sensory experience) sources. This attentive presence, be it the mother, the household or the village, offers a buffering, metabolizing function. Part of this care involves focused attention that labels, and thus transforms, distressing experience into meaning ('you're feeling hungry . . . you were startled by that loud noise'). Labelling transforms waves of eruptive affect into mental objects or images which can then become the seeds of thought. This mothering function, often referred to as 'reverie', helps the emerging self make sense of its own experience as well as of the world. In addition, such attentiveness is a primary source not only of our well-being but also of our humanity. Reverie demonstrates patience and compassion in receiving and translating external distress and internal eruptions without retaliation for the pain it has to bear. The temporal space that is part of the experience of patience is also a template for the establishment of the inner space needed for reflective thought and openness to change. External care, then, becomes the template for internal care, to which the cerebral cortex is nearly entirely dedicated. And the cortex may be thought of as the anatomic location of care.

In addition to external care, early modes of defence available to the young child attempt to evacuate distress. Denial insists that the distress didn't exist; dissociation says that nothing happened; the mechanisms of splitting and projection locate the origin of any disturbance as external to the self. These defences distort reality to offer protection to the fragile psyche. In the more mature mind, however, such defence mechanisms actually sheer away the truly stabilizing capacities of reflective thought. Mechanisms for handling difficult realities which do not distort reality nor fracture the psyche involve remaining open to pain and the modulation of dissonance. Utilizing patience and compassion, these defences face rather than deny intense negative emotion. In doing so, they strengthen whole-minded functioning. This is in marked contrast to the splitting mechanisms, which lead to the fracture of the mind, a crucial loss that can be reversed only when integration can be valued and re-instated.

Reversion to tribal mentality is also defensive against the complexities of reality in that loyalty to the group is key, and cohesive, like-minded perception (group-think) predominates. Although it was important for cohesion among our ancestors, in current times the power of this tribal mentality may also shift the entire group toward an unassailable conviction. This shuts out inconvenient facts, such as those of science, that are not in accord with that conviction. This tribal function may also support the authoritarian figure who promises that he/she alone can offer salvation.

So, when we are not in the full embrace of external or internal care, we easily resort to early modalities. The mechanisms of splitting and projection are efficient efforts by attempting to rid ourselves of unwanted aspects of experience and relocating them in fantasy into someone 'out there'. In doing so, however, one slips into an endangered-seeming mental world, feeling now threatened by those external persons who are felt to harbour the 'bad' qualities that we have just disowned. Similarly, those targets of our projection are now felt to rob or harm us due to our feeling diminished by the very act of projecting away a part of ourselves. Actually, of course, when we utilize splitting and projection, we do fracture and diminish our minds. We shear away not only our fears and uncertainties but our spacious, thoughtful selves, which embrace the very capacities for the transformative understanding and thought that can offer rescue (Anderson, 2019).

Shame

Shame can be viewed from many perspectives. In general, it is considered as one feeling small or inadequate in the eyes of others, as 'not up to expectations' in one's own eyes. For some, shame is universal and omnipresent. It may be useful to consider several ways shame may be manifested:

- In projection, the act of attributing aspects of oneself to others triggers shame because one then feels diminished in one's own eyes. Idealization, which involves attribution of goodness to others and simultaneous devaluation of the self, is one such example.
- Doubt is another trigger. When doubt aims to realistically evaluate an aspect of the self, it can be considered to be creative or informing. But when it is linked with a relentlessly harsh inner voice, it is more accurately functioning as erosive in nature because it is felt to be constantly demeaning and thus shaming of the self.
- In our considerations here, shame is involved whenever our whole-mindedness is threatened; the greater the fragmentation, the greater the shame. Part of the daunting task of re-integration of the mind depends on the violence involved in the splitting processes. In our efforts to re-integrate our minds, whether we can face the shame originating in fragmentation or, rather, feel entrenched in our polarized positions may depend in part on how loyal we feel to the entrenchment but also how courageous we are in facing the violence incumbent in the re-integrative efforts.

Once cleavage has occurred, such as in reversion to the tribal state of mind, the pressures toward reunification of the mind are feared to be dangerous and destabilizing. Out of touch with care, the cleaved mind is then at war with itself: pressures toward reunification are countered by pressures to re-enforce the conviction that all doubt, uncertainty and danger lie outside and must be kept at bay or in some way subdued. Otherwise, the fear contends, the disowned elements in the form of tormenting doubt (an internal tormentor) or the now-hated other (an external danger) may return violently to overwhelm the fractured mind. The feared repatriation of disowned aspects, then, in the absence of patience and reflective thought, may become a feared collision of catastrophic proportions. Polarization – staying frozen in one binary or black/white position – often comes into play to ward off such a feared clash with the seeming enemy, that is, those warded-off parts of ourselves that we have so effectively projected elsewhere.

The forces for unchanging stasis, or polarization, can, then, entrap the mind for years, lifetimes or generations in this altered reality, where appearances and unquestioned traditions comprise 'all there is'. Here, any new idea is considered as betrayal or heresy. Slavery in North America and the myth of white supremacy are enduring examples of this toxic, seemingly untouchable polarized/polarizing situation.

Myths

Myths are created by the idealization of certain fantasies and imaginings as attempts to supplant unwelcome truths. The myth of white supremacy in the American South before and since the Civil War may be seen as one such example. To obscure the brutality and dehumanization of slavery, which seemed so important for the success of the Southern agrarian economy, a myth of white supremacy was established and held in place for generations prior to the American Civil War (1861–1865). This myth, based purely on appearance, held that the planter and slave-owning class, comprised of worldly, generous, genteel patricians, provided care for all in their household and community. Unspoken, and indeed unspeakable, was the underlying truth that a black enslaved underclass was essential for the continuance of this myth (Wyatt-Brown, 1982).

Such a fable, challenged by the Civil War, would not easily be relinquished. Instead, shame-based honour, underpinning the myth, could only trigger outrage and vengeance. Brutal violence and persecution of the black man, thought of among many Southern whites as 'putting him back in his rightful place' following this war, was felt to be patriotic to the old myth of white supremacy as well as the new myth of the Lost Cause. That it has lasted more than 150 years following the war demonstrates the intransigence of this myth and the virulence of the hatred stirred following the defeat of the South, which led to the abolition of slavery. Several historians of the American South have suggested that the photos of seeming pride in the faces of white witnesses of the lynchings of black people expresses the Southern feeling of brutal righteousness in 'setting the world aright'. The brutality and hatred triggered by splitting and projection echoing through the generations can be found in the degree of abject humiliation felt as deliberately imposed by Northern victors. The North's intention of raising the status of the black man was felt by many in the South as cruelly pulling the white man down, an intolerable situation according to the persisting myth of white supremacy.

The intensity and persistence of the myth may be seen in the fact that Civil Rights legislation giving equal rights to blacks could not be passed for 100 years following the Civil War. More contemporary echoes of this same sentiment some 150 years on may be seen in the response of the Republican Party to the election of a black president. Astonished and chagrined by Barack Obama's election in 2008, the Republican-led Congress felt that it must oppose all cooperation with him, that it was more important to frustrate and defeat this president than to do the business of the country. Continued hatred of progressive policies has heightened polarization in current American politics, where loyalty to an idealized (and non-existent) past ('Make America Great Again') galvanizes many voters who still feel diminished by so-called coastal elites, whom they feel (sometimes accurately) look down on them. The relative values of those conservative Americans who place high value on pride of place, family and honouring the past versus progressives who value change and inclusiveness – these different value systems do polarize, partly due to seeming differences that divide rather than inform. These intensely held positions may lead to descent into our inhumanity where difference disturbs, often mightily.

The fragility of our humanity

In the 1960s, American psychologists were trying to understand how relatively normal people could commit the atrocities that so characterized Hitler's death squads. Interviews of participants verified the power of peer pressure to carry out these grisly duties. Yale psychologist Stanley Milgram (2011) developed experiments which also revealed how easily ordinary people could become blindly obedient to authority: although these experiments were in part controversial, Milgram did demonstrate that well-meaning Americans could give over their own judgement and authority to follow the firm direction of the nearby seeming authority sternly giving orders to provide the unseen 'learner' (a confederate of the experiment) with added shocks to aid that learning. Milgram reported that about 65% of subjects complied, even when the so-called learner seemed to cry out in pain and fear medical damage. The anonymity of the learner seemed to correlate significantly with the subject's compliance with the experimenter's dictate. Projecting away one's moral compass, we might say, amidst anonymity, allows one to descend into committing inhuman acts.

In 1971, Phil Zimbardo, Professor of Psychology at Stanford, set up the Stanford Prison Experiment (Zimbardo, 2017). Twenty-four healthy male students were randomly assigned to be guards or prisoners in an experiment advertised as a study of prison behaviour; it was scheduled to last for two weeks. What was stunning was that in a matter of several hours many of the subjects slipped into the assigned roles, prisoners in anonymous garb losing touch with their identity and guards in appropriate regalia often becoming overtly sadistic. Zimbardo himself also slipped into role: assigning himself as superintendent of this prison, he became quite protective of his 'interesting experiment' even in the face of some of the prisoner subjects breaking down emotionally within the first couple of days. It took a whistle-blower to call a halt to the experiment after six days instead of fourteen. It took Zimbardo years to be able to write up fully the study of what occurred, including his becoming more focused on the 'so interesting' experiment rather than the welfare of the student subjects. These are rather breath-taking examples of how easily we can descend into inhuman functioning when we are not fully and rigorously in the embrace of our whole-minded capacities.

Indeed, it seems to take concerted energy to remain self-respecting and thoughtful over time. According to the contemporary cultural philosopher Rob Riemen (2018), Alexis de Tocqueville, observing America in the 1820s, and Nietzsche, in Europe fifty years later, noted that when people are liberated from tyranny, rather than maintain the disciplined thought needed to retain that freedom, they tend to go lax, resorting to sensory pleasures and losing track of the ideals and self-discipline that led to their former independence. It is hard work to remain focused and attentive; we tend to want someone else to take the lead so that we might fall back on more sensuous pleasures. There is a great allure to join with like-minded others and to assume that someone else will do the thinking.

Further, historian Timothy Snyder (2017) as well as Riemen and others mention how resentful and envious the sensory-based mind can be of the mind which does work to operate via reflective thought. Arlene Hochschild (2016), a sociologist from Berkeley, mentions how resentful working-class Southerners can be of the coastal elites whom they feel look down upon them. She observed a basic divide in terms of values: Southern working-class Americans were seen to value pride of place and continuity within one's community, as contrasted with the Southern view of East and West Coast people as mobile, inconstant and even unfaithful to family roots. Coastal values of education and upward mobility viewed the Southern working class as staid, stodgy and even ignorant. This significant divide could be seen in tribal ways. Hochschild herself, considered a coastal elite by her Louisiana subjects, was able to bridge the divide due to her respect for the values of the Southerners she visited for over a decade and her wish to understand their experience.

The hard work of mental integration

We might also keep in mind, even within ourselves, that the sensory-based mind wants there to be no difference, no gradient to ascend; all should be equal so there is no need to put forth effort or to learn. We are all to some extent, sloths at heart! Snyder reminds us that fascism is fuelled almost entirely by such grievances. The election of Donald Trump, emphasizing such grievance and polarizing division, may be seen as contemporary evidence of this trend. In part to counter these lapsing tendencies, Riemen and others urge that education orients around the humanities and aesthetics, including transcendent ideals such as truth, equality and justice. These qualities provide external forms of containment when we are internally disturbed by doubt or intense emotion or, indeed, by internal envy toward our or others' more thought-based capacities. From the seventeenth century, Riemen reminds us, as does Spinoza, that the true enslaver of humankind is ignorance. We might paraphrase that true enslavement is our state of mind shorn of the capacities for reflective thought fostered by internal care.

An informing example of both the enslavement and the hard work of freeing the mind is found in recent American history (*American Experience*, 2020). In 1950s America, the nation was recovering from the ravages of World War II, but it was feeling anxieties about Communist intrusions into national life. Joseph McCarthy, the junior senator from Wisconsin, seeking to establish himself in the public eye, found that he could exploit these anxieties by way of fear-mongering speeches about the invasive cancer of Communism while also establishing Congressional hearings and investigations to 'rout out Communism'. McCarthy seemed to gain a momentum and a sense of omnipotence in terms of intimidation and by black-listing figures not only in government but also among academics and the arts. Governmental leaders, including President Dwight Eisenhower, were concerned that McCarthy was becoming a public menace with his near-dictatorial tactics and that he needed to be constrained. The needed containment seemed to be evident in the Army-McCarthy Hearings of 1954. Although details of these hearings may be interesting, more relevant to our considerations are the confrontative capacities of Joseph Welch, counsel for the Army, who was more angered than intimidated by McCarthy's bullying tactics. At one point in the hearings, likely to distract attention from Welch's exposure of McCarthy's having entered tampered evidence, McCarthy turned to unrelenting attempts to slander a young lawyer who had been vetted and denied participation in the hearings due to his brief association with a communist organization during law school. Maintaining his clarity about McCarthy's behaviour, Welch (1954) famously broke into McCarthy's ongoing rant and retorted:

> Until this moment, Senator, I think I never really gauged your cruelty or your recklessness. . . . Senator, you've done enough. Have you no sense of decency, sir? At long last, have you left no sense of decency?

Welch's clarity and confrontation seemed to break the spell McCarthy held over the audience and within the country. In the same time frame, the noted commentator Edward R. Murrow (1954), further commenting on the tactics of McCarthy, issued his famous exhortation to the public to resist fear but to retain clear thought, qualities also relevant to breaking the spell which McCarthy apparently had cast upon the American public.

More current history illustrates how polarized positions affect clarity and judgement. Polarization involves splitting and projection which gives rise to the emergence of sharp, blaming rhetoric. Balanced views with space for thought are minimized in such an atmosphere.

Examples from my own experience offer further illustration: shortly after the 2016 election I found myself caught up in shocked disbelief and grievance. I was so filled with these emotions that I had difficulty working. I found I had to put blinkers on my mind, as it were, to listen carefully and help my patients with their own turbulence. I could see that to do this I had similarly to pay attention to my own affects – my shock and disbelief – and to mourn, to feel the grief about what I had come to believe would be an easy win for the Democrats. An important part of this care has been the need to mourn when necessary, to let go of the outcomes I have longed for. For only then can I move forward. Otherwise, I can easily be caught in grievance and at times obsession about 'how it should have been'.

Currently I still struggle at times. Indeed, with the increased atmosphere of polarization, it can feel delicious to read the sources of news which lean in my political direction. I can feel so pulled to read only those authors with whom I agree and to bypass those with whom I disagree. And regarding the recent presidential impeachment proceedings, I could feel myself drawn to search out 'the news of the hour'. These fascinations demonstrate the allure to indulge in polarizing excitement for my team and repudiation for the other.

Deliberate effort has been required to maintain self-respect and balance. Writing a book became a project to keep me on track, and my research revealed several historical and cultural figures who have become mentors of a sort, figures offering guidance and containment when I felt beleaguered or drawn toward a polarized view. But I also have learned that holding a figure in thrall narrows the mind; even quietly idealizing another may be similar to Zimbardo's privileging his experiment over the well-being of the student subjects.

Another current challenge to clarity of thought is the pandemic of the coronavirus known as COVID-19. The edge of panic which may accompany this news threatens to dissolve patient, clear thought needed for planning. Deliberate efforts toward balanced thought for local and national navigation during this world-wide health crisis may well again be necessary.

One more example, here of a global concern, is that of climate change which most people seem to have kept to the side of the mind. Psychoanalyst Sally Weintrobe (2013) and others have written about the general tendency toward disavowal of care toward this growing crisis. She suggests that we have often engaged in the position of exceptionalism ('I can still do what I want. I do not have to be disrupted in my use of fossil fuels. I am too important to have to curb my activities'). And that this attitude of exceptionalism or omnipotence may be seen as a defence against the underlying helplessness and perhaps even terror about the growing climate crisis. Such defensiveness, Weintrobe suggests, is blatant anti-care for the planet. But she also notes that in the past few years attitudes have changed in terms of countering this dismissive attitude. In his laudatory review of Weintrobe's work, emphasizing her impact on public attitudes, Don Campbell (2019) suggests that a paradigm shift is occurring:

> It involves a new caring imagination that now sees life as a series of support systems (physical, social and psychic frameworks of care) that all interconnect. She [Weintrobe] gives examples of this paradigm shift in economics, architecture and the law; also, in social group behaviour and within the psyche. Just as insight gained on the couch needs working through and is hard to sustain, so is the shift to the new imagination.

Such a shift involves the capacity to face current reality, which involves mourning the disappointments and losses which have accompanied the relinquishing of the myth of exceptionalism. Further, such mourning fosters the capacity to move ahead with hope rather than to sink into cynicism, stasis or further myths based on denial. The hard work of mental integration, then, involves the pains of reality including our efforts to avoid it while cultivating openness to the wider learnings that this integration promotes.

Summary and conclusions

These warnings have relevance in contemporary times. On the one hand, they illustrate the liberating and orienting function of the mind capable of facing psychic truth. On the other, they demonstrate that the distortions of reality which the splitting processes[1] give rise to may be especially daunting, partly because when we have succumbed to splitting, we cannot then observe ourselves. We may feel that we are suddenly in a dangerous world, one populated by our projections. Our intensely felt stance of being good or upstanding amidst the harshness all around is a distortion of reality that we cannot observe. We are, instead, caught up in living it or, better stated, in efforts to survive it, often feeling ourselves to be either beleaguered or heroic on such a hostile frontier.

This insistent stance, felt as a truth, is likely to collapse into the sense of abject shame and humiliation when it is revealed to be a myth rather than an absolute reality. We can begin to recover from this humiliation when we can bear to suffer empathically this pain of facing difficult realities, a task which often requires aid from a patient and compassionate other. Access to empathy allows us to see this seemingly heroic stance as a myth rather than a singular truth, one viewed with compassion rather than scathing internal criticism. Moreover, amidst an empathic attitude, we can see more clearly our previous distortions: how we may have projected blame rather than take responsibility or to have imputed truth to positions which were actually based on retentions of certainty and power. So, this truth-based position, available amidst a compassionate atmosphere, widens our view and strengthens respect for ourselves as well as for others. Its rescuing potential ferries the journey from the so-called realities based on myth and power to those based on humanity.

We each will have our own ways forward as we aim to navigate these times of danger for not only our mental integration but indeed perhaps for the survival of our inhabitable planet. Facing difficult truths in open ways rather than retreating into cover-ups or denial is the likely lesson from China's hesitation in facing the coronavirus outbreak. We need similar courage to face the truths as they emerge about the even more significant global issue of climate change. As Edward R. Murrow admonished, and more recently historian Snyder, philosopher Riemen and psychoanalyst Weintrobe urge if we can keep our fears from fragmenting our whole-minded capacities, we can access our best capacities for navigating these difficult times.

I would like to conclude with a quote about the pain and dread of mental reunification which I penned earlier but which I feel is at the heart of these considerations:

> Reintegration (of the mind) . . . requires the capacity to discern intensely felt polarized constraints as products of brutal division, rather than as unassailable 'truths'. . . . This process involves the repatriation of. . . (externalized) disturbance as part of self. And, realizing that not only the . . . disturbances (themselves), but also the divisive forces that aim to disown the disturbances, are not external. Such recognition, indeed, annihilates the myth of being the power at the centre of the world and re-establishes the humbler processive to and fro involved in learning. In lived experience, this clear view and

dismantling of. . . (the hard shell of certainty) is not a gentle process. It is one that involves bearing pain and tension as one softens the hardened carapace, risking feeling (endangered and) humiliated, as one owns the disavowed elements, before feeling the relief of reunion.

In the lived moment, that pain and tension involve the risk of embracing need, which has been felt as weakness, trust taking the place of cynicism, attentive care seen as other than manipulation or domination. As mentioned, this reunification process may involve a jarring and then dis-arming shift from power to the wider awareness of vulnerability and need, as shame and humiliation trend toward humility.

(Anderson, 2016, p. 91)

Epilogue

In light of the earlier unimaginable scale of the COVID-19 pandemic, some further thoughts may be relevant.

This pandemic is likely greater than any other natural event we have encountered in our lifetimes. Having no way to adequately apprehend it, we can only feel terrified. And in terror we likely feel helplessly paralyzed.

Approaching this force of nature with science makes the most sense. Methodical thought is often diminished if not abolished in the wake of terror. So once again we are faced with the need to reclaim our whole-minded selves to make headway.

We speak of being at war with this virus, but in saying that we are most likely trying to feel strong and militant, perhaps to gird against our sense of collapsing helplessness, wherein our primal fears and fantasies may seem to entrap and even condemn us. The unseen virus, as a feared alien, may invite us to utilize splitting and projection as we try to bolster ourselves against this foe. The diminishment we may then feel as we try to rid ourselves of worries may leave us feeling more frightened and endangered. Also, in resorting to projection, we may indeed feel our now-externalized worries are equated with the virus. Thus, when we are steeped in our anxiety we may feel we are drowning in the virus, a situation which our confused minds may equate to being condemned to death.

From another view, we might wonder about how rapidly we seem to accommodate to previously unimaginable happenings: home-made face masks to accompany latex gloves in supermarkets, emergency hospitals set up in parks and parking lots, ice rinks becoming morgues, triage decisions about who receives dwindling health resources and who does not. These happenings became everyday events within just a few weeks.

We are faced with several simultaneous versions of reality: we are laced with panic and dread and the realization that our lack of immunity to a virulent agent may cut through all our would-be defences, shearing away our entitlement as well as the advantages of technology and even, perhaps, the benefits of our civilization. We are shaken to our roots, reduced from our fantasies of dominating the world to wondering whether we will survive amidst an indifferent virus. We wonder, with good cause, about the future, what the new normal may be. A related reality is that the pandemic brings us back to nature, showing us once again who is in charge. As we have not been good stewards of the earth recently, it may be important to consider the virus as another messenger, one which can cut through the noise of our busy, self-centred pre-occupations, our familiar ruts. In so doing it confronts us with the opportunity, if not the mandate, to change not only how we think but what we do in terms of respect for nature as well as for all of humanity. Still, the pull toward the familiar, the known and the noisy will be powerful. It will take courage and discipline to remain open, to listen and to learn from this significant prompting. We are undergoing a trauma whose meaning we cannot understand until we can look back from the future. Only in the manner of such a looking back, an *après coup*, can we discern the perhaps evolving meaning of the messenger now at hand.

Note

1 From Anderson, 2019, p. 11: 'Splitting and projection are early and universal mental mechanisms that seem to cleave the mind from its capacity for reflexive thought, rendering it back to the less complex state which only perceives absolutes, such as "good and bad" and "how things are". This reversion to a concrete view of reality may occur when doubt, pain or uncertainty are too much to bear. In these circumstances the mind is attracted to unquestionable certainties and anything felt to be otherwise, such as doubt, is expelled and then perceived to reside or define a 'bad or denigrated other'. Thus, the mind *splits* off its own doubted aspects, and by *projection* attributes them to others.

References

American Experience: S32E1: McCarthy. https://wwwpbs.org/wgbh/americanexperience/films/mccarthy [Accessed 1 June 2020].

Anderson, M. (2016). *The Wisdom of Lived Experience*. London: Karnac Books.

———. (2019). *From Tribal Division to Welcoming Inclusion: Psychoanalytic Perspectives*. Abingdon: Routledge.

Campbell, D. (2019). Submission of Sally Weintrobe for an IPA 2019 Community Aware for Her Work on Climate Change.

Hochschild, A. R. (2016). *Strangers in Their Own Land: Anger and Mourning on the American Right*. New York: The New Press.

Milgram Obedience Study with Videos of Some of the Actual Participants in the Original Experiments. (2011). www.youtube.com/watch?v=fCVlI-_4GZQ [Accessed 24 February 2020].

Murrow, E. (1954). "On McCarthy, No Fear." www.youtube.com/watch?v=vEvEmkMNYHY [Accessed 24 February 2020].

Riemen, R. (2018). *To Fight Against This Age: On Fascism and Humanism*. New York: Norton.

Snyder, T. (2017). *On Tyranny: Twenty Lessons from the Twentieth Century*. New York: Tim Duggan Books, Penguin Random House.

Solms, M. (2013). "The Conscious Id." *Neuropsychoanalysis*, 15, 5–19.

Weintrobe, S. (2013). *Engaging with Climate Change: Psychoanalytic and Interdisciplinary Perspectives*. London: Routledge.

Welch, J. (1954). "YouTube. Have You No Decency?" www.youtube.com/watch?v=wJHsur3HqcI [Accessed 24 February 2020].

Wyatt-Brown, B. (1982). *Southern Honor: Ethics and Behavior in the Old South*. New York: Oxford University Press.

Zimbardo, P. (2017). "Stanford Prison Experiment." www.prisonexp.org/ [Accessed 24 February 2020].

Chapter 4

From leper-thing to another side of care

A reading of Lacan's logical collectivity

Robin McCoy Brooks

Introduction

In the present essay, I conceptualize the psyche-social dynamic of *trans-subjectivity* that itself is a precursor to the possibility of a collective individuation or what Jacques Lacan obliquely referred to as "collective logic." This concept is related to what Heidegger described as "having become" (or later *Augenblick)*, Gilbert Simondon as "trans-individuation," and Derek Hook as "trans-subjectivity" (Lacan, 1945/2006, pp. 197–175; Heidegger, 2010, pp. 65–74; Simondon, 1992, p. 248; Hook & Vanheule, 2018, pp. 86–114).[1]

I elaborate a notion of "trans-subjectivity" through a reading of Lacan's, 1945 essay titled "Logical Time and the Assertion of Anticipated Certainty," whereby he delineates three iterative moments of logical time towards a culminating expression of a collective truth or "logical collectivity" (Lacan, 1945/2006, pp. 197–175). Whereas Lacan utilized the allegory of the prisoner's dilemma to illustrate his thesis, I use a clinical vignette from a Project Quest therapy retreat to elaborate the symbolic processes underlying the movement between *inter* and *trans*-subjective logic and the expression of a shared solution to the dilemma posed. Rarely does Lacan use the term "trans-subjective," and he does not do so in his 1945 essay. I borrow Derek Hook's use of this term from his own substantial reading of Lacan and trans-subjectivity (Hook, 2013; Hook & Vanheule, 2018).[2]

Self as political possibility

This essay is the second of two, the first titled "Self as Possibility: Subversive Neighbor Love and Transcendental Agency amidst Collective Blindness" (Brooks, 2018). Before fleshing out the present thesis, I must briefly summarize crucial aspects of the first on whose shoulders this paper stands. Self as political possibility, as I am viewing it here, can be seen as the enunciation of the "struggle to articulate the "*I*" with the "*we*" amidst "blind [collective] stupidity" and a relationship to an impossible future and a past that is not one's own (Ross, 2018, p. 7; Stiegler, 2019, p. 26).[3] That is, the political subject is inaugurated not only through its own becoming (psychical individuation) but also through the emergence of a novel collective individuation (Brooks, 2018).

"Self as political possibility" was in part an auto-ethnographic study of the psyche/social conditions that contributed to the birth of a non-profit clinic called Project Quest in 1989 during the height of the AIDS pandemic. I engaged the philosophical and psychoanalytic thought of Jung, Žižek, Badiou, and Heidegger in formulating my thesis for co-effective individual and collective individuations. Quest's emergence was not an anomaly but serves as an example of how encountering the singular real of the wound of contemporary existence amidst massive entropic collapse (or collective dis-individuation) may awaken us to something we truly care about, thus activating subversive expressions (thinking, actions, artistic productions) of care that may culminate in collective individuations (Stiegler, 2019, pp. 29–30). There are *basic structural elements* that contribute to self-formation in relation to others that have the potential to mobilize a group towards collective action. These collective actions resist and invert abusive dominating norms towards new expressions of care. I did not use the term "trans-subjective" in the earlier paper, nor did I conceptually develop its role towards collective individuation, which is the focus of the present essay.

I now summarize three of these elements that form the background of the present paper. First, the subject engages a singular rupture, in this case a vicious exposure to one's own situation by engaging with the reality of the AIDS pandemic. As such, the subject is affected by the collision between the contingency of his own temporality and the incontingency of existence. The subject is brought to his knees, and if he can bear the fierce libidinal tensions activated by this destabilizing reality; a new and terrifying space opens to a heightened awareness of lived time through which a singular moment of truth may be revealed in a penetrating flash. Second, if the subject remains actively engaged with the reality of his dilemma, he may grasp its significance allowing him to make a fundamental choice to act on behalf of himself *and* his world with a new sense of responsibility: "I am not alone." "There are others like and not like me who share this dilemma." Third, the subject commits to an ongoing everyday struggle of taking concrete responsibility to the object of his truth with and amongst others so that a new egalitarian ethos may emerge beyond its own future. "I am dying, but what I labour for now may contribute to a better life for those I leave behind." In other words, the coin of this realm is not directed to my personal retirement plan but towards a society of care for which I make my sacrifice.

The cost is perpetual struggle, uncertainty, the radical loss of identity and a decisive break with empty abstractions contained within a social order that condones exclusivity. The work task of the Quest community, for example, was to provide and maintain a community of care for and by the people who were socially isolated because they were afflicted with a deadly disease amidst a world health crisis devoid of sufficient authority/resources in a climate of terror and violent discrimination. The times were dark as well as illuminating. Solidarity existed only in those trans-subjective moments that lifted and informed individuals and sometimes groups of individuals towards a kind of concrete action that often enough furthered its collective purpose (Brooks, 2018, p. 68).

Connie's blood and Lacan's notion of logical collectivity

Prefatory note: Half of the individuals attending the particular retreat in the following vignette are dead, and all were HIV positive and/or living with an AIDS diagnosis. Highly Active Antiretroviral Therapy (HAART) would not become widely available in the United States until the mid- to late 1990s. The so-called working through the repercussions of the following incident of Connie's bleeding out occurred in sessions after she was taken off the island and became a focus of therapy in a variety of striking ways after the retreat. There were, of course, many trans-subjective moments that evolved in the multiple group processes of all kinds that led to the actual founding of Project Quest. What informs my clinical interpretative assumptions throughout this essay, now almost 30 years later, are culled from recollections, process notes, artefacts and other materials collected from auto-ethnographic research I conducted with my colleagues and others who attended this retreat in the early years of the plague.

Lastly, the protagonist of this essay is the *subject*. The Lacanian subject is the *unconscious discourse of and with the Other*, as we will see.[4] I use gender-fluid pronouns for the sake of narrative clarity. The composite narrative I generate about this incident is delivered in a chaotic flux congruous with the discourse of self-formation and informed by the work we did together over years.

Clinical vignette

Almost 30 years ago, I was co-leading a psychodrama residential retreat with medical psychologist Lusijah Marx, newly graduated psychotherapist Graham Harriman and 28 participants living with AIDS at Doe Bay resort on Orcas Island. During the first night, one of our members (whom I will call Constance) began to menstruate in her sleep. The blood quietly haemorrhaged out of her body onto the mattress and floor throughout the night. We found her in a coma in the morning as we were gathering for the first session of the day. Our entire community moved into action. Within moments, Constance was being carried on a mattress to one of our vans. Greg Carrigan describes the moment this way: "We could all see our own death then, and it was at the same time so healing because we were all [literally] lifting her on her mattress, over us. . . . She floated over the top of us." We headed towards a colourful van decorated with a hand-painted rainbow motif. One of the retreat participants spontaneously started to play his flute, and long, soulful notes accompanied the sombre procession to the van. We were quite suddenly thrown (in the Heideggarian sense) from the order of the everyday into a reality that we were already immersed but that had somehow eluded us. That is, the ordinariness of our lives had quite violently been punctuated by the reality of Constance's blood, what that foretold and our powerlessness and responsibility to her impossible demand. Lusijah and Deb Borgelt (friend and volunteer) drove towards the ferry that would take them to a hospital off the island. Next, I remember that Graham and I, half mad with fatigue, were sitting on a sofa preparing to gather the group, instinctively holding each other's hands like a lifeline – such a tender moment. We were all engulfed in a fierce eddy of unintelligible forces that were swirling around and through us. "Are you ready?" I asked, looking into his eyes. "Yes," he replied. We stood up and moved into the gathering storm (Brooks, 2018, p. 55).

The first structural moment of time, that of the subject

Nobody alive today remembers who found Connie's unconscious body in her bed. Dark red menstrual blood continued to drip out from under the covers, still coagulating on to little pools on the floor. At first sight, it looked like a crime scene. The smell of her blood filled the room. The sight of her bleeding out presented *each of us* with our own dilemma. Lacan's first logical gesture begins the moment the singular subject engages the evidence of an existing dilemma, what he refers to as "the instance of a glance" (Lacan, 2006, p. 204). The kind of subjectivity that develops in the first logical moment Lacan refers to as "noetic," "impersonal" and "independent" from others (ibid, pp. 204–205). Instantaneously, the sight of *Connie's blood* evokes a singular wrenching away from the banality of the everyday into "fulgurating" time (ibid, p. 167). A memory from a forgotten history may "flash up" in the Benjaminian sense in moments of danger like this one. How the subject has known himself is radically repudiated in a moment of truth. Doors to its own ruins are thrown open through the trans – "temporal index" across time to others who may share its plight (Benjamin, 1968, p. 254). The subject has encountered the *Real* through the material signifier of her blood and its bizarre and terrible gaze. At this instance "one knows that" while Connie is in serious peril, so too is the subject irrevocably stricken (Lacan, 2006, p. 204).

The traumatic effects of the Lacanian *Real* are made known to the subject by its utter resistance to symbolization. What I am witnessing is inarticulable, unintelligible and beyond my comprehension. I cannot separate myself from the material reality of what I perceive, yet the signifier of her blood would become what later Lacan refers to as a master-signifier or "the point of convergence that enables everything that happens in this discourse to be situated" (Lacan, 1993, p. 268). The signifier of her blood incarnates itself into the subject's body, making itself known through *anxiety* (Lacan, 2014, p. 88). Anxiety, for Lacan, is a "signal of the Real" and emerges when separation is in question, but separation from what? (Lacan, 2014, p. 207). The effects of anxiety open a space that demands a relating of something to something else.[5] One is required to hold sway and garner a strength to not resist the burden of such a relation. Only then does one know that one has been claimed enigmatically (Lacan, 2006, p. 204).

Vulgar repulsion, horror, vertigo and shreds of shame take form in the subject, thrusting it into another dimension of time that cannot be incorporated into a teleological narrative. We cannot shake it, as Anne Caron reminds us, because "shame lives on the eyelids" (Critchley et al., 2014, p. 8).[6] Shame greets us at the mouth of the void that is opening. The subject is radically faced with a fundamental lack, a *nothing* that is irreducible to the signifier that itself cannot be signified except through the effects of anxiety (Lacan, 2014, p. 134). Their own lack, a psychical *emptying-out* or *nothing-ness* engulfs them. In my personal situation, for example, I wanted to vomit and imagined my own body simultaneously evacuating all of its bodily fluids from their various orifices . . . a gripping memory.[7] The subject bears witness to fragments of a truth about its own existence because it now stands both "*inside and outside* of [*its*] *own* picture," no longer entirely bound to a hegemonic discourse that was instantaneously shattered by the sight of Connie's blood (Žižek, 2006, p. 17). In other words, the radical negativity of the void inherent in the subject's core that is experienced somatically in the present catastrophe serves as a vector between the subject and its world. It is here that the ethical dimension or possibility for subjectification opens up with the constitutive madness and disorientation that ensue.

Lacan, in a later work, would designate *objet petit a* as the object cause of desire from which the "sharp goad of the enigma" is produced (Laplanche, 2014, p. 96). From this perspective, *objet a* is *both* the gap (that radical core of negativity) and whatever comes to fill that gaping void in our symbolic reality (Žižek, 2008, p. 178). On the origins of *objet petit a* Lacan (2006, p. 198) states:

> The child, in his relation to the mother, a relation constituted in analysis not by his vital dependence on her, but by his dependence on her love, that is to say, by the desire for her desire, identifies himself with the imaginary object of this desire insofar as the mother symbolizes it.

Lacan locates the subject at the centre of his psychoanalytic gaze (unlike American psychologists who focus on ego formation) where it is primordially alienated from its own history and formed within and through its relationship to the impossibility of its mother's desire. The unconscious is not viewed as something "inside" the person, in contrast to Jung's problematic, but more as an inter-subjective space between people. Thus, the tiny subject is cast (castrated) into an external symbolic network of language as desire and connection are created through language. *Objet a* is not really an object at all, or a person or material reality, but a transferential placeholder for the birth caregiver, the *one I hopelessly seek in the other*. As such, *objet a* can never be obtained and as such animates the drives to seek what is lacking from my life (Lacan, 1981, pp. 76–78).

Connie's arresting predicament penetrated a void in each of us that in turn *singularly* inaugurated transferential fantasies directed towards *objet a* ("what does she want of me?") that in turn produced the production of the master signifier, meaning, for the Lacanian subject is sought through a signifying chain of language in and through its relationship to iterative loss and the impossibility of a unified psychic life. The master (signifier) is empty, however, and not part of a chain of signifiers because it is self-referential and only gestures to itself.[8] That is, no narrative about Connie's blood can provide relief about what is happening here, and so a psychical remainder hangs in the still air like raw sewage that none of us can escape. The Real of Connie's blood is *shared by all of us* and therefore becomes a hegemonic "nodal point" around which our overwhelming libidinal excess would collectively organize (Butler, 2014, p. 190). In other words, in spite of our differences, our incompatible identifications, values and life experiences, the shared enigma, or empty signifier, of Connie's blood can "only function as an *objet petit-a*" (Hook & Vanheule, 2016, p. 8).

Gripped with dawning *intuition* that there is something he *does not know* that exceeds the factual evidence, the subject reflexively turns outside himself for the key (Lacan, 2006, p. 205). He turns to the broader social field of psychical intersubjectivity to verify his existence (ibid, p. 206). This turn to a social field to find itself is a fiction generated to tourniquet the haemorrhaging of its impossible desire for reunification generated from the Real of Connie's blood.[9] Meaning, according to Lacan, can be created only as part of a signifying chain of language through encountering the Real of the Other itself rather than narrativized through egoic accounts of reality. Nevertheless, phenomenological consciousness is at this point completely unaware of *objet a*, being caught up in its own phantasmatic longings to regain its moorings within its tribe. "Are others claimed as well?" "If so, what is my place in the face of this predicament?"

The second moment of structural time, that of subject in relation to inter-subjectivity

Lacan identifies the second structural moment as "the time for comprehending" what was *seen* in the "instance of the glance" (Lacan, 2006, p. 205). The subject finds itself reflexively positioned in what Lacan refers to as the imaginal realm, where with questions regarding *who* and *what* I imagine myself to be in relation to you and others are generated. My *fantasy* of who I am to you in a given community forms the very coordinates of my identity, sense of belonging and existential purpose (Lacan, 1981, p. 235; Hook, 2008, p. 279). Inter-subjective engagements shape my narrative about what is important to believe, whom I identify with and what I must do (rules, customs, practices) to be a part of things.

The subject of this second moment is distinguished through his bafflement, doubt, continued anxiety and curiosity about what is happening in relation to his social milieu. The imaginary ego is captured by a net of signifiers contained within a socio-symbolic field (Lacan's symbolic order) through which the identity of any term (or key signifier) is determined by the historical structures that the subject has itself not created. The subject struggling for identity stands in-between the tension of recognition of others and for an identity whose frame of reference is impossible because of his place in history (Butler, 2004, pp. 150–151). A gay person living with AIDS in the height of the AIDS pandemic is in double social jeopardy. He cannot be recognized by his polity on two counts because the historical structures that determine who is valued in a society and who is worthy of care (or mourning) do not include the gay person or the person dying of AIDS (Butler, 2015; Akca, 2017).[10]

Lacan is mostly interested in the structural positionings that *underlie the symbolic order* and the contingency of symbolic values that gravitate towards a *key signifier* because the truth of the subject can be realized only through a crack in its discourse. Discourse "stands in between language and speech" or at the point in which the two intersect and is the starting point of any possible authentic speech (Hoens, 2006, pp. 94–95). However, the subject of our vignette is not yet capable of discourse and instinctually turns towards the imaginary realm of intersubjective identification because he cannot, at this point, directly identify with himself (through the haze of his own raw sewage) but only with the image of another that he feels reflects him or at least "what [he] would like to be" (Žižek, 2008, p. 105).

Elsewhere, Lacan would describe the initial actions of the subject into the social field as "egomiming" (Lacan, 1991, p. 180). Egomiming is limited to the subject's perception of others as being "like me." "Who is thinking what *I am thinking?*" "Who is feeling what I am?" Phantasmatic communications at this level may happen within a glance. With another dimension of consciousness, the subject is felt capable of role-reversing with the *other* or can imagine that the *other being* is itself an "other" and not just its pure reflection (Lacan, 1991, pp. 180–181). Communications (apperceptions) between group members from this dimension, if we could put pre-theoretical utterances into words, might be symbolically conveyed thus: "What are *you* seeing? "What am I seeing?" "What am *I* to you?" "What do you want of me?" "What do I want from you?" "What is happening?" The constituting subject continually folds back to itself to reflect, cogitate and think abstractly about the weight of these transactions. With mounting anxiety, the subject begins to perceive tentatively a "we" or can situate itself in the place of a "we." "Where do 'I' stand with "all of you?" (Lacan, 2006, pp. 207, 211–212). Nevertheless, this tentative perception of a "we" obtained by a constant recourse to the other's desire (who is thought to hold the *answer* to what I am seeking) is still inadequate. Derek Hook (2008, p. 278) adroitly outlines the futility of these non-reciprocal structural inquiries this way:

> This desire of the subject to locate itself relative to the question of the Other's desire [however] is destined to constant failure . . . an incessant querying of the Other's desire, assumption of a hypothetical answer gleaned from their gestures and actions; a gradual wearing thin of this hypothesis as inadequate; and then, once again: a renewed querying of the Other's desire.

Thus, the self is internally divided and "hemorraging," as Critchley et al. (2014, p. 7) describes it, "a kind of half-being that is splintered between different kinds of experiences of desire." The subject feels a desire to flee from the wound (a kind of *nachträglich*) that is reflected back in a gaze of Connie's blood, alongside of other contradicting affectivities such as feelings of profound tenderness towards her, oneself and others (Critchley, 2009).[11] The subject cannot penetrate the key to his mystery so redoubles to the initial sensorial awareness of Connie's claim in the first structural moment. He dares to wonder with more clarity; "What hold does *her* blood have on me, and the others?" "What am I to *her*?" and "What is *she* to *me*?" and further, "Who is *she* to *them, of which I am one*?"

The fantasy-driven inter-subjective transactions of the second moment culminate with the "growing illumination" of a singular truth that has to do with *returning to Connie's impossible claim* sustained in the first moment of logical time encountering *her blood* (Lacan, 2006, p. 168). The psychical hold of the master signifier of her *blood* in other words begins to shift to *the one* who is bleeding. "Maybe, *she* (or what my fantasy of what she is becoming to me) will have the key to what I am not finding here. . . . Maybe, *she* is the *'one who is supposed to know' what her blood foretells, for me, or all of us*." The time for comprehension concludes when the subject has objectified the very intuition that inaugurated its entrance into the second movement, born of the first that now "blazes a path" into the third (Lacan, 2006, p. 206).

The third moment of time, logical collectivity: we are not only leper-things

In this third moment of time, *who I am* is not only mediated by a second object but also by a *third*, a third that exceeds the "we," intuited in the closing of the second structural moment. The third is *the other's Other* or *objet petit a*, who is the unconscious remainder of the initial wound that formulated the subject. In other words, the child's mother first occupies the position of big Other and is traumatized through the discovery of her lack, her incompleteness or imperfection. The big Other who timelessly dominates the narrative about what matters in all levels of collective discourse is carefully sutured into significance by fantasies that are generated by our transferential relationships between the image we have of ourselves and the belief that the big Other (*or objet petit a*) is *not lacking*. Our fantasy motivations, to be absurdly simplistic, are constructed to hide *the nothing* that is *the lack* in the Other and *our own primal resonances and resistances to it* (Žižek, 2008, pp. 147–148).[12]

The subject of our narrative now turns to Connie, the third, the *other of the Other* who is the remainder of the object-cause of desire (mother), the Lacanian *objet petit a*. The claim Connie has on me, or rather the symbolic investiture I have in her as an *ego-ideal*, makes itself known through Connie's lack. *Her* lack is symbolized by the void of her womb revealed through the real evacuation of her blood. Her blood reveals her lack. Being must return to the wound of the encounter from which Connie's devastating lack is revealed. Here, the subject must face Connie's impossible demand, *to give her what she lacks* (her lost object), but now it dawns on him that what she lacks is *not his to give*. He is called to give her what *he does not have*, or is *his* to give, one of Lacan's many definitions of love (Lacan, 2006, p. 516). What Connie needs is beyond her own capability to acquire, her own lost object *or* the subject's ability to help her. The full effect of the transference is mobilized when the subject identifies with something that the Other's other is not aware of and more importantly is singularly meant for him to make use of. He cannot save her, heal her from AIDS or put her blood back into her body. Nor, can *he save himself*. He must face the two lacks, his own failure to meet the letter of Connie's impossible demand *and* his own constitutive lack, his own lost object of which he now only has a momentary glimpse. This momentary glimpse reveals an inescapable and singular poignancy, thus ushering the subject from the inter-subjective discourse of the imaginary realm into the symbolic. *This movement inaugurates what we are calling trans-subjectivity* through which a collective truth *may become known.*

Let's break this thought down further. The subject's field of psychical inquiry has now opened further beyond his discourse with an inter-subjective "we" and the egoic-guided desires that unfolded in the second movement. The discourse with the other of the Other, directed by his transferences with Connie (*objet a*), now opens him to a new, terrifying and fascinating (*jouissance*) field of desire. The subject is now compelled to face his own *timeless* shame, for *being* impotent and helpless in the first place, for *seeing* Connie in her absolute naked helplessness *and* for turning away with repulsion. "I am ashamed for my repulsion by the sight and smell of your vaginal blood." "I was repulsed looking at your bleeding vagina (yet could not look away) and at the very virus ridden blood that is killing *both of us, no, all of us*." "I am ashamed for hating myself for having AIDS, for how I contracted the virus in the first place and for turning away from my own raw helplessness."

Suddenly, a new thought flashes up that pivots the subject from the present field of desire to another psychical borderland between *two other* phantasmatic and somatic bodies. "Was this a birth or death room?"[13] In such moments, we can feel the powerful recursive pull of the Hegelian *Aufhebung*, where the subject steps backwards with a new rush of anxiety and then goes under into even deeper timeless ground, a ground that has been there all along (Giegerich et al., 2005, pp. 6–7).[14] We can almost hear the psychical churning of *prima materia*, where formlessness incarnates itself further, seeking its own logical other.

Desire for Lacan is always known through the body (Lacan, 2014, p. 216). The subject can traverse the libidinal weight of the question only so far without going up in flames. However, from this new perspective the subject can *see* Connie and himself with raw and open eyes. This occurrence reveals a new dimension of temporality through which the subject is given a present that is not cut off from a haunted past or future but contains both. The subject "opens up historicity" through the voices of others past and present to which he is now able to respond (Akca, 2017, p. 317).[15]

Another question arises. "What do '*I*' want of *myself* in relation to *your* need?" "What do you need of me that requires *me* to *exceed how you have been cared for* in our world and *how I have cared* or *been* cared for?" And further, in another stunning bolt of clarity, "She relies on *me* to know how to *be* and *what to do* no matter what." Hook, through Vanheule and Verhaeghe, gives us a clarifying summary of how the subject is mediated by its ego ideal while engaging the big Other:

> In Lacan's interpretation, ego-ideals are symbolic elements that the subject takes from the discourse of the [O]ther. This means that they are nothing but privileged discursive elements: specific traits and characteristics of others that arrest a subject's attention and are unconsciously adopted to the extent that they are considered to imply an answer to the riddle of the [O]ther's desire.
>
> (Vanheule & Verhaeghe, 2009, p. 397 in Hook &
> Vanheule, 2018, p. 132)

A new relationship between a bloodless woman and a mindless man becomes strangely animated by an *objet a* between them that is shared yet not entirely their own. New life flashes up from her bloodless body and is directed to his lifeless mind and back again to hers and so on and on. The subject can now deduce: "H*er* fate is also *mine* and *all of ours*." The logical reasoning in the third moment opens with the subject's formulation of a truth it now believes is shared by the group.

We see here another iterative manifestation of trans-subjectivity. The singularly invigorated "I" apprehends a new "we" perspective only now perceived from the collision between what is finite in being and what is not. It is here that the subject may begin to translate particularity into some kind of universality, one that levels distinctions between others by recognizing what is common amongst ourselves as people over time but, at the same time, does not disallow what remains irreparably separate (Ruti, 2013). The subject of Lacan's third moment has acknowledged to himself his own limits and culpability in Connie's dilemma and now extends this responsibility to the group through what he believes is a "shared" but yet unspoken truth (Lacan, 2006, pp. 211–212). What the subject has tremulously and still privately concluded may be formally articulated thus:

> The mortifying effects of shame I feel towards myself for having AIDS in the first place and have likewise inflicted on Connie in her nakedness can now be recognized as not *entirely* originating from my own constituent vulnerability but perpetuated by a brute and senseless reality outside of myself that I complicitly supported. *We* are participating victims in a society that condones exclusivity and "*we must conceive of ourselves as formally responsible* [and] guilty for it" (Žižek, 2008, p. 247). These societal forces that once gave us a sense of belonging, identity and hope for a future worth living have now turned against us when we became infected with HIV/AIDS. The medical

system, government and people on the street, even our own friends and family, disavow our suffering, treat us like leper-things and look at us with terror and contempt. We have to lie about our health status, or else we will lose our jobs, our sexual desirability, our families and friends, our homes or any desirable social standing within the society that we contributed to and depended upon for care. *These norms create the very criteria through which each of us is judged. They are not my own, your own or Connie's.*

The revelation, for which Connie has made her sacrifice, reveals a crucial void within the symbolic order portrayed in an *ideology of carelessness*. From this void and only from it can a new basis of care be created through novel interpretations of what matters: traditions, values and norms. Nevertheless, the subject continues to doubt why *he* has this mandate and if he is up to the task (Žižek, 2008, p. 126). When he makes a fundamental choice to act in response to his revelation, a new and terrifying space opens to everything through a heightened awareness of lived time. Lacan (2006, p. 212) describes this moment thus:

Only the slightest disparity need appear in the logical term "others" for it to become clear how much the truth for all depends upon the rigor of each: that truth – if reached by only some – can engender, if not confirm, error in the others; and, moreover, that if in this race to the truth one is but alone, although not all may get to the truth, still no one can get there but by means of others.

The stakes are high in other words, and the subject cannot be certain about what is true or if he is actually serving a shared truth.

Let's return now to the actual vignette where the tendrils of this discussion are rooted. There, I stated that our entire community moved into action, an action born by a *shared rigor*. Whoever initiated the symbolic utterance of truth into action, *"Let's all carry her together to the van,"* is not remembered. The collective gestalt born of a shared revelation whooshed out of us like a baby spinning out of its mother's bloody womb. As Greg Carrigan describes it almost 30 years later, "We could all see our own death then, and it was at the same time so healing because *we were all lifting her on the bloody mattress*, over us, she floated over the top of us." We were all engulfed in the fierce eddy of unintelligible forces swirling around and through us that somehow, as I believe, Lacan tries to articulate through the culminating movement of collective logic into a new form of *intelligibility*, a new collective organizing mandate of care. Disease was momentarily elevated from the shame stained status of the leper-thing towards another side of care analogous to love (Critchley et al., 2014, p. 7).

Notes

1 I develop early Heidegger's (2010) depiction of "having become" in relation to the phenomenon of what can also be considered collective individuation and illustration of the Project Quest community at some length (Brooks, 2018, pp. 63–67).

2 Derek Hook masterfully elaborates a theory of the trans-subjective using the illustration of the prisoner's dilemma as Lacan had done in his 1945/2006 essay. He extends his theory from a multi-disciplinary perspective. He is interested in delineating the difference of social psychical theory from Lacan's depiction throughout his collected works attempting to formulate the best aspects of either towards a fresh "extra-disciplinary" contribution that has broader applications than either (Hook, 2013; Hook & Vanheule, 2018). My focus in this work is to elaborate a psychoanalytic understanding of group phenomena as relevant not only in the formation of the subject but as co-effectively individuating as a response to the effects of real world history or one's place in history.

3 Daniel Ross (who also has a chapter in this book) explicates Stiegler's critique of Heidegger on this point thus: "If politics is the struggle to articulate the I with the we, a struggle that requires both the calculation of the future and the incalculability of the very same future, then Heidegger's failure to clearly see that the technical objects of tertiary retention are the basis of every relationship to the future, of whatever kind, proves to be the very reason for his political failure: failing to see the role of technical individuation between psychic individuation and collective individuation" (Ross, 2018, p. 7). Stiegler's primary concern has to do with a massive entropic collapse that renders us into a stupor or a "blind stupidity leading to the madness of those it strips of the feeling of existing – that is, of being themselves worthy of respect, and of understanding themselves as such" (Stiegler, 2019, p. 26). Other conceptions akin to crowd stupidity resulting in massive entropic collapse are Heidegger's "They," "das Man" or "Inauthentic man" and Jung's "soulless herd animal" (Heidegger, 1927/1962, p. 164; Jung, 1928/1931, paras. 150, 9).

4 Lacan sharpens his distinction between "the little other" or objet petit a (autre) and "the big Other" (Autre) in 1955 and later (1991, chapter 19). The little other is not other but an egoic projection activated in the transference (of all kinds) generated within the imaginary order (see what follows). Lacan would later flush out his concept of objet petit a as the object cause of desire that one seeks through phantasmatic identification's with the other. An important point to emphasize here in light of the subject of our essay is that little a transactions played out through inter-subjective identifications through one's body affects self-image. Disturbing or immature fixations that are lodged in the fantasies (imaginary order) may become dislodged through language which is structured in the symbolic order – the site of Lacan's big Other. Subjective encounters with Big Other-ness messaging are received as radically de-centering because they cannot be assimilated through imaginary identifications (Dylan, 1997, pp. 132–133). The symbolic order or socio-symbolic field is socially structured by language and cultural laws (codes) that regulate kinship, belonging through ideological messaging. Fantasies (little a) that are generated in the Imaginary realm may intersect the socio-symbolic field as the subject struggles with the paradoxes that are evident within a particular ideological situation (big Other messaging) to which one is subjugated. One example is the gay person living with AIDS in a society that does not recognize the value (significance?) of his sexual orientation or respond adequately to the effects of the pandemic (medical care, research, adequate provision for pragmatic or psychological effects on its victims). A contemporary example is the first responder who is authorized by society to treat COVID-19 victims even though they have inadequate protective equipment to do so safely. This subject's struggle to recognize itself as valid amidst societal norms that disavow his value becomes the site of trans-subjective possibilities and collective change (individuation).

5 There are certain resonances to Heidegger's discussions about the ontological difference where Dasein finds itself in a middle between being and beings and what I relay in this sentence (Inwood, 1999, pp. 211–299). See Žižek's Parallax View (2006) for another perspective of an ontological gap as the site of subject formation.

6 See Anne Caron:

> https://kenyonreview.org/kr-online-issue/literary-activism/selections/anne-car
> son-763879/ <https://kenyonreview.org/kr-online-issue/literary-activism/selections/
> anne-carson-763879/. Shame is a universal basis of the ethical relation in that
> it is the affect that accompanies our encounter with an alterity that exposes us
> to being and the movement of being's possibility. Such a subject is not self-
> constituting but is given over to the other's alterity or, in Lacan's view, the other of the
> Other. Shame is the "sharp goad of the enigma," in Laplanche's terms (Laplanche,
> 2014, p. 96).

7 Julia Kristeva refers to such moments as the "alterity of madness" as "the ground zero
of psyche . . . spasms and vomit, repulsion, the retching that thrusts me to the side and
turns me away from defilement, sewage and muck, a void . . . improper and unclean"
(Kristeva, 1987, p. 160).

8 Stephan Gullatz identifies Jung's reliance on the self as the empty master signifier
through which the terms of Jung's epistemology seamlessly "knots" its meaning into a
closed totality (Gullatz, 2010, p. 697). In my view, Gullatz conflates the Jungian master of self with the World Soul (*Unus Mundus*) as all signification in Jung's problematic comes from and toward it (pointing to itself as unitary source), not the other way
around (Brooks, 2011). The collective unconscious is only the World Soul's a-temporal
reservoir from which the archetypes emerge as messengers from its unitary source.
Giegerich's project attempts to keep his own version of "soul" relevant by intellec-
tually contemporizing it without completely abandoning Jung's vision (Giegerich,
2004). Giegerich is well read not only in continental philosophy (French and German)
but also Lacan. He once said that Jungians are "third rate" thinkers, whereas Lacan is
first rate (personal conversation, 2008).

9 I am referencing how Lacan's notion of the death drive is activated in the face of ultimate disempowerment by a constant pressure to seek oneness with a primordial lost,
displaced or imagined drive object. As I stated it elsewhere, "Think of the death drive
as a psychic first responder to a destabilizing crisis whose reflexive and deeply unconscious 'directive' is to turn inward and seek an originary oneness with [*objet petit a*] to
avoid annihilation at any cost" (Brooks, 2016, pp. 138–139).

10 See Uljana Akca's erudite and illuminating article titled "Identity as the Difference
of Power and the Difference from Being" through which she explores the connections amongst identity, difference and power through the intellectual lenses of Butler,
Heidegger and Foucault (Akca, 2017). Ladson Hinton has elsewhere warned us that
those who disrupt our illusory ideal of unity (refugees of any kind) are also vulnerable to being culturally scapegoated thus magnifying the "all-too-human tendency to
eliminate the troubling 'other,' whom we blame for disrupting our personal or social
worlds" (Hinton, 2011, p. 280).

11 Critchley follows Levinas and Lacan with his own conception of the subject who
shapes itself in relation to a demand that it can never meet that divides and sunders
itself through the experience of hetero-affectivity. Heteronomy is the determination of
the subject in another. See note 13 for further discussion on *Nachträglichkeit*.

12 From this point of view, our own blind affiliations to an empty master signifier (as Gullatz claims in note 7) can now be seen as a vector to *objet a* and our need to believe this
big Other is *not lacking*. Thus, personal wound is connected or transferred to symbolic
investments of all kinds.

13 This moment can also be conceived as a Freudian *Nachträglichkeit* or revised Lacanian *Après-Coup* insight in psychoanalytic terms when the here-and-now trauma opens
the patient to an earlier wound. See Brooks, 2016, for a full discussion on this topic and
a case illustration.

14 Giegerich actually states, "stepping backwards and going under, rather than a utopian waiting for a resolution." Giegerich strongly veers away from a dialectic that emulates Jung's transcendent function (Giegerich et al., 2005, p. 7). See also Jon Mills (2002) for an explication of Hegelian sublimation (*Aufhebung*) and its psychoanalytic application.
15 I am correlating aspects of Akca's depiction of Heidegger's moment of *Augenblick* with Lacan's account of collective logic and what I am referring to as a trans-subjective moment.

References

Akca, U. (2017). "Identity as the Difference of Power and the Differing from Being." *Researching Hermeneutics, Phenomenology and Practical Philosophy*, 10,1.

Benjamin, W. (1968). *Illuminations Essays and Reflections*. New York: Schocken Books.

Brooks, R. M. (2011). "Un-Thought Out Metaphysics in Analytical Psychology: A Critique of Jung's Epistemological of Basis for Psychic Reality." *Journal of Analytical Psychology*, 56, 492–513.

———. (2016). "The Intergenerational Transmission of the Catastrophic Effects of *Real-World History Expressed Through the Analytic Subject*." In *Ethics of Evil Psychoanalytic Investigations*. Eds. R. Naso & J. Mills, pp. 137–176. London: Karnac Books.

———. (2018). "Self as Political Possibility: Subversive Neighbor Love and Transcendental Agency Amidst Collective Blindness." *International Journal of Jungian Studies*, 10, 1, 48–75.

———. (2019). "A Critique of C. G. Jung's Theoretical Basis for Selfhood Theory Vexed by an Incorporeal Ontology." In *Jung and Philosophy*. Ed. J. Mills, pp. 109–137. London & New York: Routledge.

Butler, J. (2004). *Precarious Life: The Powers of Mourning and Violence*. London & New York: Verso.

———. (2015). *Frames of War: When Is Life Grievable?* London & New York: Verso.

Butler, R. (2014). *The Žižek Dictionary*. Durham, NC: Acumen.

Critchley, S., Bennetts, S. R. & Tutt, D. (2009). *Infinitely Demanding: Ethics of Commitment, Politics of Resistance*. London & New York: Verso.

———. (2014). "Hamlet's Nothing: Berfrois Interviews Simon Critchley." www.berfrois.com/feed

Giegerich, W. (2004). "The End of Meaning and the Birth of Man." *Journal of Jungian Theory and Practice*, 6, I.

Giegerich, W., Miller, D. & Mogenson, G. (2005). *Dialectics & Analytical Psychology: The El Capitan Canyon Seminar*. New Orleans: Spring Journal Books.

Gullatz, S. (2010). "Constructing the Collective Unconscious." *Journal of Analytical Psychology*, 55, 5, 691–721.

Heidegger, M. (1927/1962). *Being and Time*. Trans. J. Macquarrie & E. Robinson. New York: HarperOne.

———. (2010). *The Phenomenology of Religious Life*. Trans. M. Fritch & J. A. Gosetti Ferencei. Bloomington: Indiana University Press.

———. (2012). *Contributions to Philosophy (of the event)*. Trans. R. Rojcewicz & D. Vallega-Neu. Bloomington: Indiana University Press.

Hinton, L. (2011). "*Unus Mundus* – Transcendent Truth or Comforting Fiction? Overwhelm and the Search for Meaning in a Fragmented World." *Journal of Analytical Psychology*, 56, 375–396.

Hoens, D. (2006). "Towards a New Perversions Psychoanalysis." In *Reflections on Seminar XVII*. Eds. J. Clemens & R. Griggs. Durham & London: Duke University Press.

Hook, D. (2008). "Fantasmatic Transactions: On the Persistence of Apartheid Ideology." *Subjectivity*, 24, 275–297.

———. (2013). "Towards a Lacanian Group Psychology: The Prisoner's Dilemma and the Trans-Subjective." *Journal for the Theory of Social Behavior*, 43, 2, 115–132.

———. (2018). *Six Moments in Lacan*. London & New York: Routledge.

Hook, D. & Vanheule, S. (2016). "Revisiting the Master Signifier, or: Mandela and Repression." *Frontiers in Psychology* [Accessed 10 January 2020].

Inwood, M. J. (1999). *A Heidegger Dictionary*. Malden, MA: Blackwell Publishers.

Jung, C. G. (1928/1931). "The Spiritual Problem of Modern Man." *CW*, 10, 74–94.

Kristeva, J. (1987). *Woman. Alterity*. Ed. M. C. Taylor. Chicago & London: University of Chicago Press.

Lacan, J. (1981). *The Seminar of Jacques Lacan, Book XI: The Four Fundamental Concepts of Psychoanalysis*. London: W.W. Norton.

———. (1991). *The Seminar of Jacques Lacan, Book II: The Ego in Freud's Theory and in the Technique of Psychoanalysis*, 1954–1955. Ed. J. A. Miller. New York & London: W.W. Norton.

———. (1993). *The Seminar of Jacques Lacan, Book III, The Psychosis, 1955–1956*. New York & London: W.W. Norton.

———. (1945/2006). *Écrits: The First Complete Edition in English*. Trans. B. Fink. New York & London: W. W. Norton.

———. (2007). *The Other Side of Psychoanalysis: The Seminar of Jacques Lacan*, Book. XVII. New York & London: W.W. Norton.

———. (2014). *Anxiety: The Seminar of Jacques Lacan*. Book X. Ed. J. A. Miller. Trans. A. R. Price. Cambridge: Polity Press.

Laplanche, J. (2014). "Sublimations and/or Inspiration." In *Seductions and Enigmas*. Eds. J. Fletcher & N. Ray. London: Lawrence & Wishart.

Mills, J. (2002). *The Unconscious Abyss: Hegel's Anticipation of Psychoanalysis*. Albany: State University of New York Press.

Ross, D. (2018). "Care and Carelessness in the Anthropocene, Introduction to a Reading of Stiegler and Heidegger." Paper presented at the University of Canterbury, Christchurch, May.

Ruti, M. (2013). "The Other as the Face in Post-Levinasian and Post-Lacanian Ethics." Paper presented at the Psychology & the Other Conference, Cambridge, MA, October.

Simondon, G. (1992). "The Genesis of the Individual." In *Incorporations*. Eds. Jonathan Crary & Sanford Kwinter. New York: Zone.

Stiegler, B. (2019). *The Age of Disruption Technology and Madness in Computational Capitalism*. Malden, MA: Polity Press.

Vanheule, S. & Verhaeghe, P. (2009). "Identity Through a Psychoanalytic Looking Glass." *Theory and Psychology*, 19, 3, 391–411.

Žižek, S. (2006). *The Parallax View*. Cambridge, MA: MIT Press.

———. (2008). *The Sublime Object of Ideology*. London & New York: Verso.

Chapter 5

Hontologie

Lacan, shame and the advent of the subject

Sharon R. Green

In 2011, I had the opportunity to visit Cambodia, where my son and daughter-in-law were teaching English for the Peace Corps in a remote village. While in Phnom Penh, my son and I visited the genocide museum, which is housed in the buildings of Tuol Sleng, sometimes known by its abbreviated name, S-21 (Security Office 21). Tuol Sleng was the key interrogation and prison centre of the Khmer Rouge. Here, around 12,000 people branded enemies of the regime were tortured into confessing non-existent crimes before being executed. Between 1975 and 1979, close to 2 million out of a total population of 8 million Cambodians died in the genocide perpetrated by the ruling Khmer Rouge Party (Hinton, 2016).

When prisoners arrived at Tuol Sleng, each was documented in a bizarre ritual. After their handcuffs and bindings were removed, they were seated in a specially made chair with a headrest that forced them to look directly into the camera for a mug-shot style photograph.[1] Each prisoner had a number pinned to his or her chest (sometimes literally through their skin rather than clothing). Unlike the tattoos that the Nazis inflicted on their victims, these numbers were not unique identifiers. The numbers merely indicated the prisoner's position in the order of those who had arrived that day – for example, if 15 prisoners arrived, the numbers were 1–15. The next day the numbers started over again from one. Hundreds of these mug shots were on display pinned to bulletin boards that filled room after room of the museum – rooms that were once the prison cells of those photographed. The images haunted me, knowing through the uncanny temporality of a photograph, that each person gazing back at me had been executed decades earlier. It was a devastating experience. After completing our tour of the museum, my son and I sat silently for a while on the benches in the sunny courtyard where instruments of torture were displayed. I was trying to regain my capacity to think after the powerful impact of our visit. Although I had read extensively about the Cambodian genocide, knowledge of what had happened did not buffer me from the uncanny gaze of the executed Cambodians nor the brute reality of the apparatus of torture vibrating nearby.

In the course of trying to talk with my son about what I had witnessed, I blurted out, "I am so grateful to live in a country where there hasn't been a genocide." My son's startled exclamation of "Mom!" and the look of shock on his face instantly stripped me of my defensive denial – leaving me mortified with shame. In that moment, it was incomprehensible to me that I had forgotten that the United States was forged through genocide and slavery and that these crimes persist. Even as I write these words, I am burning with shame while flames of protest and outrage are burning across the United States. Our burning cities are testifying to the death of George Floyd and the countless other lives lost to colonial violence, police brutality and institutionalized racism. Crimes against humanity have been systemically hidden and forgotten. In addition to the uprising of voices demanding that we recognize racism and oppression, there is a pandemic ravaging the human population and destroying our taken-for-granted and ordinary ways of life. Some suffer more than others as we all face an unwritten future. Climate change may make the earth uninhabitable, and nuclear weapons are brandished by authoritarian strong men threatening to annihilate the entire planet.

The writings of Imre Kertész (2006), the Nobel laureate in literature who survived both Auschwitz and Buchenwald, offer a glimpse of the hidden processes operating within me at Tuol Sleng – processes that are at work in all of us to hide what we do not want to know – especially during times of transition when our familiar ways of organizing the world no longer hold:

> I don't know when it first occurred to me that there had to be a terrible mistake, a diabolical irony, at work in the world order that you experience as part of ordinary life, and that terrible mistake is culture itself, the belief system, the language and the concepts that conceal from you that you have long been a well-oiled component of the machinery that has been set up for your own destruction. The secret of survival is collaboration, but *to admit that is to bring such shame down on you that you prefer to repudiate rather than accept it* [my emphasis] . . . the fact remains that when I grasped it, my whole way of looking at things changed.
>
> (pp. 66–67)

During these times of upheaval and turmoil, what does psychoanalysis have to offer that could help us resist collaborating with our own destruction? How do we stay open to uncomfortable truths about ourselves and our society without rushing to automatic narratives that restore coherence to the fraying world order? Kertész is emphasizing that if we wish to resist those forces that would use us as "well-oiled components in the machinery" of a destructive culture, then we must recognize and learn to accept our shame rather than repudiate it. The philosopher and Lacanian analyst Joan Copjec states that in Seminar XVII, *The Underside of Psychoanalysis*, Lacan renders the goal of analysis in a distilled formula. She writes (2006, p. 91), "The final aim of psychoanalysis, it turns out, is the production of shame. The seamy underside of psychoanalysis, the backside towards which all the twists and turns have led, is finally shame." The idea that the production of shame might be the aim of psychoanalysis is provocative and generates a lot of questions – especially in the current climate of absolute shamelessness and narcissism. Although Lacan refers to shame throughout his work, he did not offer a detailed analysis as he did for anxiety in Seminar X, *Anxiety*.[2] Therefore, using a Lacanian psychoanalytic perspective in dialogue with multiple views on "shame," I will explore the relationship between the traumatic structure of subjectivity, shame and culture – especially during times of ominous transitions. Shame that continues to burn may be the only reliable compass we have when confronted with the ethical dilemmas that are emerging as the basic coordinates of our social lives are disrupted.

Varieties of shame

But what is shame? Certainly there is no definitive answer to this question! However, a brief overview may help situate how Lacanian concepts offer a unique contribution to the conversation. All but the most shameless are familiar with the embodied feelings that accompany shame: our cheeks redden and burn and so we drop our head, cover our face and avoid the gaze of others; mortification leaves us frozen in our tracks and speechless; feeling exposed, we wish we could sink into the ground to disappear. Shame is often characterized as a painful emotion where we feel that our self is defective, faulty, unworthy and vulnerable in a global way rather than for any particular action or quality. Theories of shame range from those that understand it as a toxic and pathological affect to be avoided to those theories that see shame as the fundamental sentiment of what it means to be human (Nathanson, 1987). Although it is true that the experience of shame profoundly *affects* us, others have pointed out that relying solely on a conceptualization of shame-as-affect doesn't convey the import of shame as a temporal process that reveals its relationship to being, its ontological dimension (Seidler, 2000).[3] For example, Heidegger (1992) writes that shame is an emotive tonality that traverses a person's whole being: "*Aidos* [shame] is not a feeling man possesses but the disposition, as the disposing, which determines his essence, i.e. determines the relation of Being to man" (p. 75). For Levinas shame is not about deviating from a moral norm but is understood as the crucial phenomenon disclosing to the self the fundamental insufficiency at the heart of the human condition (Zahavi & Sánchez, 2018). No matter how much we try to struggle against our insufficiency and vulnerability, which are constitutive of being, we are chained to ourselves and can never escape our lack:

> What appears in shame is thus precisely the fact of being riveted to oneself, the radical impossibility of fleeing oneself to hide from oneself, the unalterably binding presence of the I to itself. . . . It is therefore our intimacy, that is, our presence to ourselves, that is shameful. It reveals not our nothingness but rather the totality of our existence.
>
> (Lévinas, 2003, pp. 64–65)

Shame is often characterized in two broad categories depending upon which dimension of the experience is emphasized (Zahavi & Sánchez, 2018). Some characterize shame as a distinct social emotion in that it emerges as a response to the scrutinizing gaze of an actual other person or an internalized critic. Because shame is self-reflexive, others see shame as primarily an emotion of self-assessment, a self-conscious emotion:

> Shame, as one of the self-conscious emotions, differs from what has been called the primary emotions because it comes about through self-reflection. . . . self-conscious emotions require a self both to produce the state and then to experience it.
>
> (Miller, 1999, p. 1181)

For example, the psychoanalyst Broucek (1991) includes aspects of both self-assessment and the gaze of the other in his analysis of shame. Following Merleau-Ponty, he says that the "look" of the other as well as the recognition of one's reflection in the mirror results in an alienation where the self is torn from itself. He explains that this alienation occurs because the child's body is transformed from a kinesthetic instrumental presence to a visible presence, an object that is perceived via a reflexive relationship of the self by the self. Shame is activated when the person feels related to or looked at in a way that is objectifying. Because Broucek places shame in a developmental trajectory, he links future psychopathologies to the child's experiences with the degree and quantity of shame-inducing intersubjective objectifications by others during the child's development. Zahavi (2014) recognizes shame as both a self-conscious emotion and a social emotion and writes that there is no need for theoretical tension between the two viewpoints. He favours Sartre's phenomenological account of shame in that shame reveals our relationality, our being for others as well as our self-assessment. For Sartre (1943/2018), whose work influenced Lacan,[4] it is the Other that constitutes me as an object, and shame is shame *of myself before the Other* where these two structures are inseparable. A Sartrean subject becomes a subject when it experiences itself as an *object* of another subject; shame is then the inevitable experience of realizing that I am not only a being-for-myself, but I am also being-for-other.

> Pure shame is not the feeling of being this or that reprehensible object but, in general, of being *an object*; i.e., of *recognizing* myself in that degraded, dependent and frozen being that I am for the Other. . . . Thus shame is a unitary apprehension with three dimensions: "I am ashamed of *myself* before the Other."
>
> (pp. 392–393)

Although this brief review cannot do justice to the rich literature on shame, what I'd like to emphasize are the concepts reflected in these descriptions: the shame of being as well as the shame of the self experiencing another aspect of the self as an undesirable or defective object in the eyes of the other (whether an actual other person or an internalized other). Each of these terms – being, self, object and other – points to key dimensions of Lacanian subjectivity. However, with his concept of 'the Real', Lacan destabilizes the meaning of these terms as they pertain to the formation of subjectivity.

The Real

The Real is one of the three orders that structure the Lacanian psyche (the other two being the imaginary and symbolic)[5] and evolves throughout Lacan's teaching. Most importantly though, the Real is not a substance and is not to be confused with socially constructed "reality" – rather, it is the unpredictable *excess* that escapes the signifying process. In other words, the Real – as the limit of the symbolic – is that which *cannot* be formulated in speech or represented in the language – but has effects. Because the Real cannot be represented, it is experienced as trauma. The Real points to the primordial loss of being and to the enigmatic void around which subjectivity is constituted. The two primary manifestations of the Real linked to subjectivity are *jouissance* and the *objet petit a* (Vanheule, 2014).

The *objet petit a* (often referred to in English as "the small object *a*" or simply the "object *a*") is a paradoxical concept in that the object *a* is not any kind of object in the world; rather it is a negativity. It is not a substance but a *lack*. The *a* in *objet petit a* represents *autre* (other), and even when referred to in English, Lacan wanted the letter *a* to remain untranslated. In Lacanian theory, the 'other' is a central and complex term; Lacan conceptualized otherness in many ways including the big Other (*Autre*), which is another name for the symbolic order, radical alterity. The symbolic is the realm which regulates social functioning and includes the rituals and rules that structure our thoughts and actions (e.g., law, religion, education, medicine). Most importantly, the symbolic includes language, which consists of the signifiers and grammatical structure of the mother tongue.[6] Language determines our perceptions of the world. When other people are but a reflection and projection of our own ego, they are not actually "other" but merely serve as our mirror image, our alter-egos. The other as alter-ego is related to the imaginary order, which is characterized by illusions of sameness, wholeness and autonomy. And the "otherness" of object *a* is of the Real. It is linked to the limits of language and our loss of being – object *a* is "the portion of life that is lost because of language" (Soler, 2016, p. 22). With his invention of object *a*, Lacan introduced a new dimension to subjectivity by placing an enigma that is excessive, haunting and disruptive at the heart of what it means to be human.

I will return to the object *a*, but to pursue a Lacanian perspective on shame and subjectivity, there is another manifestation of the Real to consider and that is jouissance. The French word *jouissance*, like the little *a*, is also left untranslated in English because the literal meaning of enjoyment does not convey Lacan's concept:

> What I call jouissance – in the sense in which the body experiences itself – is always in the nature of tension, in the nature of a forcing, of a spending, even of an exploit. Unquestionably, there is jouissance at the level at which pain begins to appear, and we know that it is only at this level of pain that a whole dimension of the organism, which would otherwise remain veiled, can be experienced.
>
> (Lacan, 1967, p. 60 cited in Braunstein, 2003, p. 103)

Jouissance is related to those forces of the body beyond our control that generate excitation and agitation that exceed representation.[7] Jouissance, although sometimes considered "pleasure in pain," is perhaps more accurately understood as that which is "beyond the pleasure principle." The Freudian pleasure principle is the principle of mental functioning that avoids un-pleasure and seeks to safeguard homeostasis; transgressing the pleasure principle brings pain as there is only so much pleasurable intensity that we can bear. For Lacan, the pleasure principle is linked to the symbolic order, the law that attempts to regulate the agitated chaos of our fleshy body (the Real of jouissance) through our use of signifiers (language). Thus, signifiers serve as a barrier to the primal unbound jouissance of *das Ding*, which is originally experienced as the mother's body, by creating boundaries around the psyche and the soma of mother and infant. However, when the Real of jouissance is channelled through language, there is always a leftover kernel of the Real that escapes the net of signifiers – the agitating excess that cannot be translated is the object *a* – which continually destabilizes the borders and boundaries between self and other.

Shame as a barrier

The unique model of shame put forward by Sylvan Tomkins may have interested Lacan.[8] Tomkins, who has been called the originator of affect theory (Nathanson, 1987, p. 133), proposes that shame is an innate mechanism, present from birth, that is automatically elicited when there are barriers to enjoyment and excitement. For Tomkins, affects are part of our biological inheritance and form the basis of the human being's motivational system. His model is an elaboration of the Darwinian view wherein he is trying to understand the utilitarian and evolutionary nature of shame (Lewis, 2003, p. 1184). He defines affects as the biological response to the increasing, decreasing or persistent intensity of neural firing triggered by a wide variety of stimuli both innate and learned. An innate affect (a proto-affect) is active from birth but becomes amplified into more complex affective scripts with the acquisition of speech. Affective scripts are co-assembled from perceptions, cognitions, drives, intentions and memories. In other words, the individual's life experiences shape the innate affective mechanisms into a person's singular emotional patterns. Tomkins does not consider shame a primary affect but an innate auxiliary affect that operates only after the positive affect pair he names "interest-excitement" has been activated. Interest-excitement is the genetically scripted protocol that mobilizes attention to information acquisition. The interest-excitement affect protocol increases in intensity from the pole of interest to excitement depending upon the intensity and rate at which new information is acquired. Because interest is an ubiquitous and necessary feature of human information gathering, it was taken for granted as an attitude of pure attention rather than an affect. However, Tomkins (1963/2008) recognized that gathering novel information is necessary for survival and is thus a primary motivating affect for human beings. In his view, shame is inevitable because humans must maintain an interest in new situations which unceasingly arise over the course of a lifetime and "desire always outruns fulfillment sufficiently to attenuate interest without destroying it" (ibid, p. 388).

In this model, the innate activator of shame is the incomplete reduction of interest or joy when one is involved in an absorbing situation. Tomkins (1963/2008, pp. 353–354) states that any barrier to further exploration which partially reduces the smile of enjoyment will activate shame and reduce further exploration or self-exposure:

> Such a barrier might be because one is suddenly looked at by one who is strange, or because one wishes to look at or commune with another person but suddenly cannot because he is strange, or one expected him to be familiar but he suddenly appears unfamiliar, or one started to smile but found one was smiling at a stranger.

Lewis (2003, p. 1184) points out that there is confusion in Tomkins's theory as to whether the barrier to interest or enjoyment causes shame or whether shame is the cause of the barrier, but he states, "I think the term 'blocking of desire' would approximate Tomkins's meaning of shame." In either case, shame is intimately linked to barriers to excitement coupled with a desire to resume the interrupted activity or to maintain connection with the other. I am struck by the resonance between this idea and jouissance: Lacan (1970, pp. 194–195) writes,

> If the living being is something at all thinkable, it will be above all as subject of the *jouissance;* but this psychological law that we call the pleasure principle (and which is only the principle of displeasure) is very soon to create a barrier to all *jouissance.* If I am enjoying myself a little too much, I begin to feel pain and I moderate my pleasures. The organism seems made to avoid too much *jouissance.*

The original situation of (proto) shame is activated in the gaze between the mother and the infant. Tomkins (1963/2008) characterizes this first non-verbal communication as a social communion between mother and child of great interest to both, but when the interest gains in too much intensity, resulting in over-excitement, shame is activated, and the eyes are averted. However, unlike contempt or disgust, which are also auxiliary affects, an important dimension of shame is the subject's desire to return to that which created the original state of excitement; in this way, shame facilitates the restoration of relational links and the maintenance of social bonds. Tomkins believes that shame, shyness and guilt all share the same underlying biological identity at the level of affect. The failure to recognize this has created conceptual confusion regarding shame and guilt and has hindered our understanding of the magnitude and nature of the role shame plays in human functioning (p. 352). He speaks of the important role shame plays in relation to human dignity:

> Why are shame and pride such central motives? How can loss of face be more intolerable than loss of life? How can hanging the head in shame so mortify the spirit? In contrast to all other affects, *shame is an experience of the self by the self* [my emphasis]. At that moment when the self feels ashamed, it is felt as a sickness within the self.
>
> (p. 359)

Now the question arises, what is this self that experiences another part of its self in so many of these descriptions of shame?

The advent of the subject

For Lacan, there is no authentic or true self that we can ultimately achieve or discover. The self, equated with the ego, is a misrecognition – *méconnaissance* – rather than a true self because it is based on the imaginary identifications that are assigned to us from the Other, thus creating an inevitable condition of alienation. Rather, Lacanian theory posits that we exist as a *divided subject* that is constituted through lack and loss rather than through any substantial essence (Verhaeghe, 2004). The primordial loss in the formation of the subject is the loss of immortality – as soon as we are born, we are divided between eternal life and death, creating a void at the core of our being. The subject is also divided between jouissance – the corporeal Real of the body that exceeds symbolic representation (which Lacan distinguishes as "being") – and that which we can put into language ("existence" as opposed to "being"). This division between being and existence generates the fantasy of a primal loss of an unmediated relationship with the world. Only in looking backwards can we retroactively believe that we once had a state of symbiotic bliss with the (m)Other – and so we yearn for what we believe we lost – das *Ding*, the Thing of primal jouissance, poignantly and terrifyingly associated with the mother's body. In our fantasy, we imagine that *das Ding* will make us whole again by restoring our idyllic lost state of being (Lacan, 1959–1960/1997).

However, the speaking human being can never enjoy a life of harmonious self-presence. Our search for *das Ding* has always already been a lost cause because, as soon as we are born, and even before birth, we are immersed in the ocean of the Other – the Other being both the infant's actual caregiver, the mothering other, as well as the big Other. Even before we acquire the ability to speak, we are immersed in the language of our caregivers, and so the distinction between the actual other and the big Other of language/culture is not as clear as it seems. The infant, *infans*, the one without speech, emits a cry that signals the needs of the body (the biological organism, *soma*). Through an innate biological programme – an instinct (Freud's *Instinkt*) – the helpless infant seeks sustenance and is satisfied when the instinct's aim is achieved. The idea of the infant-as-organism is a mythical moment in time, however, because the infant is bathed in the (m)Other's calming or anxious words while in the womb and immediately from birth onwards. The human being who speaks (which Lacan calls the *parlê-tre*) is distinguished from other living beings by an additional dimension beyond seeking mere sustenance: The infant's cry to have an instinctual need satisfied (such as hunger) is also answered by the (m)Other through her speech and touch, both of which include the music of her response – the choice of soothing words or abrupt silence, the loving or angry tone of her voice, the tenderness or cruelty of her touch.

So, we can retranslate the scene of the crying infant: the infant experiences an internal sensation that is uncomfortable or painful – Lacan calls this jouissance. And so, in addition to satisfying a biological need, the (m)Other's bodily ministrations along with her speech initiate the first effort to symbolize and represent the infant's bodily tension (jouissance). It is this dialectic of the infant's cry *along with* the (m)Other's response that always already turns an instinct (*Instinkt*) into a drive (the Freudian *Trieb*), forever linking the infant's existence to the Other. Jouissance denotes the bodily tension associated with the drive. In the retroactive retranslation of instinct to drive, the infant's need (which can be satisfied) becomes a demand for the mother's love and recognition (which can never be satisfied). The drive is thus the infant's un-pleasurable bodily experience that has been addressed as a demand to the (m)Other for satisfaction of its need *along with* the demand for her love and attention.[9] The drives are linked to particular parts of the body (e.g., the mouth/nipple are linked to the oral drive) of the single constant force called desire. Unconscious desire moves us; it is what remains after need is subtracted from demand in the dialectic between infant and (m)Other; in other words, it is a desire for the love and recognition of the Other that can never be wholly satisfied. And so in the dialectical exchange of demand, the infant expects the (m)Other to provide the answer to its drive impulse. However, the infant, with no bodily boundaries yet established, ascribes the drive impulse to the (m)Other – although in terms of its lack, its desire – and asks: What does the Other want from me? (Verhaeghe, 2004, p. 224). This existential question sets off the never-ending dialectic of desire between the divided subject and the Other.

Once we enter into language, our desire is forever bound up in the play of words (signifiers). The installation of language into the psyche/soma is represented by the infant's first signifier, called the S_1 in Lacanian algebra. The S_1 cannot fully represent the Real of the body's drive tensions, but it indicates the first efforts at representation and regulation of the drive, linking it to both language and the body. Thus, the S_1 points to the traumatic disjunction of the divided subject: constitutionally split between living organism and speaking subject and the resultant loss – object a (Lacan, 1969–1970, 2006, p. 15). Installed at the level of both the soma (organism) and the psyche (first efforts at representation), the S_1 and object a will affect the subject's fundamental fantasies and future relationships. Because the S_1 is related to one's own body and earliest relationships, it is a unique and contingent signifier that points to the subject's absolute singularity; it is what makes each individual "one of a kind" (Miller, 2006). Our unique S_1 gets taken up into the signifying chain – the words and concepts that we use to both describe ourselves and to ascribe meaning to our experiences. Lacan represents this with the formula: $S_1 \rightarrow S_2$, where S_2 represents the infinite flow of signifiers. Because language inevitably fails to represent the totality of experience, efforts at symbolization endlessly persist. When we speak, jouissance is drained from the body and connected to the flow of signifiers. This is why words plays such a vital role in regulating the body's agitations and arousals (Vanheule, 2014, p. 153). Thus, in addition to meaning, signifiers are laden with drive – jouissance – and serve as the basis for our affective experiences (ibid).

Despite our unceasing efforts to regulate our arousal by draining jouissance from the body through symbolization, there is always an untranslated remainder of jouissance, an agitating kernel of the Real generated through speech – the object a. As discussed, object a is a component of libidinous corporeality (the Real) that is created by using signifiers but is not represented by a signifier or transformed into the symbolic (Vanheule, 2014, p. 127). It is the enigmatic dimension of our being that forever eludes our grasp, the uncanny excess that haunts us generating our endless efforts to contain, regulate and represent our experiences.

The barred and embarrassed subject

To confound our ordinary ways of thinking, Lacan created his own "algebra" wherein he uses symbols to formalize his ideas. This method troubles our immediate understanding so that we have to slow down and work with the symbols rather than believing we have easily grasped a concept. For example, the description of the installation of language into the world of the infant should not be read simply developmentally, which is perhaps most intuitive. Lacanian psychoanalysis is not a developmental psychology trying to restore so-called mental health based on preconceived ideas of what is good for the normal individual (De Kesel, 2009, p. 55). Rather, Lacan is interested in our singular stance towards the Real – the contingent and accidental events that will have affected our process of becoming via the retroactive and anticipatory temporality of *Nachträglichkeit*.[10]

In Seminar X, Lacan (1962–1963, 2014) represents the advent of the barred or divided subject – which I have described in a narrative form – through a quasi-arithmetical graph based on the European form of division. Through the use of symbols to represent the advent of the subject, the (pre)ontological structural dimension of subjectivity is emphasized. The diagram is meant to highlight the dialectical tension between the subject of jouissance (the mythical infant-as-organism already discussed) and the Other that constitutes our divided subjectivity (Vanheule, 2014):

$$\frac{O \mid S}{\underline{S \mid}}$$
$$a$$

In this scheme, O is divided by S, the subject of jouissance. O represents the symbolic order (the big Other) through which the Real of bodily jouissance (S) is transformed (ibid, p. 130). In the European form of division, the quotient is written under a bar. When O is divided by S, the *barre* (the typographical slash /) creates the always already barred subject ($) divided between its living being (S) and speaking existence (O). Lacan plays with the etymological relationship between the *barre* and *embarras* (a form of shame), saying embarrassment is "quite precisely the subject S decked out with the bar, $ . . . When you don't know what to do with yourself anymore, you look for something behind which to shield yourself" (ibid, p. 11).

Although the diagram illustrates structure, the advent of the barred subject ($) is not something that is acquired and then remains static (Neill, 2011).[11] If this simplified scheme included counter-clockwise arrows moving from *a* to S to O to $ to *a*, it would illustrate how the advent of the barred subject ($) – divided between living being (S) and speaking subject (O) and excess (a) – is a *temporal* process. Human temporality is not an entity, a sequence of self-contained 'now's moving from future to present to past in linear succession but is the distinctively human capacity to be at once ahead, behind and alongside oneself (Green, 2018). The divided subject is always in relation to *future* possibilities, which means that "the subject is what it is not yet, in order not to be what it is" (Hyldgaard, 2003, p. 231). Lacan sometimes calls the subject of the unconscious a *manque-à-être*, a lack-of-being or a lack-towards-(a-future) being. By being able to distance myself from myself ($) in time – via memories of the past or anticipation of the future, which is possible because of language (O) – we are freed from a merely biological life of continuous bodily need and gratification (S). It is the Real (*a*) that endlessly drives us to make sense of what has been to anticipate what will be in light of our constantly unfolding present. Because of this uncanny temporality, there is always an element of uncertainty generating anxiety because speech – which is infused with jouissance – always eludes our conscious control and desire for mastery.

However, rather than an opportunity for reinterpreting the past through our anticipation of the future, chains of signifiers can become the automatic and uncritical ways we think about and talk about ourselves and our world. Lacan (1964/1998) refers to this aspect of signifiers as the *automaton*. The structure of the unconscious follows certain logical rules (similar to the way language is ordered by grammatical rules), and once these rules are set into motion, the structure itself 'remembers' chains of signifiers without the necessity for an intentional subject. Thus, *automaton* refers to the insistent movement of the signifying chain and belong to the deterministic, mechanical model of existence (Miller, 2013; Verhaeghe, 1998). Reflecting back on Imre Kertész (2006), it is the insistent automatons of the big Other that set all of us up to be "a well-oiled component of the machinery" of culture (pp. 66–67). However, our automatic thinking can be interrupted by an encounter with the Real that disrupts the chain of signifiers.[12] In the diagram, O divided by S also leaves a remainder, the object *a*, surplus jouissance. As a piece of the Real, the object *a* disrupts the automatic functioning of the signifying chain; although encounters with the Real are often experienced as traumatic, it is the Real that saves us from determinism allowing for our limited human freedom.

Object *a* is not to be equated with those objects of the world that we (falsely) believe will complete our lack. It is the disturbing remainder that testifies to the traumatic disjunction between our soma and psyche, the living organism and the speaking subject. Lacan calls the object *a* the "object-cause of our desire" because as the agitating remainder of the Real rooted in our corporeal bodies, it "is" the lack and loss ($) that sets desire into motion. It is our lack that generates the neverending process of trying to make sense and meaning of our lives. However, since object *a* is untranslatable, we can never master nor fully understand our existence. This little (virtual) object consigns the speaking being to a life marked by temporal disjunction and affective disequilibrium, which is our shame.

Hontologie

I have detoured through the advent of the Lacanian barred subject to come to some thoughts on shame in its intimate relationship to our traumatic subjectivity. In Seminar XVII, Lacan (1969–1970, 2006) creates the neologism *hontologie* when he combines the French words for shame (*honte*) and ontology (*ontologie*) and says that the correct spelling of *ontologie* would be *hontologie* (p. 180). Later he says, "*l'ontologie . . . est une honte*" – ontology is a shame (Lacan in Soler, 2006, p. 92). To me, Lacan is emphasizing that – in contrast to Heidegger and Levinas, who link shame *with* being – the barred subject *lacks* essence and ontological substance, and this is the shame of human being. As Verhaeghe (1998) writes, the divided subject "comes down to a pre-ontological, indeterminate non-being which can only give rise to an identity, an ego, in retrospect" (p. 178). The (pre)-ontological lack that we are is a primordial facticity of being human. This is why the philosopher Hyldgaard (2003) – writing on the Real as the cause of the Lacanian subject – asserts, "shame is the definition of being human" (p. 238). Tomkins (2008, p. 371) recognized the role of shame in our lifelong process of coming to be, and although he uses different concepts, he expresses the relationship between the coming-to-be of the subject, shame and temporality:

> The importance of the individual's struggles with his shame, the incessant effort to vanquish or come to terms with the alienating affect, his surrenders, transient or chronic, have too often been disregarded by personality theorists in their quest for a static structure which will describe a personality.

Giorgio Agamben (1999), in *Remnants of Auschwitz*, calls shame the *fundamental sentiment* emerging from the human being's divided nature: "We can therefore propose a first, provisional definition of shame. It is nothing less than the fundamental sentiment of being *a subject*. . . . Shame is what is produced in the absolute concomitance of subjectification and desubjectification" (p. 107). As the barred subject we are always already divided between living being (desubjectification) and speaking subject (subjectification). and what is produced is shame. However, what is also produced in the advent of the barred subject is the remainder – the object *a*. Shame involves an encounter with a real, living bit of jouissance (object *a*) that remains traumatic because it cannot be symbolized (Faye, 2003, p. 250). In that logical instant when being (jouissance) is mortified by the signifier of the Other, we shamefully come face-to-face with the leftover remainder, the excess of the subject's impossible being, the object *a*. Faye goes on to say that,

> Shame, as testimony to the mark of 'the inhuman' in 'the human', thus broadcasts, from a Lacanian perspective, the irruption of a jouissance that drowns the (human/speaking) subject. It testifies to, in other words, the signifier's failure to do its job.
>
> (p. 250)

Faye's observation that shame testifies to an irruption of jouissance that drowns the speaking subject has a haunting similarity to Tomkins's model, which posits that shame is a barrier to "too much" excitement. We rely on the signifier to act like a dam that keeps the "too much" of jouissance from breaking in on and drowning the subject; thus, both shame and the signifier act as a barrier to jouissance.

Ominous transitions

Like the barred subject ($), the Other is also lacking (Ø). This is expressed in the phrase "There is no Other of the Other," which means that there is no ground that guarantees a correspondence between the mysteries of life (being/the Real) and the ways in which we understand and talk about the enigmas of life (existence/the symbolic). "The only thing the Other provides to the living being is a medium by means of which a subject can be articulated. What it does not offer is a standard against which this articulation can be tested" (Vanheule, 2014, p. 131). In other words, there is no ultimate truth that can be articulated in language and no final authority to whom we can turn during troubled times. We yearn for the Other who is *not* lacking, who purports to know the answers to the questions of life – whether it be the parent, priest, teacher, celebrity, scientist or authoritarian leader. "It is only to the extent that a person has faith in a Father figure or master figure that his rules and explanations function as a law whereby sense can be made of desire" (ibid, p. 136). Especially during times of historical tumult, frightened people uncritically accept the answers of whoever promises safety and security, happiness and wholeness.

Because the Other is lacking, the signifiers that create the barriers to jouissance do not represent final truths but rather social mores, the agreed-upon rules and conventions of culture. In our day to day lives, "master signifiers" (S_1) are those that organize our psychical reality.[13] Master signifiers play a key role in the way we make meaning and understand the world because they orient an entire chain of signifiers; however, the master signifier itself has no positive content – it is a signifier without a signified (Žižek, 1989, p. 103). For example, COVID-19 has become a master signifier orienting radically different signifying chains depending on whether they are discourses of religion, science, economics, politics or entertainment. There is a frantic rush to tame COVID-19 into something understandable by generating endless narratives. However, the virus that ravages the body is of the Real and resists our efforts to tame it; it can never be adequately represented. Master signifiers preside over the values and duties of the social order; they are passed down to us through the big Other, which is composed of our families, the institutions that shape us such as schools, church, the media and the laws that govern us as well as unwritten conventions.[14] They are the hidden assumptions that we take for granted until there is an eruption of the Real.

For Lacan, the law is not the legal system but those signifiers that organize our everyday reality into a social system (Cauwe et al., 2017, p. 611). In Seminar X, Lacan (1962–1963, 2014) writes, "Desire and law – are but one and the same barrier to bar our access to the Thing" (p. 81). "The Thing" is jouissance that has not been mortified (sublimated) through signifiers (Miller, 2019, p. 60). When there are no longer shared master signifiers, that is, no shared understanding of the law, we are at risk of being engulfed by lethal jouissance and shamelessness. Adrian Johnston (2018, Section 2.4.2, para. 6) describes lethal jouissance that is not bound by the law:

> The *jouissance* presumably lost to the speaking subject returns only in the guises of what might be labeled "limit experiences," namely, encounters with that which is annihilating, inassimilable, overwhelming, traumatic, or unbearable. Similarly, *jouissance*, in this vein, is related to transgressive violations, the breaching of boundaries and breaking of barriers.

As eruptions of the Real (e.g., the global pandemic) disrupt our ordinary customs and discourse, the symbolic order, which serves as the barrier to lethal jouissance, is changing. As Žižek (1989) explains, "The very existence of the symbolic order implies a possibility of its radical effacement, of 'symbolic death' – not the death of the so-called 'real object' in its symbol, but the obliteration of the signifying network itself" (p. 147). As the events of the 21st century unfold, we are indeed confronting the obliteration of the signifying network. All too often, people rush to create new discourses confident that their master knows the answer rather than tolerating uncertainty. During times of upheaval and change, we yearn to make sense of things so that we can return to the illusion of coherence and wholeness; it is hard to resist the urge to prematurely create narratives to pin down what is still evolving. There are those of us who embrace the death drive and rush in to limit experiences that offer the ecstasy of lethal jouissance. Instead of identifying with either side of our division, we must remain unsettled in the gap between being and existence long enough to tune in to the haunting and uncanny aspects of the unfolding events. Otherwise, we risk erasing that which is alien or unrecognizable to our everyday ways of thinking (Hinton, 2016).

When the symbolic network itself is undergoing radical effacement, there is a paradox to consider: What happens when the shared mores of society no longer reflect one's own values? What happens when you realize that your culture has benefited from rules and rituals that facilitate forgetting – just as I forgot about our country's genocides while visiting Tuol Sleng? If our friends and family accept social injustices to create an illusion of societal harmony, and if our educational and religious institutions remain blind to maintain power, where is the shame? In his sociological research, Michael Lewis (2003, p. 1202) demonstrates that by three years of age, children are able to evaluate their own actions and have the cognitive capacities to show self-conscious evaluative emotions. "The emergence of shame as part of this complex of new emotions acts to inhibit children's actions, thoughts, and feelings *that do not conform to the internal standards learned through socialization*" (my emphasis). It is sobering to realize that shame – as an integral component of socialization to the norms of culture (the big Other) – is already established by age three.

During times of ominous transitions, it is necessary to question the ways in which we have been socialized to conform. Shame can stop us in our tracks, but then as the painful burning slowly subsides, it allows us to take the necessary time to reflect on "the belief system, the language and the concepts that conceal from you that you have long been a well-oiled component of the machinery that has been set up for your own destruction" (Kertész, 2006, p. 66–67). When we feel shame, we must assume it rather than narcissistically converting it into rage directed at the other to regain whatever illusions we harbour about our ideal selves. We must have the discipline to empty ourselves of preconceived ideas and wait so that new answers can emerge from our singular S_1 rather than falling back on uncritical thinking – our *automatons*. Psychoanalysis as a clinical practice has always recognized the importance of silence and waiting to allow the necessary time for reflection and change. Following Agamben (1999), I think of silence and waiting as the ethos of testimony:

> It is precisely because the relation (or, rather, non-relation) between the living being and the speaking being has the form of shame, of being reciprocally consigned to something that cannot be assumed by a subject, that the ethos of this disjunction can only be testimony.
>
> (p. 130)

And he adds, "What testimony says is [that] human beings are human insofar as they bear witness to the inhuman" (p. 121).

In his seminar on ethics, Lacan (1959–1960/1997, p. 21) says that psychoanalysis can take us to the door of moral action, but it does not provide us with a set of norms or moral principles. We must walk through the door alone. Shame maintains social bonds and shared values, but it also encourages conformity and unquestioning obedience. As Kertész (2006, pp. 66–67) wrote, once he grasped the shame of his collaboration with the machinery of culture "my whole way of looking at things changed." Analysis is the process through which we have the opportunity to experience our fallen, divided subjectivity in its singularity rather than uncritically accepting the master signifiers of society – what Heidegger calls "the They" (*das Man*) – the gaze of the anonymous crowd. It is the gaze of the Other that elicits shame. For Lacan (1959–1960/1997, pp. 84–89), the gaze is experienced when we project the objec*t a* (that little piece of the Real) outside of ourselves and attribute it to the Other and then imagine, based on our own fantasies, what the Other is thinking about us or how the Other is judging us:

> The gaze that surprises me and reduces me to shame . . . is not a seen gaze, but a gaze imagined by me in the field of the Other. If one does not stress the dialectic of desire, one does not understand why the gaze of others should disorganize the field of perception. It is because the subject in question is not that of reflexive consciousness, but that of desire.

It was the gaze of my son that reduced me to shame in the courtyard at Tuol Sleng. But as Tomkins reminds us, shame is different from self-contempt and disgust because the desire to restore the interrupted communion defines shame. As the shame receded, I became motivated to explore what had happened in that exchange between myself and my son which evoked such disorienting shame. To live ethically means assuming responsibility for our fractured subjectivity and becoming our own master, living from our unique S_1, the primordial signifier that links jouissance to our singular and unceasing (re)interpretation of the world. Sometimes we must risk being labelled shameless to speak our own truth and to act from the values that make life worth living. Rather than repudiating shame, we must strive to be those ethical fools always precariously balanced on the edge of the abyss.

If we deny our constitutional division and seek wholeness by endlessly writing coherent narratives to cover over the void at the core of our being, we risk psychic deadness. And if we embrace the death drive, moving beyond the pleasure principle and seeking unbound lethal jouissance, we risk losing our shared humanity and our capacity to care for the radically Other – the neighbour. The shame I experienced at Tuol Sleng set me on this journey and remains a haunting presence – shame evoked by the gaze of my son but also by the gaze of those looking at me from the past – those who were photographed, objectified and executed in the Cambodian genocide – along with all of those forgotten Others who have died from our lack of shame.

Notes

1 Susan Sontag (2001): "To photograph people is to violate them . . . it turns people into objects that can be symbolically possessed." *On Photography*, p. 14.
2 Shame in French includes *honte*, *pudeur* and *vergogne*; in this paper I am working with shame as *honte*. For discussion see Johnston & Malabou, 2013; Bernard, 2011.
3 See also: Agamben, 1999; Bernard, 2011; Heidegger, 1962; Lévinas, 2003; Sartre, 1978; Seidler, 2000; Slaby, 2015.
4 See Lacan's Seminar XI, pp. 82–85, for his discussion of Sartre and shame.
5 The Lacanian psyche is described through the interwoven movement of three registers or orders – the imaginary, the symbolic and the Real. For an introduction to these concepts, see: Evans, 1996; Bailly, 2009.
6 Signifiers are the basic units of language and can be a syllable, a word or even a phrase. A signifier has no inherent meaning; it is only through its difference from other signifiers that it becomes a constituent in a process of meaning making. For example, "cat" signifies a furry creature because (in a closed system) it is *not* a "dog" and *not* a "mouse" and *not* a "goat" – that is, there is no essential meaning underlying "cat" that anchors these letters or this sound to the concept of a particular living, furry creature. For Lacan, language is a system of signifiers, and the effects of the signifier on the subject constitute the unconscious and thus the field of psychoanalysis. A succession of signifiers that produces meaning through their interaction is called a signifying chain or chain of signifiers. The production of meaning through the use of signifiers is referred to as "the signifying effect" to emphasize that meaning results from the difference between the signifiers and is not inherent in the signifier itself (Pluth, 2007, p. 30).
7 Throughout Lacan's oeuvre, the specifics of jouissance evolve; see Miller, J.-A. (2019). *Six Paradigms of Jouissance*.
8 Tomkins (1911–1991) studied psychology and philosophy at the University of Pennsylvania and then pursued post-graduate work in analytic philosophy and logic at Harvard. It is especially interesting to note that in 1958, the first publication of Tomkins's theory of affect was translated into French and appeared in the Premier Volume of *La Psychanalyse*, edited by Jacques Lacan. This allows us to assume that Lacan was at least familiar with Tomkins's work and possibly even influenced by it. At the same time that Lacan was returning to and revising Freudian theory, Tomkins was developing his affect theory in response to what he saw as the limitations of Freud's drive theory for explaining human motivation.
9 It is this recurring movement of sending and receiving messages to and from the Other that perpetually troubles the binary of inside-outside in Lacanian topology. Our most intimate interior comes to us from the outside (the Other); in Lacanian terminology this is represented by the neologism "*extimité*." See Miller (2005).

10 *Nachträglichkeit* has been translated into English as *deferred action* by Strachey and *afterwardness* by Laplanche. In French it is *après-coup*. *Nachträglichkeit* is a psychic dynamic that interweaves past, present and future such that memories are in constant temporal flux, with meaning always deferred into some indefinite future, with no final ground or presence. See Green (2018), *Lacan: Shame, Nachträglichkeit and Ethical Time*.

11 *Advent* comes from the Latin words *ad-venire* "to arrive."

12 An encounter with the Real that interrupts the chain of signifiers is called *tuché*. Lacan borrowed (and revised) the two concepts – *automaton and tuché* – from Aristotle. In Aristotle they relate to chance happenings in nature and chance happenings that we consider lucky or unlucky. See Harris (2017).

13 In the Lacanian algebra, the master signifier is denoted by the symbol S_1. The primal S_1 installs the dialectic between being and existence; the master signifiers are those signifiers that the subject most deeply identifies with and so play a key role in meaning making.

14 Another example of a master signifier would be "freedom." Recently, those aligned with the far right have used the S_1 freedom to demand the right to bear arms, the right of free movement despite shelter-in-place orders and the right to disregard public health advice such as wearing face masks during the novel coronavirus pandemic. However, for those who have been oppressed by the practices of American police that have resulted in the disproportionate and unjust deaths of Black men (as I am writing, protests are going on within earshot of my window demanding justice for George Floyd), freedom as a master signifier orients historical discourse rooted in trauma and slavery.

References

Agamben, G. (1999). *Remnants of Auschwitz: The Witness and the Archive*. New York: MIT Press/Zone Books.

Bailly, L. (2009). *Lacan: A Beginner's Guide*. London: Oneworld Publications.

Bernard, D. (2011). *Lacan et la honte: De la honte à l'hontologie: étude psychanalytique*. Paris: Éditions du Champ lacanien.

Braunstein, N. (2003). "Desire and Jouissance in the Teachings of Lacan." In *The Cambridge Companion to Lacan*. Ed. Jean-Michel Rabaté, pp. 102–115. Cambridge, UK: Cambridge University Press.

Broucek, F. J. (1991). *Shame and the Self*. London & New York: Guilford Press.

Cauwe, J., Vanheule, S. & Desmet, M. (2017). "The Presence of the Analyst in Lacanian Treatment." *Journal of the American Psychoanalytic Association*, 65, 4, 609–638. https://doi.org/10.1177/0003065117721163

Copjec, J. (2006). "May '68, the Emotional Month." In *Lacan: The Silent Partners*. Ed. S. Žižek, pp. 90–114. London & New York: Verso.

De Kesel, M. (2009). *Eros and ethics: Reading Jacques Lacan's Seminar VII*. Trans. S. Jottkandt. New York: State University of New York Press.

Evans, D. (1996). *An Introductory Dictionary of Lacanian Psychoanalysis*. London: Routledge.

Faye, E. (2003). "Being Jewish After Auschwitz: Writing Modernity's Shame." *Australian Feminist Studies*, 18, 42, 245–259.

Green, S. R. (2018). "Lacan: *Nachträglichkeit*, Shame and Ethical Time." In *Temporality and Shame: Perspectives from Psychoanalysis and Philosophy*. Eds. L. Hinton & H. Willemsen, pp. 74–100. London: Routledge.

Harris, O. (2017). *Lacan's Return to Antiquity: Between Nature and the Gods*. London: Routledge.

Heidegger, M. (1992). *Parmenides*. Bloomington, IN: Indiana University Press.

Hinton, A. L. (2016). *Man or Monster? The Trial of a Khmer Rouge Torturer*. Durham, NC: Duke University Press.

Hyldgaard, K. (2003). "The Cause of the Subject as an Ill-Timed Accident: Lacan, Sartre and Aristotle." In *Jacques Lacan: Critical Evaluations in Cultural Theory*. Ed. S. Žižek, vol. 1, pp. 228–242. London: Routledge.

Johnston, A. (2018). "Jacques Lacan." In *The Stanford Encyclopedia of Philosophy* (Fall 2018 Edition). Ed. Edward N. Zalta. https://plato.stanford.edu/archives/fall2018/entries/lacan/.

Johnston, A. & Malabou, C. (2013). *Self and Emotional Life: Philosophy, Psychoanalysis, and Neuroscience*. New York: Columbia University Press.

Kertész, I. (2006). *Dossier K: A Memoir*. Brooklyn, NJ: Melville House Publications.

Lacan, J. (1970). "Of Structure as an Inmixing of an Otherness Prerequisite to Any Subject Whatever." In *The Structuralist Controversy: The Languages of Criticism and the Sciences of Man*. Eds. R. Macksey & E. Donato, pp. 186–200. Baltimore, MD: Johns Hopkins Press.

_____. (1997). *The Seminar of Jacques Lacan, Book VII: The Ethics of Psychoanalysis*. Trans. D. Porter. London & New York: W.W. Norton (Originally published 1959–1960).

_____. (1998). *The Seminar of Jacques Lacan: The Four Fundamental Concepts of Psychoanalysis: Vol. XI*. Ed. J.-A. Miller. Trans. A. Sheridan. London & New York: W.W. Norton (Original work published 1964).

———. (2006). *The Seminar of Jacques Lacan: The Other Side of Psychoanalysis*. Trans. R. Grigg. London & New York: W.W. Norton (Original work published 1969–1970.)

———. (2014). *Anxiety: The Seminar of Jacques Lacan, Book X*. Ed. J.-A. Miller (English Edition). Cambridge, Oxford & Boston: Polity Press (Original work published 1962–1963.)

Lévinas, E. (2003). *On escape – De l'évasion*. Trans. B. Bergo. Stanford: Stanford University Press.

Lewis, M. (2003). "The Role of the Self in Shame." *Social Research: An International Quarterly*, 70, 4, 1181–1204. www.muse.jhu.edu/article/558609.

Miller, J.-A. (1999). *Paradigms of Jouissance*.

———. (2005). "A and a in Clinical Structures." *The Symptom*, 6. www.lacan.com/symptom6_articles/miller.html.

———. (2006). "On Shame." In *Jacques Lacan and the Other Side of Psychoanalysis: Reflections on Seminar XVII*. Eds. J. Clemens & R. Grigg. Durham, NC: Duke University Press Books.

———. (2013). "The Other Without Other." *Hurly-Burly*, 10.

_____. (2019). "Six Paradigms of Jouissance." *Psychoanalytical Notebooks*, 34, 11–80.

Nathanson, D. L. (Ed.). (1987). *The Many Faces of Shame*. New York: Guilford Press.

Neill, C. (2011). *Lacanian Ethics and the Assumption of Subjectivity*. London & New York: Palgrave Macmillan.

Pluth, E. (2007). *Signifiers and Acts: Freedom in Lacan's Theory of the Subject*. New York: SUNY Press.

Sartre, J.-P. (2018). *Being and Nothingness: An Essay in Phenomenological Ontology*. Trans. S. Richmond. London: Routledge (Originally published 1943).

Sedgwick, E. K., Frank, A. & Alexander, I. E. (Eds.). (1995). *Shame and Its Sisters: A Silvan Tomkins Reader*. Durham, NC: Duke University Press.

Seidler, G. H. (2000). *In Others' Eyes: An Analysis of Shame*. Madison, CT: International Universities Press.

Slaby, J. (2015). "Affectivity and Temporality in Heidegger." In *Feeling and Value, Willing and Action: Essays in the Context of a Phenomenological Psychology (Phaenomenologica)*. Eds. M. Ubiali & M. Wehrle, pp. 183–206. New York: Springer International Publishing.

Soler, C. (2016). *Lacanian Affects: The Function of Affect in Lacan's Work*. London: Routledge.

Sontag, S. (2001). *On Photography*. New York: Pan Macmillan/Picador.

Tomkins, S. S. (2008). *Affect Imagery Consciousness: The Complete Edition*, vol. 1–2. New York: Springer Publishing (Original work published 1963.)

Vanheule, S. (2014). *Subject of Psychosis: A Lacanian Perspective*. New York: Palgrave Macmillan.

Verhaeghe, P. (1998). "Causation and Destitution of a Pre-Ontological Non-Entity: On the Lacanian Subject." In *Key Concepts of Lacanian Psychoanalysis*. Ed. D. Nobus, pp. 165–189. New York: Other Press/London: Karnac Books, 2017.

———. (2004). *On Being Normal and Other Disorders: A Manual for Clinical Psychodiagnostics*. New York: Other Press.

Zahavi, D. (2014). *Self and Other: Exploring Subjectivity, Empathy, and Shame*. Oxford: Oxford University Press.

Zahavi, D. & Sánchez, A. M. (2018). "Unraveling the Meaning of Survivor Shame." In *Emotions and Mass Atrocity: Philosophical and Theoretical Perspectives*, pp. 162–184. Cambridge, UK: Cambridge University Press.

Žižek, S. (1989). *The Sublime Object of Ideology*. London & New York: Verso.

Chapter 6

Nihilism and truth

Tarrying with the negative

Michael Whan

By way of an introduction

In this study, I explore Nietzsche's concept of 'nihilism', especially what he termed 'incomplete nihilism'. Whether one accepts Nietzsche's interpretation of nihilism or not, what he has described has in many ways come to pass. What he termed incomplete nihilism especially has a fundamental significance. Our age appears to be one of 'meaninglessness', although with much simulacra, fabrication and seeming *excess* of 'meaning'. There are many reactive, indeed, reactionary responses to 'meaninglessness', taking the form of a 'search for meaning'. A common complaint within and outside psychotherapy is: 'I don't feel any meaning in my life', 'I feel like I'm nothing, a nobody', 'I just feel empty'. The feeling of the loss of meaning and value for many is profoundly painful and disturbing. Mostly, the simulacra of 'meaning' fall under Nietzsche's term of incomplete nihilism. They are attempts to find 'positive' modes of thought that will rescue us from this 'uncanniest' of guests (the *Nihil*). Incomplete nihilism is, on the surface, a kind of 'positive psychology', an attempt to ameliorate and counter the prevailing pessimism and loss of meaning and value. Nevertheless, the search for meaning is in fact the opposite of itself: *a refusal to tarry thinkingly with the negative*. To engage with Nietzsche's notion of nihilism is to question *his interpretation* of it. Rather, we need to read Nietzsche against Nietzsche whilst *holding to* the prevailing climate of *negativity*. Nihilism may be but the first *immediate* face of *negation* in an unfolding dialectic. Indeed, the ominous mood may have more to do with the way incomplete and reactionary nihilism interprets nihilism *as* nihilism. Nihilism's growth out of its Christian soil, according to Nietzsche's brilliant analysis, means that *the interpretation of nihilism remains in some way a Christian interpretation*. We pay respect to the iconoclastic Nietzsche by learning from him to, in turn, direct an iconoclastic questioning of his interpretation. For, to *think* is, etymologically, also *to thank*.

The advent of the uncanniest guest

Nietzsche, in his posthumously published *The Will to Power*, announced what he called *the coming of nihilism*:

> What I relate is the history of the next two centuries . . . what is inevitable: *the rise of nihilism*. . . . The whole of our European culture has long been in an agony of suspense . . . like a torrent, restlessly, violently rushing *to its end*, refusing to reflect, afraid to reflect.
>
> (Nietzsche, 1968a, aphorism 2, p. 3)

Key in this passage is how 'the rise of nihilism' affects *thinking*. The passage points to an intensifying of anxiety: 'an agony of suspense'. Nietzsche forecasts this prevailing anxiety as 'the history of the next two centuries'; the 'suspense' casts its disturbing shadow over our capacity to *think* for we are afraid to do so. Anxiety is never a good place from which to think.

To be afraid to think means a failure to address this historical condition in which modernity finds itself: a failure to think through nihilism. Incomplete nihilism is that failure. In a passage, headed 'Toward an Outline', Nietzsche intimates more deeply whence comes this anxiety that affects our thinking. He writes, 'Nihilism stands at the door: whence comes this uncanniest of all guests?' (Nietzsche, 1968a, aphorism 1, p. 7). The advent of nihilism, the arrival of the uncanny guest, marks Nietzsche's statement on the *death of God*. His pronouncement is given in a passage from Section 125, Book Three, of his *The Gay Science*, titled 'The Madman': 'The madman jumped into their midst and pierced them with his eyes. "Whither is God? he cried; I will tell you. *We have killed him* – you and I. . . . The feeling of the loss of meaning for many is profoundly painful and disturbing. . . . Gods, too, decompose. God is dead. God remains dead. And we have killed him"' (Nietzsche, 1974, p. 181).

Nietzsche's words are a watershed in the history of Western religion and metaphysics. Even so, there is a questionable melodrama or hysteria about them. Is not Nietzsche's shrill feeling-tone similar to all who react to the death of God, the end of metaphysics, with a form of histrionic emotion? Others, too, have spoken of the death of God and the gods. In his early work, *The Birth of Tragedy*, Nietzsche wrote: 'I believe in the ancient German saying: "All gods must die"'. And earlier, the young Hegel, in his treatise, *Faith and Knowledge*, spoke of the 'feeling on which rests the religion of the modern period – the feeling God himself is dead. . . . In the ancient pagan world, Plutarch told of the cry, "Great Pan is dead"' (Heidegger, 1977, pp. 58–59). For Hegel, then, before Nietzsche, the 'religion' of 'the modern period' is God-less. The feeling-tone of Hegel's words though is more measured.

Nietzsche's insights proclaim the advent of the uncanny. Hence, in *The Gay Science*, he describes humankind as 'straying as through an infinite nothing' (Nietzsche, 1974, p. 181). With this event, according to Nietzsche, Christianity has come to the end of itself. This is an internal rupture *within* Christianity itself; it broke with itself, with its metaphysics. Further, Nietzsche's nomination of nihilism as *the uncanny* signals the mood that lies at the heart of modernity. The term uncanny ('*unheimlich*' in German) was later employed by both Heidegger and Freud although with radically different meanings: '*Die Unheimlichkeit*' literally translates as the 'unhomely', interpreted by Heidegger as a condition of profound existential *homelessness*. For Freud, the uncanny signified the repressed maternal body, our original 'home'.[1] The sense of being firmly embedded in the world, of *feeling at home* in it, of being contained either, as in ancient pre-Christian times, in myth, or subsequently in Christianity and metaphysical thought, has foreclosed. With the death of God, the metaphysical order of the world has seemingly crumpled. Nietzsche describes human beings as cast adrift, as living under the mood of the uncanny, of a nothingness. The expression 'the uncanny' invokes something disturbing, uncertain. For Nietzsche, then, existence discloses itself through the anxiety-ridden mood of the uncanny, the advent of nihilism. Such a feeling was brought sharply into focus with the worldwide 'lockdowns' during the coronavirus pandemic, when the cities of the world became almost entirely devoid of human beings; they became uncanny places, manifestations of a *void*, of an eerie nothingness.

Heidegger, commenting on the profound impact of Nietzsche's thinking on Western metaphysical and theological thought, writes (1977, p. 61):

> This realm of the suprasensory has been considered since Plato . . . to be the true and genuinely real world. In contrast . . . the sensory world is only the world down here, the changeable, and therefore the merely apparent, unreal world.

Nietzsche's critique of Platonic-Christianity undoes the foundational underpinnings of meaning. We are left with no grand, overarching meaning with a big M. His critique though does not only undermine metaphysics and Christianity, the loss of the 'Real', the 'true', 'meaning' but also the 'apparent, unreal world'. For, if the suprasensory realm has been undone, then likewise, is not the notion of the lower, 'apparent' realm undone? In his *Twilight of the Idols*, in the briefest of sections titled, 'How the "Real World" at Last Became a Myth: History of an Error', Nietzsche (1968b, pp. 40–41) declares:

> We have abolished the real world: what world is left? The apparent world perhaps? . . . But no! *with the real world we have also abolished the apparent world!*
>
> (Mid-day moment of the shortest shadow; end of the longest error; zenith of mankind; INCIPIT ZARATHUSTRA.)

Unmoored from its Platonic-Christian tradition, thought finds itself in a radically different world. Today, the world is dominated by simulacra, simulations, semblance and fabrication: the media age. The widespread social symptomatic of narcissism puts the highest value on 'appearance': 'I am my appearance', 'What is my social media status?' What Nietzsche called the 'apparent world' has been abolished or eclipsed by semblance, simulation. Social media and the internet entice multitudes into their webs of fabrication. Psychic interiority, the depth dimension, is emptied out into the preening one dimension of the narcissistic surface. We have learned to be entrepreneurs of ourselves, to self-market. This puts a premium on 'success'. Fear of 'failure' then threatens with anxiety, psychological breakdown, despair or the stigma of shame and suicide. Or else, we void ourselves of shame and adopt shamelessness as our strategy to negotiate the market, media world, ourselves and others. Interior *life* and aliveness give way to emptiness, deadness, and the *nihil*. Further, the technologies of social media and the internet efficiently facilitate the worldly communication of the *nihil*. On the other side of the inflated 'self-made' man ('Become the Giant Within!') looms the feeling of 'I am nothing'. The *nihil* wanders in and out of our being, oppressing us with alternative moods of mania or despair.

What brought this about? Nietzsche refutes *external causes*:

> Nihilism stands at the door: whence comes this uncanniest of all guests? Point of departure: it is an error to consider 'social distress' or 'physiological degeneration' or, worse, corruption, as the cause of nihilism. . . . Distress, whether of the soul, body, or intellect, cannot of itself give birth to nihilism (i.e., the radical repudiation of value, meaning, and desirability). Such distress always permits a variety of interpretations. Rather: it is in one particular interpretation.
>
> (1968a, aphorism 1, p. 7)

With remarkable dialectical insight, Nietzsche understands the advent of nihilism has come about from *within* Christianity itself, from being faithful to its spirit of *truth*. It results *internally*, from *within* the historical unfolding of Christianity itself: 'The sense of truthfulness, developed highly by Christianity, is nauseated by the falseness and mendaciousness of all Christian interpretations of the world and of history: rebound from "God is truth" to the fanatical faith "All is false". . . . Everything lacks meaning'. All meaning then becomes untenable, uncertain, suspect (ibid, aphorism 2, p. 7).

The 'truth' of metaphysics, the philosophical 'beyond' of Christianity, these Nietzsche understood as the source of the nihilistic spirit. Heidegger observes that the death of God is not a matter of 'unbelief', for that is still to think nihilism theologically (1977, p. 63). The truthfulness fostered in Christianity culminated in a 'hermeneutics of suspicion' (Ricoeur, 2012, p. 72) that turned upon Christianity itself. It wasn't 'the madman', it wasn't 'we', that brought about the death of God rather a radical change of consciousness that took place within Christianity itself and unfolded historically, culturally, into the whole world.[2]

The implication of this is spelled out remarkably by Heidegger and bears upon our present historical condition: 'Through the overturning of metaphysics accomplished by Nietzsche, there remains for metaphysics nothing but a turning aside into its own inessentiality and disarray. The suprasensory is transformed into an unstable product of the sensory' (1977, pp. 53–54). With the loss of the suprasensory, the distinction between itself and the sensory 'culminates in a "neither-nor" in relation to the distinction between the sensory . . . and the non-sensory. . . . It culminates in meaninglessness' (ibid., p. 54). To escape from this, we seek out meaning and assign meaning ourselves, which in the climate of simulation, essentially takes the forms of incomplete nihilism. Thus, the 'place' emptied of God needs to be filled with different, novel ideals and meanings and has to be preserved (Heidegger, 1977, p. 69). The loss of the *difference* between the suprasensory (the metaphysical) and sensory (the empirical) results, says Heidegger, in meaninglessness, therefore in 'blind attempts to extricate itself from meaninglessness through a mere assigning of sense and meaning'. The 'suprasensory' as an 'unstable product of the sensory' *is* incomplete nihilism. The historical error is to mistake the 'appearance of nihilism itself', our understanding of it remaining superficial (Heidegger, 1977, p. 66).

Incomplete nihilism

Taking nihilism at face value means our response is not informed by a true confrontation with it but from a failed understanding and thus opposition. Nietzsche defines it thus: 'Incomplete nihilism, its forms: we live in the midst of it. Attempts to escape nihilism without revaluating our values so far; they produce the opposite, make the problem more acute' (Nietzsche, 1968a, aphorism 28, p. 19). Nietzsche shows how attempts to escape nihilism deepen it. Incomplete nihilism replaces the former ideals, but it posits them in the same 'empty place' of the suprasensory and so fails to think through its own actions. Attempts to escape nihilism, although seeming to counter it, in fact *act it out*. Indeed, with the collapse of the critical *difference* between the suprasensory and sensory realms, with their conflation and confusion, in the 'mere assigning of sense and meaning', those who assign in this way bolster their claims with a fabricated suprasensory, a fabrication *by the sensory realm*, as with so-called new age 'thinking' and 'spirituality' or, indeed, as with all forms of fundamentalism (with their covert and overt violence). The 'empty place' lends specious authority to the counterclaims that assert themselves against the meaninglessness and pessimism holding sway in the modern age. Such forms fail to recognize the *nihil* in their own heart. Despite these fabrications, the 'empty place' does not *really* get filled. It becomes the *void* of the nihil; it's the abyss, the groundlessness of modern existence:

> The "black hole" is a floating signifier . . . varying greatly in the ways it has been 'languaged'. It involves a cluster of experiences involving acute anxiety

and terror. . . . Such experiences are enigmatic, uncanny, they are the gaps and
holes in experience, lacking language, representation.

(Hinton, 2007, p. 435)

Experiences of the *nihil* permeate the historical, cultural level and, hence, enter
the psyche of individuals.

Nietzsche himself itemized several forms of incomplete nihilism. Their purpose
is to give answer in the historical present to the question 'for what?' They serve,
from Nietzsche's perspective, to give purpose and meaning, to fill the metaphysical vacuum with substitutes of 'authority'. He lists them as socialism, systems of
morality, music (Wagnerian), nature such as the idea of 'natural man', 'his belief
in the dominion of feeling', romanticism, the valuing of 'extreme states in general
and [seeing] in them a symptom of strength, the 'cult of passion', 'the dominion
of the feelings of unbridled *ressentiment*, devised as a banner of strength', 'the
morality of *ressentiment*' – these and others, such as today the worship of the
unbridled so-called free-market capitalism, become the new 'God-terms', the sovereign ideals and 'supreme fictions' holding sway in the manner of the displaced
metaphysics (Nietzsche, 1968a, aphorism 1021, p. 528). 'The nihilistic question
"for what?" is rooted', Nietzsche asserts, in the demand for '*another* authority that
can *speak unconditionally* and *command* goals and tasks' (1968a, aphorism 20,
p. 16). How prescient Nietzsche was concerning *ressentiment*, which in the 20th
and 21st centuries, has become the emotional engine for politics and political conflict. Even in the intimacies of psychotherapy, *ressentiment* rules, fuelling emotions and feelings of victimhood, hurt and the need to blame, whilst the internet
provides a world-wide system for the transmission and acting out of *ressentiment*,
accelerating and amplifying it.

One major reaction to nihilism takes the form of the need and search for meaning and yet entails an inherent self-contradiction. Ignoring this self-contradiction
comprises a flight from nihilism, deepening its grip. The aversion to meaninglessness takes the form of an oppositional stance that in its very opposition remains
deeply tied to what it denies. The search for meaning seemingly *negates* the
absence of meaning. Active searching, however, brings into play a second negation, raising meaninglessness to a higher level of duplicity, namely, to a *covert*
meaninglessness having the appearance of meaning. The *fabrication* of meaning
is but the duplicitous sublation of meaninglessness. Negating the loss of meaning
itself entails a negation of the search for meaning, a negation concealed behind
the rhetoric of 'affirmation'. Loss of and search for meaning are two sides of the
same. For the affirmation of meaning points back to, tries to escape from, what it
is asserting itself *against*. The search for meaning opposes itself. It makes reality
itself senseless; why otherwise search for meaning? It is

itself that symptom or illness the cure of which it claims to be. The longing
for meaning is deluded about itself. . . . Meaning . . . is first of all an implicit

fact of existence . . . embeddedness in life, of containment in the world . . . the logic of existence *as such.*

(Giegerich, 2010, pp. 191–192)

Nietzsche called nihilism a most *uncanny of guests.* If meaning is embedded in life, nature, God or the gods; it is a state of *in-ness.* Then the *unhomeliness* of existence signifies the *loss* of in-ness:

> If in the 19th century the question of the meaning and worth of life all of a sudden – or by and by – became impossible . . . a radical change in man's being-in-the-world must have taken place. Man must have stepped out of his previous absolute containment in life . . . enabled and forced to view life as if from the outside.

(Giegerich, 2010, p. 192)

With *the unhomely of nihilism,* humankind is thrown out of embedded existence. The search for meaning is a desperate search to experience being-in-*in-ness,* namely, to feel at home *in* the world. When the need to feel oneself in an in-ness, 'to belong', prevails, displacement overshadows existence. The search for meaning takes many forms, not only in the 'Mind, Soul, Body' sections in bookshops, with their mental exercises, 'thinking positively' programmes and self-help creeds but also neo-shamanisms, 'spiritual' practices, cults, born-again Christianity, pagan rites, other religious beliefs and practices, political- and eco-activisms, 'the return of religion' and not least psychology itself with its promises of 'depth' and finding again a 'meaningful life' or 'personal myth'. The key is whether any of these truly confront the nature of nihilism, the uncanny, or merely set up an oppositional ideology. The failure to do so then marks them out, ideologically, as consumerism, for what they offer is a kind of 'supermarket pick and mix' of 'meaningfulness': 'The search for meaning unwittingly has to construe that which it desires to be the logic or *syntax* of life as a *semantic content* . . . ultimately as a commodity' (Giegerich, 2010, p. 193). The *syntactical truth* of these commodities of meaning simulates the appearance of meaningfulness.[3] Faithful to the consumerist ideal, such commodities of meaning have a built-in obsolescence; they last a short while, innovating further searches for meaning. The syntax of consumerism requires we go on consuming, go on searching for meaning and thereby deepen the senselessness of our lives *as actually lived.*

The critical point about such incomplete nihilism consists of the way it can show itself as its opposite. Unless one recognizes this, one takes up the struggle against nihilistic thought and develops a self-sabotaging approach. What is crucial in this is the relation between form and content, syntax and semantics.

Where is Jung's psychology in this question of syntax and semantics? Jung did appear to recognize the prevailing mood of meaninglessness, its nullity in the desolation and absence of symbol, myth and religion. In an essay, 'Archetypes of the Collective Unconscious', notably published in German in 1934, he identifies this loss of meaning in contemporary consciousness. At the same time, he warned against the temptations of irreality and flight from the nihilistic condition:

> The growing impoverishment of symbols has meaning. It is a development that has an inner consistency. . . . It seems to me that it would be far better stoutly to avow our spiritual poverty, our symbol-lessness, instead of feigning a legacy to which we are not the legitimate heirs at all. . . . Anyone who has lost the historical symbols and cannot be satisfied with substitutes is certainly in a very difficult position today: before him yawns the void, and he turns away from it in horror.
>
> (1959/1968, *CW* 9i, para. 28)

Rather, it is better, against this recoil from

> the void . . . to renounce the false riches of the spirit in order to withdraw not only from the sorry remnants . . . of a great past . . . in order, finally, to dwell . . . alone, where, in the cold light of consciousness, the blank barrenness of the world reaches to the very stars.
>
> (ibid, para. 29)

This is the world of Wallace Stevens's poem, 'The Snow Man', in which 'One must have a mind for winter' and become 'the listener, who listens in the snow/ And, nothing himself, beholds/Nothing that is not there and the nothing that is' (Stevens, 1984, pp. 9–10). In this symbol-less time and place, witnessed by a wintery consciousness, says Jung, one should confront the void stoically, looking without self-deception. Seemingly, then, Jung appears to hold fast to remaining truly conscious of this 'blank barrenness', the 'nothing that is not there and the nothing that is'.

Despite Jung's statement, however, there remains a contradiction between the *syntax* of Jungian psychology, its form of consciousness, of reflection and, as in the preceding passages, the *semantic* reference to nihilism and its void of symbols as the *content* of its *form* of consciousness. This passage from Jung indicates a recognition on his part of the prevailing nihilism, the 'symbol-lessness', of the modern age. He goes further and advocates we accept our 'spiritual poverty' and not turn to 'substitutes', accept the loss of 'the historical symbols' and not deceive ourselves with *simulacra*, that is, 'feigning a legacy' which is not ours historically and culturally. And, Jung concludes, what matters is a consciousness open to 'the blank barrenness of the world'. To 'dwell . . . alone . . . in the cold light of consciousness' means to take the burden and responsibility of one's existence on one's own shoulders, to learn to cut one's own cloth.

Yet, the passages, written in an essay, which in its title, 'Archetypes of the Collective Unconscious', point away from negation and nihilism, rooting itself in an *archetypal positivism*, that is to say, 'archetypes' are positive-factual, empirical realities imparting meaning with a big M. So, the *positivistic syntax* of Jung's psychology, with its notion of positive-factual, subsisting meanings contradicts a true recognition of the loss of meaning explicitly stated in the statement about the 'symbol-lessness' of the modern age. Additionally, in an important passage in *Memories, Dreams, Reflections*, Jung, having asked himself whether people still live *in* myth, answered that modern people, including himself, 'no longer have any myth'. Jung suddenly reverses his direction of thought, putting a contradictory question to himself: 'But then what is your myth – the myth in which you do live?' To put this question in such a way immediately calls into question his previous one, whether in modernity there could be authentic myth. It implies the actual possibility of mythical being today, thereby our being placed back *inside* myth. Jung here regresses the logic of psychology – from *logos* to *mythos*. Thereby, Jung finds his *in-ness*. Then, he states, 'At this point the dialogue with myself became uncomfortable, and I stopped thinking. I had reached a dead end'. Yet, again contradicting this last question, Jung recalled that in this same 'dialogue' with himself, he had a moment of 'unusual clarity', asserting, 'Now you possess a key to mythology' (Jung, 1963, p. 171). Such a claim could be said only from a standpoint that had long ago surpassed mythic being in the world. The syntax of such a question differs radically from the syntax or form of consciousness of true myth. Its syntax is of the logos (*psycho-logos*). Namely, it is a firm *theoretical* claim. To make such a claim, Jung situates himself irrevocably in psychology; his approach to understanding myth is inescapably psychological. With this sentence about having 'a key to mythology', Jung seemingly acknowledges the temporal, logical rupture from any mythical mode of being in the world. Psychology belongs to a different age and form of consciousness. The philosopher Ernst Cassirer wrote in his *Philosophy of Symbolic Forms*, 'The world views of myth and theoretical knowledge cannot coexist in the same area of thought. They are mutually exclusive: the beginning of one is the equivalent to the end of the other' (1957, pp. 78–91). As a theoretical, speculative discipline, psychology therefore cannot lay claim to a mythical foundation, a grounding in 'gods' and 'goddesses' in everyman and everywoman. As a 'discipline', that is, as a rigorous mode of thinking, psychology carries within itself the logical and historical rupture between *mythos* and *logos* – which had already happened in ancient Greece.

Psychology itself, resulting from a centuries' long process of internalization and complexification of the psyche, has been an important driving force in demythologization, in the 'disenchantment of the world', as when Jung spoke of the 'despiritualization of nature'. Here again, there is ambiguity. Psychology's claim to having 'a key to mythology' is a claim rooted in theory, which thereby cancels out any notion of psychology as rooted in a primordial, mythic ground, an *ur-existence*. The *theoretical* claim of Jung's psychology to a mythic groundedness remains a retrospective, re-projection by the self-same psychology of its supposed 'origin', an after the fact, an 'after-thought', a claim that in its *theoretical* nature contradicts its claim of mythic embeddedness. Such a claim derives from the very ego psychology it purports to overcome and not from the deeper soulful hinterland:

> It is the insistence on being an actor in the divine drama, the sons of the Sun, the Father . . . or "age-old son of the mother," "the old man," the "ancient" . . . who has always been and always will be. . . . It is the insistence on a meta-physical or mythical garment . . . a higher status.
>
> (Giegerich, 2010, pp. 204–205)

Hence, the claim of Jung's psychology of an archaic, a 'sacred *ur*-experience' derives utterly from the modern form of consciousness. From Nietzsche's perspective, the psychological assertions made here represent a form of incomplete nihilism. The logos of psychology has arisen out of the historical rupture with *mythos* yet, with Jung's psychology, asserts its 'origin' in and continuity with *mythos*. Such an assertion *implicitly expresses* the *opposite* of what it *explicitly claims*. For the *logos*, whilst claiming itself as 'psychology as mythology', as 'personal myth', is in fact 'feigning a legacy', denying its logical and historical *discontinuity* in the form of an archaic, mythic trace.

Jung makes the point in these passages that one cannot be 'satisfied' with recourse to 'the historical symbols'. What is lost is lost. History does not flow backwards, as Jung well knew. This means remaining with *what is* in the historical present and owning up 'to the new situation into which history has placed us and allow oneself to be taught by it about how to think' (Giegerich, 2010, p. 203). In an early paper, 'The Theory of Psychoanalysis', Jung, critiquing psychoanalysis in relation to neurosis, argued,

> The further we get away, in analytical investigations, from the epoch of the manifest neurosis, the less can we expect to find the real *causa efficiens*. . . . In constructing a theory which derives the neurosis from causes in the distant past, we are first and foremost following the tendency of our patients to lure us as far away as possible from the critical present. *For the cause of the pathogenic conflict lies mainly in the present moment.*
>
> (1961, *CW* 4, para. 373)

For Jung, neurosis was essentially a 'regressive phenomenon', activating 'reminiscences' from the past which served only to mislead: 'Those reminiscences determine only the form, but the dynamic element springs from the present' (ibid, para. 372–374). Apply this thinking on the aetiology of the present to the matter of incomplete nihilism, and it becomes evident how it expresses a *recoil* against the historical present and an attempt to restore, or regress to, 'the historical symbols' or to institute 'substitutes' – what Jung called at the individual level 'reminiscences'. This attempt at restoration entails seeking the in-ness of the historically former soul truths and containment in some mythic, religious, or metaphysical existence. Such attempts deprive us of the in-ness in the real, historical present, truly being in the historical situation of meaninglessness. Being truly in it, it is the very truth of the historical present that teaches us to think (Giegerich, 2010, p. 203).

What Jung names as 'the void' is precisely the realm of 'the uncanniest guest'. It is 'who' now stands 'at the door'. How one responds to that presence, as Nietzsche has shown, reflects how one responds to truthfulness, for that is the 'whence' from where the uncanny guest has come. Nietzsche's analysis tells us how Christianity, faithful to its truth, has undergone a self-negation. The 'void' is indeed 'the sense of truthfulness', its *telos*. Christianity has emptied itself, *Kenô-sis*. As Hegel put it, when the Son dies on the cross, so does the Father, hence Christ's cry of *forsakenness* with his last words on the Cross. With the death of the Son and the Father, what is left is the Holy Spirit, which is not a personified person of the trinity but the *radically different, unfolding of historical conscious-ness* (Spirit, *Geist*). Incomplete nihilism is thus a turning away from 'the void', from the historical 'sense of truthfulness' that Christianity has bequeathed to us, *Kenôsis* (the self-emptying of divinity). In the passage from Jung, he describes how in facing 'the void', facing the loss of 'the historical symbols', one 'turns away from it in horror'. That means that one turns away from *the truth of our his-torical condition*. Giegerich observes Jung's statement as 'scaremongering'. For Jung, the loss of meaning was the cause of psychic illness, the cause of neurotic suffering. To threaten 'with the horrors of the void' speaks from an *insistence* on meaning (Giegerich, 2010, p. 204). It is to hold *the principle* that there *must be* meaning and that remains *absolute*. That meaninglessness could stand uncannily before one is unbearable and, even more so, *unthinkable*. Thus, says Nietzsche, our 'refusing to reflect, afraid to reflect'.

Another response, and one that much psychology and psychotherapy actively promote, is

'a psychology of blame and self- or other-shaming'. The loss of meaning is *our* fault:

> Our hubris, our neglect and forgetfulness. It is all our guilt. The West has *squandered* its spiritual heritage. . . . We have been too rationalistic, too patri-archal, too one-sided. So now, this conception claims, we have to . . . turn again to the ignored unconscious as the true source of meaning.
>
> (Giegerich, 2010, p. 204)

Nevertheless, the psychology of blame and self- or other-shaming is itself a reac-tionary acting out against nihilism, no less rooted in incomplete nihilism and cul-tural regression: the 'return to traditional values'.

Negation, nihilism and truth

As has been argued all along, incomplete nihilism, with which we have been essentially concerned, as Nietzsche stressed, deepens the thrust of nihilism. It is a defence against allowing oneself, or rather *consciousness*, to be truly penetrated, to take fully to heart. This, too, belongs to the impact of 'the uncanniest guest', to our 'refusing to reflect, afraid to reflect.' Therefore, in following Nietzsche, does one not *have to think* through this condition of meaninglessness with all its talk of 'the void', of turning away 'in horror'? That is, do we have *not* to refuse to reflect, *not* be afraid to reflect, tarrying with its uncanny? And what in our experience and thought might provide an openness to reflect upon it without immediately taking flight into the *simulacra* of commodified meaning and symbol? Nietzsche observed how nihilism grew out from Christianity and its adherence to truth. Thus, nihilism points to a truth, but a notion of truth, as it were, born out of Christianity, a truth which is itself born out of the rupture with any containment in the in-ness of Christianity. Nihilism is a surpassing of any need for refuge in any 'beyond' or Christian innocence. For Nietzsche, it comprises an 'interpretation', one Christianity has produced out of itself: 'one particular interpretation'. Nihilism is how the self-negation of Christianity looks from within as *it* looks deeper into itself.

Nietzsche describes his own thinking as 'one particular interpretation'. To speak of nihilism as nihilism therefore speaks *interpretatively*. Christianity and its self-negating, self-sublating product, nihilism, have opened a space of reflection to understanding *as interpretation*. Hence, if what has been called 'the void' issues out of the truthfulness bequeathed by Christianity, that 'void', that emptiness, allows *truth as interpretative understanding*. The conception of thinking *as* interpretation has its roots in the intellectual history of Christianity and metaphysics. It is the transference, transmission, of *Christian hermeneutics*, the interpretative study of the Bible, the Scriptures, the incarnation, the trinity, the second coming, and so on to other disciplines of thought, not only theology but the human sciences at large, including history, psychology, philosophy and others. Of course, it is but one part of the intellectual legacy Nietzsche has bequeathed to us. We have in some part Nietzsche to thank for bringing interpretation as a discipline of thought to the consciousness of our times.

What has happened entails a shift in consciousness to a new logical status and mode of being in the world. Allowing the term *nihilism* to be itself an interpretation opens it to the fluidity of dialectical thought. This itself is hinted at in Nietzsche's hyperbolic description when he speaks of it as 'a torrent, restlessly, violently rushing *to its end*'. Although we do not have to follow Nietzsche in his overblown language, dialectical thought does not have the character of being 'violent', 'rushing' and a 'torrent'. It is quieter, gentler, patient, slower. Nihilism, as Nietzsche describes it, is a psychological transformation of consciousness, but that transformation raises a critical question concerning his interpretation of nihilism:

> The idea of nihilism is a trap into which Nietzsche and those who followed him have walked. The problem we are faced with is not nihilism; our problem is the *interpretation* of our situation as nihilism. This interpretation is

a defense against the decisive rupture from one level of consciousness to another, deeper or higher one that has long taken place. It is the attempt to account for an undeniable and radical, earth-shaking change without suffering it as our logical and psychological transformation, as our death and resurrection, i.e., the death and resurrection of our consciousness.

(Giegerich, 2005, p. 226)

Many suffer Nietzsche's interpretation *personally*. This is felt often not in any thoughtful, intellectual sense but rather as a mood, a feeling, a despair or an affliction. They personalize the loss of meaning as *their* loss of meaning. If there is an engagement, it is to activate a search for and finding of meaning; engagement here means reaction, opposition, an allopathic remedy or turning away 'in horror'. Resisting the notion of meaninglessness and nihilism consists of consciousness holding out against these notions as the immediacy of the appearance of truth *as* emptiness, *as* the 'void'. What is seen is the surface appearance, the sense of abyss, of an absence, a 'void'. The loss of *meaning* obscures the *truthfulness* given with 'the cold light of consciousness':

We have to learn to *suffer* our hands to be empty. . . . For is it not the empty hand, and the empty hand alone, that can be filled? As long as we cling to our religious traditions, we pretend to be in possession of something. We thereby prevent the advent of what can come, if at all, only as the free gift of the real world to him who is ready to receive because he has nothing whatsoever of his own accord, as the gift to him who no longer, with a modesty that is disguised arrogance, denounces our poverty as nihilism, but comprehends it as the presence of an unknown future.

(Giegerich, 2005, p. 231)

As this passage shows, what is fundamental consists of *how we interpret emptiness*. There needs to be a release from that to which we cling. But this does not require a programmatic response; it does not require new-fangled rituals, meditation, transpersonal psychologies and so on. The emptiness, the 'void', the truth these bring before us are objectively already here: 'We only need to own it, to allow it to *be*' (Giegerich, 2005, p. 230). Nihilism is an interpretation from within Christianity itself; it is its own interpretation of its self-negation, of bringing itself to its end. Seeing it as truth allows us to see the search for meaning and the loss of meaning, of meaninglessness, as belonging together, both sides of the coin which have served as the currency of our existence. Truth, the 'empty hand', 'the cold light of consciousness', show us meaning and meaninglessness in a different light. They no longer serve the former logic of being in the world; consciousness has moved beyond them, even if *we* have not yet caught up with it. What Nietzsche speaks of as nihilism acts rather as the alchemical corrosion of both the concept of truth and the acid test of the real world. The *nihil*, its experiences of emptiness, the void, generate anxiety, despair and disruption in individual and cultural life.

But there can be a different moment in the dialectic of nihilism, if one is able to traverse the abysses of one's life to tarry with the negative: 'Encountering the "black hole" in its various significations can be at the core of shifts in awareness, the creation of new signifying elements . . . of radical changes of perspective on individual and culture' (Hinton, 2007, p. 436).

Approaching nihilism from a psychological position renders a different sense of the phenomenon. Jung recognized the radically different nature of psychology when he wrote: 'Psychology is doomed to cancel itself out as a science and therein precisely it reaches its scientific goal. Every other science has, so to speak, an outside; not so psychology, whose object is the inside subject of all sciences' (1960/1969, *CW* 8, para. 429). Jung's English translator, R. F. C. Hull, in the preceding passage, employs the term 'to cancel itself out' to translate the German '*aufheben*'. But the German term has a far richer philosophical meaning. In the original German, Jung writes: '*Sie muß sich als Wissenshaft selber aufheben*'. The word '*aufheben*' was employed by Hegel to describe the dialectical movement of thought, its self-contradictory moments. Here, Jung negates the positivist notion of psychology, with its 'inner' and 'outer' at the level of empirical reality, and takes it to a different, more complex level of meaning as *absolute interiority*. Dialectically, psychology contains its own 'outside' inside itself. Jung also describes this notion of psychology's interiority as an 'absolute subjectivity and universal truth' (1960/1969, *CW* 8, para. 439). Such an 'absolute subjectivity' cannot refer to the empirical individual, and so he cannot represent absolute interiority. Such a claim would be misguided and inflationary. Psychology, as *implicit* in Jung's statement, involves a shift from one logical status of consciousness to another. Psychology is no longer at the same level and logical status of consciousness as the sciences and religion: 'Because psychology has the job of understanding, it must stand under, on a lower, deeper level than the sciences. It goes to the ground out of which, the sciences came forth, the psyche' (Giegerich, 2005, p. 222). The same goes for religion, for its believers, theologians *and critics* such as Nietzsche. That Jung felt he suffered the burden of Christianity, and that this was the task of psychology, shows it was experienced 'on an entirely *new level* of consciousness' (Giegerich, 2005, p. 223). Nietzsche's interpretation of nihilism, since it emerged out of Christianity, keeps the old level of consciousness intact: 'By admitting that nihilism is prevailing . . . we manage to hold fast to the very categories and values as the dominants informing our *thinking* that overtly we admit having lost their validity in our *objective situation*' (Giegerich, 2005, p. 226). Nietzsche's nomination of nihilism as 'the uncanniest guest' signifies the *unhomely*. This term expresses the shift out of the known, the being 'at home in', that is, the shift to a different logical status of consciousness, a different logic of being in the world. Consciousness has long ago shed its old, familiar form, but in *not accepting and resisting* that releasement, that loss of being 'at home in' the world, we experience ourselves caught in the nihilistic, neurotic interpretation of nihilism *as* nihilism.

By way of conclusion

Nietzsche's insight was correct; the rupture of Christianity with itself (the death of God, Christ's self-negation) came from within Christianity, not externally. Nietzsche's term nihilism was but the first immediacy of an unfolding dialectic of *historical consciousness*, the sublation of Father and Son into Spirit. It is Christ's *Kenôsis, the self-emptying of his divinity*, the *absolute voiding, surpassing*, of divinity and becoming fully, forsakenly, ineluctably *human, suffering a truly human death*, that releases the Third *from* the Trinity into its own – *Geist, Spirit, historical mindedness*.

Notes

1 'The Uncanny' is a study by Freud of the German word, *'Das Unheimlichkeit'*, an English equivalent to the literal German being the 'unhomely' and which carries the meaning of something 'eerie', something frightening (Freud, 1919, 2003). Freud writes 'that the uncanny is that species of the frightening that goes back to what was once well known and had long been familiar' (2003, p. 124). Freud traces the word in a number of languages and theorizes the real meaning of the word in terms of its opposite, *'heimlich'*, meaning 'belonging to the house, not strange, familiar, tame, dear and intimate, homely, etc.' (ibid., p. 126). He bases his study on a tale by E. T. A. Hoffman, 'The Sandman', about an animate doll and other uncanny happenings. The motif of the 'Sandman' is the one who throws a handful of sand into the eyes of children who refuse to go to bed, 'so their eyes jump out of their heads, all bleeding' (ibid., p. 136). Freud understands the motif of 'The Sandman' as that of being robbed of one's eyes, which he interprets as the fear of castration. But Freud goes further, stating that 'the uncanny' points to the once familiar, but then repressed, mother's genitals, the 'homely'. Lacan (2008) considers this essay by Freud to be his seminal one on *anxiety*.

2 That nihilism emerged out of Christianity appears a contradiction. But it is to Nietzsche's dialectical sensibility we owe the insight that Christianity's faithful pursuit of truth led to this seeming reversal. The contradiction was a dialectical one, a self-contradiction. The absolute pursuit of truth meant that Christianity – in its consciousness – had to turn upon itself, subject itself to its own truthfulness. In the history of Christianity, there was the initial question of Christ's second coming, which was taken at first in a literal sense. The failure of this expected arrival led to the development of different readings of the Bible. Non-literal ways of reading and understanding the Bible emerged, more complex and at higher reflective levels. In other words, the literal gave way to interpretive understanding, *hermeneutics* – the theory and practice of interpretation. The notion of interpretation then served to question literal, absolutist ideas of truth; more symbolic modes developed, namely, the hermeneutic base from which Nietzsche could account for nihilism, that it arose from 'one particular interpretation', Christianity (ibid., 1968, aphorism 1, p. 7). Nietzsche conceived this hermeneutic underpinning of all claims of knowledge, 'truths' and understandings as nihilistic, that they derived from the 'will to power', the internal drives in human nature which struggle amongst themselves to assert their 'point of view' and not attributable to any metaphysical reality. Nietzsche perceived Christianity as having been 'Platonized', thus was metaphysical, which he considered, he had successfully brought to its demise.

3 The terms *semantic* and *syntactic* (linguistic concepts), as employed here, express the difference between the *content* and the *form* of consciousness. When we speak a

sentence, the concern is with its meaning, what it says. To the syntactic aspect belongs the abstract, formal, structural internal relations of the sentence, irrespective of its sense. Psychologically, the difference is between the contents of our subjective, personal inner life, its psychic level. To the psychological proper belongs the form of consciousness, the soul's logical life, the historical-cultural mode of being-in-the-world *as which* life is actually lived. Jungian psychology, for instance, speaks of 'living myth'. Of course, there is a great knowledge of myth, its figures, images and motifs, but these are only the content of consciousness. Modernity's form of consciousness – to which psychology ineluctably belongs – has long ago surpassed any authentic mythic mode of being-in-the-world. Take the *Star Wars* film series, which is plotted on mythological themes. These mythological themes are solely its content, its semantics. The form, the syntax, in which they are presented is wholly technological, media and cinematic. These are the powers that govern the historical logic in which life is really lived. The mythic is but *simulated* content.

References

Cassirer, E. (1957). *Philosophy of Symbolic Forms*, vol. III. Trans. R. Manheim. New Haven: Yale University Press.

Freud, S. (1919). *The Uncanny. SE XVII*. London: The Hogarth Press.

———. (2003). "The Uncanny." In *The New Penguin Freud*. London: Karnac Books.

Giegerich, W. (2005). "Rupture, or Psychology and Religion." In *The Neurosis of Psychology, Primary Papers Towards A Critical Psychology, Collected English Papers*, vol. 1. New Orleans: Spring Journal Books.

———. (2010). "The End of Meaning and the Birth of Man, an Essay About the State Reached in the History of Consciousness and an Analysis of C. G. Jung's Psychology Project." In *The Soul Always Thinks*, Collected English Papers, vol. 4. New Orleans: Spring Journal Books.

Heidegger, M. (1977). "The Word of Nietzsche: 'God Is Dead'." In *The Question Concerning Technology and Other Essays*. New York: Harper and Row.

Hinton, L. (2007). "Black Holes, Uncanny Spaces and Radical Shifts in Awareness." *Journal of Analytical Psychology*, 52, 433–447.

Jung, C. G. (1959/1968). "Archetypes of the Collective Unconscious." In *The Archetypes of the Collective Unconscious. CW* 9i. London: Routledge and Kegan Paul.

———. (1960/1969). "The Structure of the Psyche." In *The Structure and Dynamics of the Psyche. CW* 8. London: Routledge and Kegan Paul.

———. (1961). "The Theory of Psychoanalysis." In *Freud and Psychoanalysis. CW* 4. London: Routledge and Kegan Paul.

———. (1963). *Memories, Dreams, Reflections*. Trans. R. & C. Winston. New York: Random House.

Lacan, J. (2008). *Le Séminaire. Livre X: L'Angoisse*. Paris: Seuil.

Nietzsche, F. (1968a). *The Will to Power*. Trans. W. Kaufmann. New York: Vintage Books.

———. (1968b). *Twilight of the Idols*. Trans. R. J. Hollingdale. London: Penguin Books.

———. (1974). *The Gay Science*. Trans. W. Kaufmann. New York: Random Books.

Ricoeur, P. (2012). *On Psychoanalysis*. Trans. D. Pellauer. Cambridge: Polity Press.

Stevens, W. (1984). *Collected Poems*. London: Faber and Faber.

Chapter 7

Towards a metacosmics of shame

Daniel Ross and Ouyang Man

Prefatory remarks arising from our current epidemiological context

Writing in the midst and from the depths of a global pandemic, the ominousness of our time can hardly be overstated, precisely because the unprecedented character of the events currently unfolding combine calculable and incalculable tendencies in a way that greatly increases the chances of an unforeseeable cascade of consequences leading to a potential transition to . . . who knows what? In this moment of extreme uncertainty, the politics of borders and locality seems to be thrown into confusion, with those who previously descried openness now excoriating the failure to close borders, whereas those who wanted to close things down and build walls call for everything to be opened back up again as quickly as possible. The political virtues of freedom, democracy, authority and security all suddenly seem fraught and uncertain as the speed and quality of collective decision-making and collective behaviour become the overwhelming imperative.

Well before the pandemic, it was clear that the global systems in which we live were rushing headlong towards their threshold limits and that the systems involved in this crisis situation were not just economic or ecological but also mental and social. Given this background, the political, sociological and economic meaning of what we are experiencing right now cannot be understood without a profound psychosocial framework, and this is shown not just in the behaviour of politicians or individuals but in the perspectives of experts and the inclinations of populations and markets: from attributions of blame to advice about the benefits of wearing masks and fears about being infected or infecting others – all this involves feelings of shame and guilt that are often unconscious, even if they are magnified by the network effects of social media. They can be clearly observed in the cultural and national variations of the response to the present crisis (and in particular, a vast gulf between 'Eastern' and 'Western' perspectives – and great reluctance of Western 'thinkers' to even acknowledge that this is a question, itself a symptom of a kind of arrogance, that is, a kind of shamelessness).

At such a moment of emergency, the real cost of 'post-truth' in the era of 'viral transmission', 'filter bubbles' and other algorithmic network effects is starkly revealed, both in terms of the statistics of illness and death and in terms of the propensity for shame and shamelessness and their reactive expressions, from guilt and denial to resentment and scapegoating. What follows is an attempt to conceive a new basis for the understanding of shame in relation to a new philosophy and politics of locality. We undertake this here, at a moment of intense and ominous risk, because we believe it forms a crucial element of the psychic and collective therapeutics that will be required if the significant dangers we currently face are to have any chance of becoming an opportunity to navigate towards new horizons and safer shores.

Introduction: Derrida, Sloterdijk, Stiegler and Winnicott

More than twenty years ago, the French philosopher Jacques Derrida (2002) reflected on the notion that borders and frontiers can be likened to the immunological systems of the organism and on the fact that, in the age of globalization and 'teletechnologies', these threats to the localized character of social systems can produce autoimmune social crises such as xenophobia and demands for closed borders. Almost twenty years ago, the German philosopher Peter Sloterdijk (2011, p. 187) saw the threat of delocalizing technologies as giving rise to 'troubles of belonging' that he, too, saw in terms of the metaphor of immune systems. For nearly as long, Bernard Stiegler (2020b) has been concerned to address the 'pharmacological' (both curative and poisonous) conditions leading to the kinds of social crisis we see rising today, but despite his close affinity to Derrida, he has consistently avoided 'immunological' accounts, instead favouring an 'organological' description of the relationships amongst the individual, the collective and the technical.

For Stiegler, reactive phenomena such as scapegoating (designation of the *pharmakos*) have their ultimate root in the fact that human existence involves a circuit between the living and the non-living, that is, the artefact (the *pharmakon*) (2018c, p. 151). More recently, Stiegler has turned increasingly to the question of locality itself, couched in the language both of exosomatization (Lotka's name for technical life, that is, life equipped with the artefactual *pharmakon* – see Lotka, 1945) and of entropy and negentropy, that is, in the questions that arise from considering systems as localized, temporary and temporal processes of differentiation and diversification that resist the overall tendency towards disorder characteristic of physical processes in general but where the negentropic effects of such localized phenomena always lead to an overall increase of entropy in the physical universe (Stiegler, 2018a). But this focus also begs the question of whether and how Stiegler's 'neganthropological' account can be integrated with the 'immunological' accounts of Derrida and Sloterdijk.

The forms of nationalist autoimmunity and xenophobic scapegoating with which these authors deal are all *reactive* phenomena in the sense that their roots lie in *other* social and psychic crises in relation to which they amount to *counter*-formations. Yet they are also reactive in the sense of the distinction between reaction and reflection, which means that they are politically reaction*ary* and psychosocially *regressive*: their roots lie in people's relationships to the primordial conditions of the psychosocial existence of their exosomatic life. Among those psychic roots is shame of all kinds, provided that we interpret this affect in a fundamental sense as a proto-affect or a *Stimmung* (in Heidegger's sense) connected with the sense of one's own finitude, which opens up virtuous forms of reserve but which can also regress into guilt and, paradoxically and *reactively*, into shamelessness (Stiegler, 2013a; Ross, 2018). Stiegler has described reactions of this kind with respect to disorders of desire, drawing upon psychoanalysis but without pursuing in any specific way how these are also questions and disorders of sexuality. Given the centuries-long history of sexuality as a locus of shame, the question of how best to conduct such a pursuit from within Stiegler's general organology remains open and perhaps surprisingly so.

One key source of Stiegler's organology is the work of the British psychoanalyst Donald Winnicott. Stiegler borrows Winnicott's famous account of the transitional object, which the mother knows how to share with the child, which she enchants and through which she opens up a transitional space for the infant to enter a diverse and differentiated world. He generalizes and extends this account to describe how every artefact bears this 'spiritual' potential, from which ideas in general arise as enchanted possibilities and the potential for realizable dreams (Winnicott, 2005). But in Stiegler's pharmacological interpretation (2013b), artefacts, and especially *hypomnesic* artefacts dedicated to the retention and transmission of memory and ideas, always *also* contain the possibility of disenchantment and the destruction of knowledge.

Stiegler's pharmacological reading of Winnicott thus makes possible his account of the 'immense regression' (2018b) that occurs in computational capitalism thanks to the network effects produced by the algorithmic artefacts of platform capitalism. This regression (of what Stiegler calls the noetic soul) is characterized by the destruction of psychic and collective individuation (in Simondon's sense) in favour of 'group psychology', that is, herd behaviour. But faced with a psychosocial crisis that, in the West at least, nowadays concerns regression (and shamelessness) much more than repression (and guilt), and where this crisis arises from out of the most recent forms of the hypomnesic artefact or transitional object, the question becomes, in Heideggerian terms, how to identify the source of any possible 'saving power' in this situation.

We will argue that in this regard profit can be drawn from a distinction made by Winnicott but not referred to by Stiegler: between *regression* and *withdrawal*, where the latter is precisely the withdrawal *from* the positive potential *contained* in the *shame* of regression. Winnicott enriches this distinction through his use of the concept of 'holding', distinguishing between, on the one hand, the positivity of therapeutic holding *within* regression in a way that opens out onto the potential for individuation, and on the other hand, the negativity of a withdrawn state in which the patient is *holding themselves back* from individuation (Winnicott,

1975, pp. 255–261). More generally, all of these analyses and perspectives, coming from Stiegler, Derrida, Sloterdijk and Winnicott, can and must be integrated to elaborate a new account of shame as a *proto-affect* or *Stimmung* arising from what Stiegler calls an originary default because it is above all shame and its originary truth of finitude that one holds oneself back from acknowledging and living with, thereby putting oneself in need of the *care* of holding. Conceiving shame in relation to holding and the originary default leads to a new understanding of the emergence of immune and autoimmune phenomena in psychosocial systems and opens the possibility of new therapeutic conceptions of the role of shame in treating and healing psychosocial pathologies, which are also, inevitably, psycho-*sexual* pathologies.

Outline of a metacosmics: from negentropy to neganthropy

Our intention is thus to outline an account of the fundamental place of shame within a new conception of the existence of the kinds of being that we ourselves are, a conception that, drawing fundamentally on the work of Stiegler, we propose to call 'metacosmic' (see Ross, forthcoming, esp. ch. 9). First, we will describe Stiegler's account of technical life as both negentropic (genetic, biological, *endosomatic*) and neganthropic (noetic, technological, *exosomatic*), but we will interpret this through the concept of *resonance*. Second, we will reinterpret the relationship between information and knowledge in terms of this concept of resonance, and in relation to the specific character of libidinal energy. Third, we will understand the transmission and sharing of information and knowledge not just as the circulation of material signals but as the propagation of waves, where the 'recursivity' of such waves invites, for the case of neganthropic beings, the introduction of a new futural and phenomenological concept that we propose to call 'procursivity'. Fourthly, we will draw attention to a neglected fact about immunological systems, which is that they are always themselves retentional, opening the way for a new understanding of how Stiegler's account of exosomatic-noetic locality can be married to Sloterdijk's account of anthropotechnical co-immunity. This all too brief presentation of the basic tenets of metacosmics will then open on to a theoretical account of shame as a proto-affect, which will be followed by a reinterpretation of Winnicott as a means of suggesting the fundamental place of shame within a therapeutics of neganthropic life.

As mentioned then, we propose to call this new conception 'metacosmic' (see Ross, forthcoming, esp. ch. 9), in a sense that implies a distinction from (but not an opposition to) metaphysics, in turn implying a non-oppositional distinction between the (physical) universe and the (sur-real) cosmos (Stiegler, 2017, p. 94). This distinction is premised: *firstly*, on the 'scientific' notion that what distinguishes 'cosmics' from physics is the advent of persistent improbable localities characterized by a strong interrelatedness of component elements, which are not just ordered but *organized*, and which through that resist the probabilistic tendency that consists in the progressive erasure of the past; *secondly*, on the 'philosophical' notion that we thus need a new conceptual language going beyond the traditional opposition of being and becoming; and *thirdly*, on the 'exorganological' (i.e., Stieglerian) notion that improbable negentropic life, which struggles against entropy through the evolution and organization of endosomatic organs, is doubled by the advent of improbable *exosomatic* processes for what Stiegler proposes to call neganthropic life.

All negentropic beings are localized: bounded but open dynamic systems constituted by a set of strongly resonant elements, where this form of life arises from an originary default and where the conservation and organization of improbabilities combines with a process of diversification that together produces a dynamic that tends to increase in complexity across time. 'Originary default' means that such a system always gets going through an event of accidental and improbable co-implication that results in a singular struggle against entropy – and which, in the case of *neganthropic* life, that is, exosomatic life that gets going with the complication that is the exteriorization of memory in the artefact, also thus becomes a struggle against '*anthropy*' in Stiegler's sense. In the case of the kinds of beings that we are, therefore, this originary default arises from the fact that *our* existence is never *just* biological but must also be supplementarily prosthetic, that is, technological – exosomatic. It is worth noting, here, that just as Stiegler insists that this originary default must be distinguished from any lack, instead constituting more an originary freedom (Stiegler, 1998, p. 122), so too Sloterdijk rejects any notion that our neotenic quality implies that human being is a deficient being, insisting that it is, on the contrary, a *luxury* being (Sloterdijk, 2016, pp. 651–662). Luxury is something like the *différance* of deficiency, and it is *between* and from *out of* the tension between deficiency and luxuriation that the proto-affect of shame originates.

No negentropic system is ever truly stable. Metastability refers to a degree of synchronic orderliness achievable by a system so long as it remains within its threshold limits, which when crossed produce a diachronic upheaval that either leads to a new metastability or to the collapse of the system. 'Resonant', here, means that this struggle for metastability operates through a proliferation of interdependent recursive operations (feedback loops) both within the system and between the system and its environment. It is the recursivity of these operations that delineates their bounded and open spatial character, as well as facilitating their dynamic temporal character, because within this recursivity there is also change – that is, *différance*. This is what produces the possibility of a distinction between interior and exterior, where interiority refers to the internal resonance that is dynamically maintained as a cohesive tension and where exteriority refers to the porosity of the bounds of a system (cell membrane, skin, city wall, national border, etc.), regulating the border crossings and sensitivities occurring at and across the edges of a system's spatial limits. This is the basis, for example, of the sensorimotor loops that Jakob von Uexküll identifies as the fundamental recursive mechanisms of animal life (von Uexküll, 2010) and which, in neganthropic life, involve recursive loops not just between organism and milieu but between organism, physical milieu and that 'third area' which is simultaneously that of transitional space, the space of the transindividuation of knowledge and the space of the circulation of libidinal energy, that is, of all forms of sublimation as the *différance* of the drives.

Stiegler's exorganological perspective means that information and knowledge must always be conceived in relation to their *material* (or *hyper*-material) supports and in exosomatic life always as a question of what André Leroi-Gourhan (1993) calls the 'exteriorization' of memory, where what circulates through these supports are 'particles' of information. At the same time, however, another set of terms is possible: 'resonance', 'tension' and 'recursivity' imply something like a 'medium', subject to *wave* propagation and return effects. We therefore propose that information and knowledge *always* have, in an undecidable and pseudo-quantum manner, dual properties of particles and of waves, depending on the standpoint from which they are being examined.

Outline of a metacosmics: information, knowledge and desire

Unlike those who maintain that 'everything is information' or that the universe 'itself' is informational in character, we maintain that whatever information is, it can be a material and energetic property *only* of negentropic and neganthropic systems, that is, bounded dynamics in which improbabilities structurally persist and even become probable, whether endosomatically or exosomatically, and at the perpetual risk of closing off the possibility of new improbabilities. The recursivity of operations characteristic of negentropic systems means that signals are sent and exchanged both 'internally' and between the organism and its milieu: in either case, informational exchange is always local and counts as informational only within a localized context in which signals can be *significant*.

The recursive operations of informational systems involve not just matter but energy. In negentropic systems, the energy circulating through recursive processes is the biophysical energy with which endosomatic life is sustained. But in *neganthropic* systems, it becomes necessary to make a distinction between the 'messages' that circulate within and between organisms, the cultivation of *knowledge* among localized groups and the *information* that is the condition of possibility of knowledge as well as of its impossibility. The fundamental possibility of knowledge is that it can be externalized in technical forms that are not lost with the death of the individual: 'human beings disappear; their histories remain' (Stiegler, 2011b, p. 131). In this way, every artefact is accidentally a form of memory, but when artefacts become *deliberately* memorious, as with painting, symbolization and writing, the lessons acquired through living become essentially shareable within a localized context and transgenerationally cumulative – this is knowledge in the strict sense.

Such accumulations in turn lead to further technical innovations, which always contain the potential to become a threat to ways of living, requiring new knowledgeable accumulations that lead to new innovations. Consequently, neganthropic beings cannot live without localized technical systems but they also cannot live without localized knowledge systems prescribing how to take care of technical systems and the endosomatic and exosomatic beings who live within them. Stiegler refers to such neganthropic beings no longer as organisms but as *exorganisms*: a human being and its hammer, a human being and its books, a human being and its dwelling, a human being and its smartphone, which by this stage can no longer be separated from planetary technological systems that turn the biosphere into a technosphere and include an exospherical belt of telecommunications satellites.

This circuit with the outside means that knowledge is always exposed to the threat of becoming dead information, losing its value over time by disconnecting from what Whitehead called the function of reason (Stiegler, 2017, pp. 83–87). This function, as Whitehead describes it, enables an attack on the environment that consists firstly in living (biologically, i.e., negentropically), secondly in living well (neganthropically) and finally in living better (transforming existence by realizing new neganthropic dreams, i.e., anti-anthropically) (Whitehead, 1929, p. 5).

What this association with Whitehead's function of *reason* shows is the irreducible connection between the neganthropic knowledge stored, shared and transmitted exosomatically and *desire*. Hence the energy that circulates in this cultivation and transformation of every kind of future-oriented knowledge, on every scale, from the couple to the tribe to the nation to the civilization, is no longer just the biophysical energy of negentropic life but *libidinal* energy. The latter is understood, à la Stiegler, as the *différance* of the drives.

Desire cannot be reduced to the laws of thermodynamics, which is why watching a good movie on a boring Sunday afternoon can mean that 'we come out of it less lazy, even re-invigorated, full of emotion and the desire to do something, or else infused with a new outlook on things' (Stiegler, 2011b, p. 10). In fact, as Stiegler shows, libidinal energy always involves exorganological relationships of this kind (ibid.): In the example just given:

The cinematographic machine, taking charge of our boredom, will have transformed it into new energy, transubstantiated it, made something out of nothing – the nothing of that terrible, nearly fatal feeling of a Sunday afternoon of nothingness.

This *increase* of energy amounts to *both* sublimation in the sense of the différantiating postponement of the drives *and* restoration that comes from *luxuriating* in the neganthropic wealth of what Stiegler calls the noetic necromass (2018b, p. 107). What occurs between the moviegoer and the movie itself involves thousands upon thousands of recursive operations that produce a resonance between this projection and the exorganism, and a tension within the psyche of this exorganism, also known, variously, as an individual, a subject, a citizen or a consumer. At the same time, not every movie offers itself as a neganthropic treasure: many, if not most, present themselves as anthropic temptations, ultimately depleting libidinal energy. We may enjoy them shamelessly but in the end risk being left with a feeling of malaise and a sense of guilt. Whatever the case, all this is played out in a field lying between exorganisms and their symbolic emanations or cosmetic adornments, or between one exorganism and another, or between collections of exorganisms, a field characterized by this production of resonating and tensing recursive operations, which we could call the 'aether' of an exorganic system (deliberately playing on the anachronistic physics of both ancient Greece and the nineteenth century).

Outline of a metacosmics: recursivity and procursivity

When that plurality of operations combines and coheres in what (looking ahead) we can call a mutually holding way, it tends to keep the system in a state of dynamic tension, and these resonant waves then function to generate signification and significance. Significance is thus produced from the dynamic potential of such recursive waves to introduce new variations into this exorganic aether, where such potential arises from the wealth and diversity of recursive operations, a potential that Georges Canguilhem (1991, pp. 206–207) calls 'propulsive'. Neganthropic recursions have the potential to produce new propulsive effects, even if they always also have the pharmacological potential to fall into empty anthropic repetition that, precisely, diminishes difference and diversification.

Propulsive dynamism is thus what enables exorganic systems to maintain their negentropic, neganthropic and anti-anthropic struggle. For neganthropic beings, this propulsive character contained in the resonant tension of recursive operations is always *in excess* over the recursive operations of negentropic life: we call this the *procursivity* of the exorganic system. We propose that this resonant propagation of recursive and procursive waves, within a singular locality in tension with an exterior milieu and traversed by a technical milieu suffused with symbolic and affective adornments, and involving the sharing, transmission, cultivation, creation and transformation of information, knowledge and significance, amounts to the production of singular and localized exorganic systems that can justly be referred to as *cosmoses*.

Within such cosmoses, which can arise only in the dynamic open systems of neganthropic life, the brain and the sense organs are all always already adjusted to and by prostheses that condition the relationship *between* these psychic systems, opening up behavioural possibilities such as cooperation that is based on mutual understanding and animated by the possibility of invention. A cosmos, which always arises from out of a singular default of origin, is always also something *more than* a universe: it is excessively and surrealistically *luxuriant*. It is because of the cosmic character of neganthropic relations within exorganic life that we refer to the theory of the conditions of possibility of such deficient but luxuriant cosmoses as a metacosmics.

What Leroi-Gourhan describes in terms of the relationship between instruments and knowledge during the process of human evolution is, by extension, precisely what Winnicott describes in relation to the way in which the good-enough mother opens up transitional space between herself and her child through the introduction of the transitional object, an object that, as mentioned already, she must *enchant* through her maternal knowledge and through the resonance of neganthropic operations she conjures between herself and her child, mediated by that object and traversing the transitional aether. Enchantment transforms the object from something existing finitely (as a real technical artefact) into something that *consists* infinitely (as a surreal cosmological adornment). It describes the character of the relationship between knowledge and desire in every exorganic cosmos, and hence the procursivity of neganthropic systems always involves processes of enchantment and re-enchantment, often given names like belief, faith and certainty. Such a potential for enchantment amounts to our originary potential for *luxuriation*, which is also a child's 'wanting more' that must be transformed through primordial shame into *also* being, for example, a *willingness to postpone* – which is precisely a question of the *différance* of the drives through their transformation into desire.

Outline of a metacosmics: on the retentional-immunological

The human and social sciences have found themselves perpetually caught on the oppositions of nature and culture, animal and human. Crucial to any extrication from this metaphysical trap is recognition that all recursive and procursive processes and operations are *retentional* and that retention has an ongoing history of epochs and eras. In other words, although rejecting oppositions, we must insist on the need to make *distinctions* between retentional systems and their accompanying retentional aethers, and first of all, those of genetic memory, nervous memory and artificial memory.

All of these retentional systems involve recursive processes, through which they improbably retain past improbabilities to open chances for improbabilities yet to come. They are, in this way, what Husserl called, with respect to time-consciousness, protentional. In the case of the neganthropic beings of exorganic systems, this protentionality is procursive in the sense that these new improbabilities aren't just new chances for biological selection to combine favourably with genetic mutation but opportunities for new improbable relationships to the adorned cosmos to be built and fashioned, both technologically and cosmetically. Such opportunities always involve the dynamic release of tensional aether through the liberation of repressed potentials, which Stiegler describes in terms of the relationship between stereotypes and traumatypes (2015b, paras. 48–49).

In addition to being retentional and protentional, recursive and procursive operations are also *immunological*. But this assertion depends on first recognizing a neglected fact: *all* immunological processes are *always* retentional. We can understand this by reading the scientific work of Jean Claude Ameisen (2003, p. 76) and the philosophical work of Francesco Vitale (2018, pp. 178–180). The physiological immune system, for example, retains a material part of a pathogen by literally cutting it out, through the retention of which it can distinguish between what is proper to its own locality and what is foreign, triggering a response aimed at preserving negentropic metastability. The physiological immune system is in a literal way an archive of the history of the organism's encounters with an internalized externality (so to speak), which the organism consults over the course of its journey through the microbial aether.

This endosomatic immune system must thus be counted as a *fourth* retentional system in addition to the three great kinds of memory that Stiegler, reading Leroi-Gourhan, identifies as the genetic, the nervous and the artificial. From this perspective, we can re-conceive nervous memory as the internalized archive of the history of the organism's encounters with what lies beyond the borders of its endosomatic frontier (outside its own skin). More generally, all retentional processes can be re-conceived as being in some way immunological: the local character of all negentropic and neganthropic recursive processes and operations means that they involve relationships of boundedness and openness, tending to maintain the dynamic of a system through various degrees of hospitality and exclusion, where these *must* compose because too impenetrable a barrier will prevent the immune system from acquiring the archive without which it cannot function, leading it eventually towards auto-immunity, that is, its turning in upon itself destructively.

In extending the immunological to exosomatic retentional processes, we must stress that this hospitality and this exclusion, this fight against the foreign that can turn against the self, do not concern individuals or peoples, as it does with the xenophobic use of the metaphor of immunity. Instead, it concerns the character of retentionality itself: information, knowledge and significance. It is information and knowledge that may always lose their significance or become, in fact, auto-immune. Here, Stiegler's pharmacology of technological retention meets up with Sloterdijk's anthropotechnical account of co-immunity and Derrida's account of the auto-immune tendency that any immunological system always contains.

All of these are fundamental elements of what we are calling a metacosmic perspective, which presupposes that all counter-entropic phenomena and all future-directed recursive processes operating in open and local dynamic systems arise from the interaction between retentional processes. These retentional processes are necessarily also immunological in character, whereas retention as the recursive maintenance of improbability within a localized system is the only possible source of protention as the procursive propulsion towards new beneficial improbabilities. With such a metacosmics in mind, it becomes possible to understand cosmic resonance as the totality of and interaction between the recursive and procursive processes and operations within a singular, local and open cosmos.

They are *always* a question of retentional systems and their economies, always possessing an immunological character and a protentional orientation. With these foundations, it becomes possible to build an account of shame as a proto-affect for those deficient-but-luxuriating beings that are neganthropic exorganisms and that must always strive to build, think and dwell within a resonant and surreal cosmos.

A metacosmic understanding of shame

Let us say that the protentional and procursive transindividuation processes occurring between the simple exorganisms that together form a complex exorganism amount to a kind of cosmic inflation, where knowledge builds upon knowledge and desire upon desire in a cumulative and enriching way via the mediation of the transitional and exomnesic aether. Such neganthropic life, always open to the luxury of enchanted inflation, is nevertheless perpetually exposed to the risk of disenchantment and cosmic *deflation* – a collapse of the resonance and tension of that aether, which is always a composition of every kind of endosomatic and exosomatic retentional system. It is only through such 'symphonic' compositions within and between exorganisms that the enchantment animating knowledge and desire is possible. Such compositions are not a question of some natural harmony of the spheres, however, but rather of endless struggle to draw nutrition from the accumulation of cosmetic resources that Stiegler calls the noetic necromass but which can always turn out to be not a life-giving humus but a lifeless desert.

If such is the character of the neganthropic exorganisms we ourselves are or hope to be, then we can conclude that such exorganisms are stretched, in their transitional and exomnesic aether, between inflationary potentiality and deflationary risk. We could thus characterize the feeling of shame in a manner akin to the *Stimmung* of *Angst* that Heidegger describes as accompanying the mortal knowledge of *Dasein* and opening up the possibility for a 'voice of conscience' that in turn enables an 'authentic' existence that is 'existentially only a modified grasp of everydayness' (Heidegger, 1996, p. 179, German pagination). Shame would then be describable as a kind of proto-awareness of, or pre-conscious relationship to, the cosmic finitude that consists in this being stretched between the tensed striving to luxuriate in enchantment and the perpetual risk of its loss. Shame would have its fundamental source in the sense that the struggle against entropy and anthropy can never be victorious, that in some way it is always a striving for what one cannot 'have', that its local pursuit always has entropic and anthropic consequences here or elsewhere (for oneself or others) and thus that the boundedness and openness of our exorganological and immunological systems are only ever local and temporary phenomena.

All of our noetic and exosomatic efforts in the face of this struggle could then be interpreted as amounting to a response, to paraphrase Primo Levi, to the proto-feeling of the shame of being an exorganism. My cosmos exists and can exist only in relation to other psychic cosmoses, and my own inflationary tendency (towards enchantment and luxuriation) can either contribute to a diachronic co-inflation with others or on the contrary crowd them out through my synchronic tendency to take power, which disenchants and deflates others. Shame is thus in part that reserve or restraint without which the tendency towards arrogance, narcissism and crime, and more generally the tendency towards taking power, will lead to discord and ultimately to war: it is shame that makes possible all those forms of politeness, respect, dignity and care that arise not just from a consciousness of their necessity but also from a feeling of the danger of my own and others' *hubris*.

Stiegler's account of *aidōs* and *dikē* can thus be read as an allegory of the immuno-logical need for a metastability between synchrony and diachrony, and between boundedness and openness, in the articulation of endosomatic and exosomatic retentional systems. For Stiegler, these proto-affects of shame and justice, distributed by Zeus (via Hermes) after the Promethean theft and gift of fire and Epimethean forgetfulness in failing to give to exorganisms any specific qualities, are the only possible basis for learning to live together, with exosomatic instruments, in peace and civility, and which thus involves what can only be a *political knowledge* (Stiegler, 2015a, p. 217):

> It is this political knowledge that, according to Protagoras, will be brought to mortals by Hermes: a knowledge founded on the feelings of justice and shame, *dikē* and *aidōs*, which are also techniques, says Hermes, and which constitute the bases of what must be understood as a *hermeneutic therapeutics*.
>
> A therapy, or a therapeutics, is the care we take of that of which we *must* take care. In this case, it is a matter of taking care of the *pharmakon* that technics proves to be, as a power that is also the scar of a *deficiency of being*, that is, of a *default of origin*, a deficiency of the *pharmakon* that can become poisonous but which, through the care we must take, may become *the necessary default*.

This 'becoming necessary' of the default is what happens through 'quasi-causally' (in Deleuze's sense) *adopting* it (or any new instrument or technical system) rather than merely adapting to it. The capacity for the deficient being to exist metastably as a luxury being then stems from the possibility for a quasi-causal adoption *in shame* of that deficiency, which becomes the accidental necessity of finding a path to one's own cosmic inflation (with others). We can also see that this 'political knowledge' is equally a question of care and, more specifically, care of the domestic realm symbolized by the figure of Hestia (ibid., p. 219):

> The fire of the hearth is as such also the *pharmakon* of which Hestia takes care, which she maintains while preventing it from spreading beyond the hearth; she thus contains it in its very intimacy, which is the meaning of *aidōs*, that modesty and shame . . . through which this intimacy is accomplished (i.e. individuated) as 'desire remaining desire' . . . . And we must

here relate Hestia, of whom Pandora is the hidden face, to Winnicott's 'good enough mother'.

Shame is therefore both an irreducible and defining characteristic of the kinds of technological beings that we ourselves are *and* the basis of an immunological function possessed by exorganisms, without which coupling, familial harmony, group cooperation and collective peace are bound to remain fantasies rather than shared dreams believed in and pursued singularly. This function consists in responding to this awareness of our limited, entropic and anthropic character as finite and exposed pharmacological beings and of the irreducible *risk* entailed by the unavoidable *necessity* of struggling to quasi-causally adopt our default and to strive to be luxuriously more than we actually are: what the *Stimmung* of shame makes possible is precisely a *response*, the *temporality* of sublimated responsibility rather than the drive-based spontaneity of reaction, *answering* to a threat or a challenge but *mindful* of the risk that luxuration can turn auto-immune.

In the case of the endosomatic immune system, the *sensitivity* of the immune retentional system arises from the *difficulty* of correctly identifying and distinguishing what is proper and what is harmful to one's body in something foreign that one has encountered and retained or that one has never encountered before. This difficulty corresponds to that of the gauging and measuring of the *level* of response necessary to maintain the metastability of the whole organism. These combined difficulties lead Canguilhem to describe the dysfunctioning of these systems as normal functioning whose auto-immune effect happens to be an under-reaction or an overreaction in terms of the healthy metastability of the organism rather than as pathological behaviour *as such*.

Exorganisms, too, face this difficulty of identifying and distinguishing between what is proper and what is harmful in whatever is received by their retentional systems at all levels but with the added *complication* that the *truly* foreign cannot be recognized at all, and only those *recognizable but stereotypically unrecognized* foreigns capable of traumatypically liberating repressed potentials bear the possibility of diachronically leading us to new exomnesic arrangements. For exorganisms, the healthy 'normal' is not *set* by the recursive operations of the endosomatic organs, which vary according to the internal and external operations of the exosomatic organs forming the exomnesic aether. This leads to constant changes in what counts as the propulsive constants of new 'normativities' (in Canguilhem's terms) of the exorganism, that is, of new metastabilities of ways of living for the forms of technical life that we constitute. This *capacity* for the formation of new constants and new norms, however, paradoxically arises *from* our proto-awareness of the finitude that opens us to exorganic pathologies; in other words, it depends on our traumatypical potential that is also our shameful '*temptation* to fall sick' (Canguilhem, 1991, p. 200; italics added).

Just as physiological immune systems are sensitive, that is, delicate, prone to dysfunction, so too are the immunological systems of the exorganism, operating with exosomatic forms of retentional and inherently pharmacological apparatus.

These systems are sensitive first and foremost because they necessitate the *interpretation* of what is retained, or, in other words, because knowledge and reason are required to gauge the *significance* of what has happened to us. Such significance always depends on the relationship between the calculable and the incalculable, and between the probable, the improbable and the utterly singular. Exosomatic immunological processes and the sensitive instruments of which they are composed are therefore always at risk of underreacting – amounting to tendencies towards shamelessness and denial, failing to appropriately weigh the gravity of threats or the significance of events – or overreacting, tending to hypostasize the proto-*Stimmung* of shame into the concrete prison of guilt, a psychic state in which the immune processes of the exorganism may be ferociously turned inwards. Such underreactions – because of an *insensitivity* of immunological interpretation – and overreactions – because of *over*-sensitivity – are both forms of autoimmunity, and the ultimate risk entailed by a lack or surfeit of sensitivity is therefore the production of reactions that are no longer in any way responses contained within the bounds of *aidōs*. They are instead regressions from shame, failures of sublimation amounting to psychosocial forms of what Canguilhem calls *anaphylaxis* – individual, marital, familial, social, political or civilizational collapse.

If we consider psychosocial metastability in the terms we have here, as involving the resonance and tension necessary to maintain cosmic inflation against the perpetual risk of deflationary tendencies, then it is this loss of tension or resonance that can lead our sensitive immunological instruments to under- or overreact, to forget shame in favour of shamelessness or conversely to rigidify it in the form of guilt. This loss of procursive resonance amounts to *dissonance*, where the waves of the noetic and exomnesic aether tend to produce disharmony, disrupting cosmic relationships in regressive, desublimating ways that, in the absence of a careful therapeutics, are bound to leave the psychic or social cosmos exposed to the entropic universe and our own anthropic, all too anthropic, stereotypical prison.

Such dissonances, however, are *also* those disharmonic faults that must quasi-causally be adopted as the necessity of new resonances. Shame bears a fundamental function in those sensitive and interpretive noetic immune systems that alone allow exorganic life to be metastably maintained or propulsively transformed. Between its de-calibrated concretizations as shamelessness and as denial or guilt, shame is the possibility of systemic self-awareness in the midst of crises of metastability. Far from eliminating shame, the function of a therapeutics of shame is to allow it to resonate without falling into either of its perpetual anthropic risks: the vacuum of shamelessness or the frozen solidity of guilt. At the national or civilizational level, for example, one might well argue that hyper-modernizing China, by still retaining previous forms of exosomatic life with significant sclerotic guilt elements, is experiencing high levels of psychic dissonance, even though it is usually suppressed precisely because it is an excessive form of shame. This will either have increasingly reactive consequences or else lead to forms of response that navigate a path between the Scylla and Charybdis of shameless empty freedom and guilt-based obsolescent authoritarianism.

In short, resonance and dissonance are not opposites, and the latter may have propulsive characteristics, facilitating neganthropic diachronies. Put another way, no system involving the relative motion of two or more bodies is ever completely stable; the relationship between them can thus be understood in terms of the composition of gravitational (attractive) and centrifugal (repulsive) tendencies that determine whether a system holds together or breaks apart. Mixing this metaphor into the metacosmic dough we are preparing, the task of a pharmacology and therapeutics of shame is to take advantage of these competing and compositional tendencies so that dissonant tensions can have propulsive effects, and shame can facilitate the quasi-causal adoption of deficiencies that in this way become necessary and realizable luxuries. But allowing this dough to rise involves reflection on the Winnicottian concept of 'holding'.

Reinterpreting some Winnicottian concepts in terms of a metacosmics of shame

Stiegler (2011a, pp. 132–137) often talks about regression as a perpetual possibility for the noetic soul. He interprets Aristotle's account of three kinds of souls – vegetative, sensitive and noetic – and insists that these three kinds, corresponding to the souls of plants, animals and human beings, not be understood oppositionally but compositionally. He also emphasizes, via Hegel, that they are to be understood in terms of the relationship between potential and act. In other words, the sensitive soul bears within it the vegetative soul and is often in a vegetative state rather than in the actuality of sensitivity, and the noetic soul is often in a sensitive state, only *intermittently* achieving noeticity. At the same time, when it *is* acting noetically, the noetic soul *remains* sensitive through and through, but its sensitivity has a noetic character, which Stiegler calls sensational. The noetic soul, therefore, is, unlike the merely sensitive soul, capable of exclaiming symbolically its sensational relationship to, for example, a beautiful sunset. But it can also fall prey to the temptation of the regressive sensational*ism* conveyed on, for example, those retentional supports of shamelessness that are the 'media', today algorithmically driven. Consequently and conversely, when the noetic soul *regresses* to being merely sensitive, this is not a question of returning to some animal state but to a kind of regressive stupidity or beastliness that is *specific* to the kinds of noetic souls that we ourselves are (see also Ross, 2009).

For Stiegler, the 'exclamatory' possibility of the noetic soul and its corresponding irreducible capacity for regression both ultimately derive from the fact that what moves it, what sublimates its drives and animates its desire, is a circuit through the outside and, in particular, through those noetico-aesthetic technologies that may enlarge that soul but also contain the potential to exploit the perpetual *temptation* to regress. Already in 2004, Stiegler diagnosed a generalization of regression leading to 'a West that is achieved, that is, finished, dead, given that capitalism fulfils itself as the advent of nihilism'. In the same year he anticipated the destructive rise of social networks (Stiegler, 2014, ch. 3). Fourteen years later, after the advent of so-called platforms, he will continue to see the anthropic decomposition of psychosocial existence as amounting to an 'immense regression' (Stiegler, 2018b).

In light of Stiegler, how might we *re*interpret the fact that when Edgar Morin, like Stiegler, explains that entropy and negentropy are not oppositional principles, he does so by describing entropy as a regression but negentropy as a 'regression of regression through regression' (Morin, 1992, p. 297), a 'regression of regression in and against this regression' (ibid., p. 302)? Morin adds (p. 303):

> Progress is born from a regression of regression and is effected through regressions. [It] returns and deviates the latter against the current, like an eddy or whirlpool . . . inscribed in what *physis* and cosmos have most fundamental in their being and their becoming.

If there is a positive clue contained in Morin's thought that can open up beyond Stiegler – and beyond Morin's own deficiencies with respect to the interpretation of entropy and negentropy – the understanding of the anti-anthropic and therapeutic significance of regression for the noetic soul, that is, the neganthropic exorganism, we argue that this depends on reinterpreting the non-oppositional distinction that *Winnicott* makes between regression and withdrawal.

In 1954, Winnicott made the distinction between *regression* and *withdrawal* in the clinical situation and specifically 'in the transference in the course of analysis', defining the former of these concepts as 'regression to dependence' and the latter as 'momentary detachment from a waking relationship with external reality' (1975, p. 255). With this thought, he intended to go beyond the common understanding 'that there is some danger in the regression of a patient during psycho-analysis': the distinction between regression and withdrawal is not exactly a characteristic of the individual but rather of the tension occurring in the space between patient and therapist, which could also be described in terms of the co-immunity involved in the cosmos of the analytical situation (ibid., p. 261):

> The danger does not lie in the regression but in the analyst's unreadiness to meet the regression and the dependence which belongs to it. When an analyst has had experience that makes him confident in his management of regression, then it is probably true to say that the more quickly the analyst accepts the regression and meets it fully the less likely is it that the patient will need to enter into an illness with regressive qualities.

In Winnicott's account, then, regression *keeps open* the dynamic therapeutic cosmos, whereas withdrawal *closes it off*, and the difference between them can be expressed in terms of a difference between two forms of 'holding'. These two forms correspond to two variations of the relationship between boundedness and openness, differentiated in terms of their capacity to establish a situation of co-immunity – a cosmic situation held in the suspense of a neganthropically tensed transitional aether:

> I would say that *in the withdrawn state a patient is holding the self* and that if immediately the withdrawn state appears *the analyst can hold the patient*, then what would otherwise have been a withdrawal state becomes a regression.
>
> (ibid.)

Regression, therefore, is the bearer of therapeutic potential precisely as a kind of regression of regression in and against this regression, as Morin argued in a completely different (but not unrelated) context. If the primordial origin of shame lies in the originary default of the exorganism, then the virtuous potential contained in regression lies not in the elimination of shame but in its exposure, rising to the visible surface in the midst of a crisis of metastability:

> The advantage of a *regression* is that it carries with it the opportunity for correction of inadequate adaptation-to-need in the past history of the patient, that is to say, in the patient's infancy management. By contrast the *withdrawn* state is not profitable and when the patient recovers from a withdrawn state he or she is not changed.
>
> (ibid.)

Here, Winnicott differentiates regression and withdrawal as the difference between the open possibility of a step of individuation or conversely the closing off of all potential diachronization: if therapeutic care *as* regression involves a state of co-immunity, then this is also a co-individuation. In Canguilhem's terms, withdrawal amounts to the underreactive constriction of the possibility of responding to primordial shame *propulsively*. In Stiegler's terms, the neganthropic regression of a regression conforms to the possibility of quasi-causally *adopting* a failure-to-adapt as, instead, a *necessity* of the exorganism, an adoption that consists in procursively rewriting the circuits that have formed into sclerotic stereotypes lodged deep within the retentional unconscious.

From the standpoint of a metacosmics, then, Winnicott's distinction can be interpreted as two ways in which a surrealistic cosmic exorganism reacts or responds to contingencies, accidents or events that lead to dissonance or expose the risk of dissonance or, in other words, that expose noetic souls to the irreducibility of their own shameful temptation to regress. By exposing the immunological and retentional-protentional tendency towards disharmonic dissonance, a tendency rooted in the originary default of the exorganism, regression at the same time opens up the possibility of adopting that shame and *enlisting* it in the inventive and luxurious writing of new libidinal circuits, new capacities for knowledge and desire to circulate and accumulate and thus to propagate new resonating waves in the transitional aether. Against the anti-anthropic counter-current of this regression of regression, withdrawal would consist in turning away from the *work* of regression, where that into which withdrawal withdraws often proves to be denial, resentment, guilt or shamelessness.

It is clear that the Winnicottian concept of holding *in* regression – where the therapist *holds out to the patient* the possibility of diachronic change *against* the temptation to remain locked within a closed sphere that refuses the world – corresponds to an analytical theatre that in some way *recreates* the original transitional space situation. The therapeutic process thus necessarily involves making room for new kinds of transitional objects opening up new forms of enchantment and warmth, not to eradicate the threat of disenchantment that shame perpetually poses but to take advantage of that shame for the production of new propulsive constants, new normativities and new forms of luxuriant diversity in which recursive and procursive operations enrich and enchant the individual and shared cosmoses of psychosocial life.

Regression can thus be regarded as an ambivalent phenomenon: it is an autoimmune, overreactive and hyper-sensitive response to systemic crisis that is therefore entropic and could easily turn anaphylactic, but it also contains the concealed potential of becoming the opening of a new neganthropic cosmo-immunological process. Withdrawal, on the other hand, is an underreactive reaction to this response that fails to engage genuine co-immune processes by not recognizing the quasi-causal possibility for the shameful fault to be adopted as a neganthropic necessity. In terms of Stiegler's exorganology, this implies the necessity of a pharmacology of shame with respect to a therapeutics of holding.

Conclusion: opening a path to a new critique

Compared with the exorganological standpoint already offered so cogently by Stiegler, the metacosmic standpoint proposed here additionally means that the overt political crises of our time, identified by Derrida and Sloterdijk in terms of autoimmune reactions, must also be understood in terms of their relationship to the smallest scales of immunological crisis. The pandemic through which we are currently living (at the time of writing: April 2020) is thrusting these microcosmic scales back into the forefront of visibility, thanks to the widespread confinement of vast numbers of individuals within their homes – together with their smartphones, tablets and laptop computers, and all the forms of connectivity and dysconnectivity they bring.

Without doubt, we can conclude that all of these reticulated devices will continue to function pharmacologically, and in ways that intensify the longer the crisis continues, with consequences that are bound to include new forms of psychosocial pathology and dysfunction at various scales. Yet there will also be opportunities for new familial resonance, for new reflections on the metastability between boundedness and openness of localities at different scales and on an immunological pharmacology of shame required by that metastability, and for new circuits of transindividuation and the enrichment of culture, knowledge and the noetic necromass. Even if Giorgio Agamben was right to point to what are undoubtedly

risks and dangers, his poorly measured response to the pandemic failed to recognize such opportunities by claiming that with our reactions 'the threshold that
separates humanity from barbarism has been crossed' (Agamben, 2020). Such
opportunities, however, are precisely what Stiegler describes by drawing on his
own past experience of desperation, shame and crisis (2020a, 2020c).

The disruptions of metastability that today plague our microcosms are firstly
all those libidinal crises that Stiegler identifies at the level of psychic individuation and collective individuation, resulting from the grammatization of daily
life and the proletarianization of ways of living. We would add that this requires
analysis at the level of the co-individuation of both the family and the couple.
No doubt Stiegler would not disagree. But we would further argue, *firstly*, that *specific* attention, care and therapeutics are necessary in relation to the immune and
auto-immune phenomena that we see today at those small scales involving the
co-immunity of simple exorganism and simple exorganism, *secondly*, that these
particularly involve forms of the regression of shame to guilt and shamelessness, and *thirdly*, that to think these forms, that is, to avoid *withdrawing* from this
regression, including into contemporary symptoms of de-sexualization and hyper-
sexualization, new concepts and new analyses will be required.

These crises of familial, romantic, libidinal and sexual metastability involve the
interaction of all the forms of retentional system – genetic, nervous, immune and
technological. They do so at an *intimate* level, where they demand to be understood in relation to specific forms of guilt, shamelessness, denial and repression
produced by platforms connected not just to so-called social media but to pornog-
raphy, 'dating sites', fan culture and other forms of the digital culture industries,
noticeably including, recently, the rise of some new types of sensationalism aimed
particularly at girls, especially in Asian countries. These forms of grammatization
and proletarianization are mostly premised on the algorithmic exploitation of the
perpetual temptation of noetic souls to fall sick and, more specifically, to fall into
addictive spirals.

The upshot, for increasing numbers of especially young people, is an increasingly thoroughly disenchanted libidinal universe – no longer a cosmos, lacking the
warmth of a resonant aether of co-individuation and sexual transindividuation –
in which they find it almost impossible to luxuriate. Hence if, as Stiegler has
recently argued, what we are currently (barely) living through indeed amounts to
an immense regression, then the therapeutic response to such a sociopathological
process can neither be to guiltily confess our shame nor to shamelessly refuse to
admit we have a problem: *our* goal must firstly be to turn that problem into a question, that crisis into a critique. We must enter into our irreducible shame of being
an exorganism more profoundly and in conditions of resonant 'holding', which
is to say, warmth and care in a shared cosmos, to locate and quasi-causally adopt
the possibilities shame offers for the development of new propulsive tendencies.
This development comprises real systemic transformation, at the psychic, sexual,
libidinal, noetic, technological, civilizational and, ultimately, biospheric scales. In
short, the depletion of libidinal energy rightly diagnosed by Stiegler may demand

not just new forms of the long circuits of transindividuation that he well argues are what makes life worth the effort of being lived but also new circuits of the transindividuation of sexual life. This requires an analysis and critique that we might half-jokingly describe as no longer just exorganological but sexorganological.

References

Agamben, G. (2020). "A Question." https://itself.blog/2020/04/15/giorgio-agamben-a-question/?fbclid=IwAR2KXeVNVwl8_CN4nxAx-TaDe-l17AlqUgjxiPDIiGIad0WA_W8LV_zjsFE.
Ameisen, J. C. (2003). *La sculpture du vivant. Le suicide cellulaire ou la mort créatrice.* Paris: Seuil.
Canguilhem, G. (1991). *The Normal and the Pathological.* New York: Zone Books.
Derrida, J. (2002). "Faith and Knowledge: The Two Sources of 'Religion' at the Limits of Reason Alone." In *Acts of Religion.* Ed. Gil Anidjar. New York & London: Routledge.
Heidegger, M. (1996). *Being and Time.* Albany: State University of New York Press.
Leroi-Gourhan, A. (1993). *Gesture and Speech.* Cambridge, MA & London: MIT Press.
Lotka, A. (1945). "The Law of Evolution as a Maximal Principle." *Human Biology,* 17, 167–194.
Morin, E. (1992). *Method. Towards a Study of Humankind, Volume 1: The Nature of Nature.* New York: Peter Lang.
Ross, D. (2009). "Politics and Aesthetics, or, Transformations of Aristotle in Bernard Stiegler." *Transformations,* 17. www.transformationsjournal.org/wp-content/uploads/2017/01/Ross_Trans17.pdf
———. (2018). "The Pharmacology of Shame, Promethean, Epimethean and Antigonian Temporality." In *Temporality and Shame: Perspectives from Psychoanalysis and Philosophy.* Eds. Ladson Hinton & Hessel Willemsen. London & New York: Routledge.
———. (Forthcoming). *Psychopolitical Anaphylaxis: Steps Towards a Metacosmics.* London: Open Humanities Press.
Sloterdijk, P. (2011). *Neither Sun Nor Death.* Los Angeles: Semiotext(e).
———. (2016). *Spheres, Volume 3: Foams. Plural Spherology.* Los Angeles: Semiotext(e).
Stiegler, B. (1998). *Technics and Time, 1: The Fault of Epimetheus.* Stanford: Stanford University Press.
———. (2011a). *The Decadence of Industrial Democracies: Disbelief and Discredit,* vol. 1. Cambridge: Polity Press.
———. (2011b). *Technics and Time, 3: Cinematic Time and the Question of Malaise.* Stanford: Stanford University Press.
———. (2013a). *Uncontrollable Societies of Disaffected Individuals: Disbelief and Discredit,* vol. 2. Cambridge: Polity Press.
———. (2013b). *What Makes Life Worth Living: On Pharmacology.* Cambridge: Polity Press.
———. (2014). *Symbolic Misery, Volume 1: The Hyper-Industrial Epoch.* Cambridge: Polity Press.
———. (2015a). "Literate Natives, Analogue Natives and Digital Natives: Between Hermes and Hestia." In *The Public Sphere from Outside the West.* Eds. Divya Dwivedi and V. Sanil. London & New York: Bloomsbury Academic.
———. (2015b). *Symbolic Misery, Volume 2: The Katastrophē of the Sensible.* Cambridge: Polity Press.

————. (2017). "The New Conflict of the Faculties and Functions: Quasi-Causality and Serendipity in the Anthropocene." *Qui Parle*, 26, 79–99.

————. (2018a). *The Neganthropocene*. London: Open Humanities Press.

————. (2018b). *Qu'appelle-t-on panser? 1. L'immense régression*. Paris: Les Liens qui Libèrent.

————. (2018c). "'We Have to Become the Quasi-Cause of Nothing – of *Nihil*': An Interview with Bernard Stiegler." *Theory, Culture & Society*, 35, 137–156.

————. (2020a). "Covid-19: Insight from the Angle of Memory." www.academia. edu/42827840/Bernard_Stiegler_Covid_19_Insight_from_the_Angle_of_Memory_2020_.

————. (2020b). "Elements for a General Organology." *Derrida Today*, 13, 72–94.

————. (2020c). "Turning Confinement into the Freedom to Create an Experience." www. academia.edu/42802435/Bernard_Stiegler_Turning_Confinement_into_the_Freedom_ to_Create_an_Experience_2020_.

Vitale, F. (2018). *Biodeconstruction: Jacques Derrida and the Life Sciences*. Albany: State University of New York.

von Uexküll, J. (2010). *A Foray into the Worlds of Animals and Humans, with A Theory of Meaning*. Minneapolis: University of Minnesota Press.

Whitehead, A. N. (1929). *The Function of Reason*. Princeton: Princeton University Press.

Winnicott, D. W. (1975). *Through Paediatrics to Psycho-Analysis*. New York: Basic Books.

————. (2005). *Playing and Reality*. London & New York: Routledge.

Chapter 8

Hineni, Hineni

Answering to other through disaster and exile, shame and temporality

Kenneth A. Kimmel

Introduction

We live in a time when society has seemingly been thrown onto a path with no ultimate ground, with no 'True North' to guide the way. Haunting, shameful images of emigrant children caged in holding pens on the southern border of the United States bring to mind the Nazi 'staging areas' in France before the Jews were shipped in freight cars to Auschwitz. There is nothing new about such shameless acts. Since archaic Roman times, sovereign powers could enact 'exceptions to the law' whereby human beings were stripped of all legal status and transformed into 'bare lives' with no rights, exposing them at any time to *legalized* murder. Flight to new, often unwelcoming lands would be the only escape for these 'accursed' ones (O'Donoghue, 2015).

Hierarchical and binary oppositions are prevalent in authoritarian states that institute practices of exclusion, eradication and/or appropriation of differences. Sovereign states making the ominous return to totalitarianism today continue scapegoating practices towards vulnerable minorities. History teaches how these lead to exile, diaspora or genocide, as predictable, 'final solutions'.

How can we unbind ourselves from hypnotic obedience to sovereign authority and the relentless, unmediated dangers carrying us blindly into the future? The question posed by the poet, singer Leonard Cohen reflects profoundly the ominous transitions in which we find ourselves. "You want it darker?" He answers, "*We* kill the flame" (Cohen, 2018, p. 143). The implication in his indictment awakens shame in recognition of *our* responsibility for the torment of the other in our midst and for all human suffering. In this writing, the capacity to bear shame is considered our great teacher, one that deepens our humility and guides our humanity.

Cohen's response reverberates from the ancient call of *Hineni*, translated from the Biblical Hebrew as "Here I am!" (Jerusalem Bible, 1992, Genesis 22:1) – that of 'presenting' or 'offering' oneself faithfully, whether it be to serve one's God, or the human being suffering before us. (At this moment, I think of the nurses and doctors, at great personal risk, coming out of retirement to meet the call to fight COVID-19). *Hineni* is memorialized 'inter-textually' where later texts absorb, transform and continually build upon the original idea over time. In this text, the

Biblical text of 'Abraham's binding of Isaac' is the origin story from which all others derive (ibid).

The authors of these later inter-textual, religious and secular works of theology, philosophy and literature – from Fyodor Dostoevsky and Søren Kierkegaard, to Emmanuel Levinas and Maurice Blanchot – use the language of *dialogic imagination* (Bahktin, 2001). Here, *alterities* – all perspectives, normally muted by the privileged author/authority, are given voice.

In this time of burgeoning authoritarian dominion, the profound act of *Hineni* brings the deepest ethical significance to what we face today in the community as well as in psychotherapy. *Hineni* has come to reflect, in Levinas's thinking, an 'infinite' responsibility and "answerability without reservation" to the other (Putnam, 2002, p. 38). Levinas's oeuvre attempts to describe our relation to the human *other* who is enigmatic and irreducible to categorization, in whose face one glimpses a trace of the infinite beyond being and comprehension, which he designated as the *Other*.

Holocaust accounts in the psychoanalytic work of Häydee Faimberg and Samuel Gerson embody the analyst's paradoxical 'presencing' and witnessing of an absence often too horrific and incomprehensible for either victim or witness to bear witness to. In the mutual space of such unspeakable memories that one cannot – must not – remember, we are left with only silence. In the dialogic dance of transgression and transcendence, testimony and silence, the call of *Hineni* arises in the midst of disaster and acts of faith, and in fortunate cases, redemption and revelation.

Two events affected me on the morning following the November 2016 American presidential election. They are the germ seed and impetus of this enquiry. I begin there.

The dream

This dream startled me awake on the morning of November 9, 2016.

> *I'm sitting facing a garden window in an old mountain lodge somewhere up in the Rockies, peacefully gazing out at the majestic peaks and forest surrounding the lodge. Bursting suddenly out of the brush is a gigantic, golden, grizzly bear. He's rampaging down a path. I think how relieved I am that I can observe him from the (relatively) safe confines of the lodge and won't have to confront him head-on. I shudder to think what would happen if someone was in the direct path of this primal beast – they'd be ripped apart!*

I have spent many hours attempting to penetrate this enigmatic dream and, in hindsight, its prescience (not least of which, the 'rampaging' global pandemic confronting us in 2020). I will, instead, focus my remarks on my fear upon the waking of the ominous future that lay ahead in the coming years post-election.

The relentless animal embodies for me the 'face of the monstrous', an unstoppable force ripping through the fabric of time and space. Does my view from the safe confines of the lodge imply an avoidance of real human engagement in dangerous times, like turning away from a violent act inflicted upon another to save one's own skin? Or does it suggest how vital the capacities for witnessing and reflection are when confronted with nature's all-consuming, raw violence? Both interpretations have merit.

But what if these extremes of nature's deadliness, embodied in the grizzly, simply defy all human understanding or ability to respond? Is it possible for us to bear the depth of the violence and catastrophic changes of our times? The truth is that the future is unknowable. *Survival is not certain.* And what then?

The dialogic imagination of Leonard Cohen

The same morning of the dream, news outlets announced the death of beloved poet, songwriter and singer Leonard Cohen. His family had chosen to suppress the news of his passing over the weekend until after the election. On that day I came across the cover song for his recently released, final album titled *You Want It Darker?* (Cohen, 2016).

In Cohen's's creative process – as in all texts I draw upon – a dialogic process is intrinsic in the narratives. The most enigmatic line from his lyric reflects the deep influences of Kabbalah, the mystical interpretation of Jewish tradition: "If thine is the glory then mine must be the shame" (Cohen, 2018, p. 143). In a dialogic meeting, human experience of *shame* lives on the border of its theological opposite, *Glory* – the 'Divine Indwelling Presence'. The Hebrew *Torah* tells how the Glory, as a fiery glow, rested over Mount Sinai while the Commandments were revealed to Moses.

Modern Kabbalistic thinking recognizes that shame has a close interrelation with selfhood, as "a significant component of the religious self, indeed part of the existential human condition" (Garb, 2015, p. 89). Implied here, shame reaches to the depths of who we are overall and assumes a role in the redemption and humility in our character (Morgan, 2008, p. 50). Emmanuel Levinas eschews the Kabbalist's goal of mystical oneness with a numinous Divine. Nonetheless, he assaults the borders of mysticism by appropriating its language to describe an "un-representable identity, there prior to all beginnings" that he calls the "*Glory* of the Infinite". Bringing *anarchy* down upon the "ego stripped by the trauma of persecution of its . . . imperialist subjectivity. . . [the ego becomes] reduced to the 'here I am' [*hineni*]" (Levinas, 2008, p. 146). For Levinas the trace of the Other is not located in the heavens but always within proximity to the face of the *human* other. Wouldn't the depths of shame be revealed in such a subject? Wouldn't he possess the eyes to comprehend the shattering revelations about his own complicity in the suffering of others? Does the indictment in Leonard's last line – "You want it darker? We kill the flame" – imply that we ourselves are the origin for all coming evil in the world (Cohen, 2018, p. 143)?

Leonard's chorus ends in the songful, revelatory prayers of *Hineni* performed by the cantor and choir from the Montreal synagogue of Leonard's youth. The song was released in September of 2016, as he faced imminent death two months later. I imagine the chorus was his reply to the world's ominous changes described as "a million candles burning for the love that never came" (ibid). In turn, the chorus expressed my own source of existential anxiety reflected in the 'grizzly bear dream'. In the face of potential, senseless destruction, my paranoia mushroomed into thoughts such as, "What if the dire forces set in motion during this epoch are reaching a critical mass and we soon will lose the capacity to prevent our extinction?" In Leonard's faithful answer at the moment of his own reckoning, he surrenders to something beyond his ken. Confronted by the 'wholly Other' in the guise of the spectre of death, his words are simple: "*Hineni, hineni,* I'm ready, my lord" (Cohen, 2018, p. 143).

In a profound act of confession and answerability to the other, Leonard's dialogic verse negates the binaries that divide 'us from them,' the same from the other, 'our' goodness from 'their' evil. Each of the opposites is reflected in one another. Implied from these lines are echoes of the famous words repeated throughout *Brothers Karamazov* (Dostoevsky, 1970, p. 384) that Levinas often paraphrases, "Each of us is guilty before everyone for everyone, and I more than the others" (Levinas, 2008, p. 146).

According to Mikhail Bakhtin, 'dialogic' writing dislodges and undermines the single standpoint of the guiding narrator by evoking the 'multitudinous voices' of the unmerged characters (Bahktin, 1984, p. 6). Their unique perspectives and the ideas conveyed remain unresolved and without closure. In Dostoyevsky, for instance, every character inhabiting his novels "lives on the very border of its opposite" (ibid, p. 176). Each verges "*on the threshold* of a final decision, at a moment of crisis, at an unfinalizable, unpredeterminable turning point for their soul" (ibid, pp. 61–62).

Bakhtin memorializes the medieval European tradition of 'Carnival' (the 'return to flesh', prior to Catholic Ash Wednesday) to illustrate the 'temporal threshold' where all social roles and hierarchies between nobles and peasants dissolve and conventions reverse. "[O]pposites come together, look at one another, are reflected in one another, know and understand one another" (ibid, p. 176). Carnival plays in the in-between, suggesting that *this* is its 'fertility'. In the dialogic opening 'in-between', the force of disaster brings undoing to the guiding stars maintaining these fixed binaries and totalizing hierarchies that forsake the multitudinous voices of unique human otherness. A simple ray of light coming in through a fracture in the world beautifully reimagines the opening (Cohen, 1992).

The concept of a *dialogical self* transcends the "monological, egocentric versions of the self that have come to be shrined in much of contemporary psychology" (Hermans, 1996; Hermans et al., 1992). Perhaps the old idea of an internal, unified self is such a totality in need of revision. Instead, the dialogical self inhabits multiple places, as an *internal* otherness; an *exterior* otherness drawing one into proximity to temporal, historical and cultural spheres; and in the relational and *inter-subjective*.

'I am here' expresses a singular presence now in this time and place, coming into being through the shattering or profound disruption of one's identity, one who is subject to – or reflexively adheres to – our socio-symbolic investments. What could galvanize this upstart, disruptive action allowing the emergence of singularity? Similar to Levinas or 'post-humanism', French psychoanalyst Jacques Lacan would say that it arises from the *Real* – an unconscious remainder that can never be known, something forever missing, a before that is un-representable, drawing one to a 'character' beyond the expectations of society (the *symbolic*) or the narcissistic mirroring of a heroic ideal that is *imaginary*[1] (Rutti, 2010, p. 1128).

The *symbolic order*, the 'Name of the Father,' governs social thought and interaction and the very linguistic structure of the culture we are thrown into at birth. Reflexive adherence to the *symbolic* or *imaginary* may lead to submission to the extremes of totalitarianism. However, Lacan cautions that without the symbolic 'Name of the Father', we would have barbarism. Therefore, in his later writings, he described the real, the symbolic and the imaginary discourses as a complex 'knot'. From this perspective, the three are always inter-related.

The existential Danish philosopher Søren Kierkegaard brings this process into crystal clarity through his protagonist, Abraham of Genesis.

Through fear and trembling . . . *Here I am*

> The singularity of the believer constitutes a remainder that *cannot* be comprehended by reason and *cannot* be assimilated by morality.
>
> (Taylor, 1987, p. 345)

In *Fear and Trembling*, Søren Kierkegaard peers into what he imagines is the state of mind of the Jewish Patriarch, Abraham. Driven by his deepest obedience and faith, regardless the price, Abraham assents to what seems to be an ominous command of the unknowable Other to sacrifice his beloved son, Isaac. Outwardly perceived as insane and monstrous, the 'attempted murder' is thwarted only in the last moment by an unknown hand. Regardless, he lives forevermore in unspeakable agony and despair (what Levinas would call shame), cast out into a *psychological* desert as a solitary wanderer and exile. After all, how could he ever return to the world he knew before, and who would believe him? He bears alone his utter, moral *transgression*, despite his *transcendent* act of faith that collapses all reason and in the end promises great blessings upon him and generations to come. Kierkegaard's writings lay bare our deepest existential anxieties, fears and dread over things such as death's fatal sting, concrete concerns that idealist philosophy sought to transcend. The heart of his work attempts to reveal "[our uniquely human] despair over who we are, the very thing that defines our being, the very thing that orients us toward our future, hence our possibilities" (Mills,

2014, p. 71). The response of *Hineni* is found throughout the sacred *Torah*, but never have its utterances been surrounded in such enigma and paradox as those of Abraham, in the *Akedah* – "The binding of Isaac". In Genesis (22:1–2), God tested Abraham's faith, calling his name: In response he answered for the first time, "Here I am!"; God said, "Take now thy son, thy only son, Isaac, whom thou lovest, and get thee into the land of Moriyya; and offer him there for a burnt offering". After three days' travel Abraham sees the distant mountain summit God had told him of. The two gather wood for the altar, fire and knife for the final trek. Then Isaac calls, "My father": Abraham responds a second time, "Here I am, my son". "Where is the lamb for a burnt offering?" the boy asks. His father tenderly assures him, "God . . . will provide himself a lamb for a burnt offering" (22:7–8). They set off. Abraham's third and final utterance of *hineni* is quoted here:

> And they came to the place which God had told him of; and Abraham built an altar there, and laid the wood in order, and bound Isaac, and laid him on the altar. . . . And Abraham stretched out his hand and took the knife to slay his son. And an angel of the Lord called to him out of heaven, and said, "Abraham, Abraham": and he said, "Here I am." And he said, "Lay not thy hand upon the lad, neither do anything to him: for now I know that thou fearest God, seeing thou hast not withheld thy son, thy only son from me".
>
> (22:9–12)

At that instant a ram appears, his horns caught in a thicket, and Abraham offers it up as a sacrifice in place of Isaac. For his absolute faith God heaps great blessings upon Abraham and his future generations, promising to "multiply [his] seed as the stars of the heaven" (22:17).

In his dialogic imagination Kierkegaard writes, "Abraham was the greatest of all, great by that power whose strength is powerlessness, great by that wisdom whose secret is foolishness, great by that hope whose form is madness, great by that love that is hatred to self" (1983, pp. 16–17). Kierkegaard perceives from Abraham's story, "the prodigious paradox of faith, a paradox that makes a murder into a holy and God-pleasing act, a mad paradox that gives Isaac back to Abraham again, which no thought can grasp because faith begins precisely where thought stops" (p. 53).

Further thoughts on Abraham and Isaac

Through the eyes of Kierkegaard, Abraham is crushed between irresolvable contradictions and disjunction in thinking in an unbearable 'too muchness of what is' – what is called *aporia*. Kierkegaard, Lacan contends, first recognized the *Akedah's* psychological meaning. This is not just the story of a nomadic Hebrew who undergoes trials of faith. Far greater, his initiation exemplifies the condition every human suffers whose subjectivity is thrown into disorder when faced with a traumatic reckoning. This is a condition of powerlessness from which a singular individual might emerge enduring and following a thread of the future, carrying the weight of the sufferer in acknowledgement of their own shame for *their* hand in their suffering.

For Levinas, shame breaks the spell negating the 'I' enthralled in its solipsism. Egoic refuge, mirrored in the comfort and security of familiar socio-symbolic investments, is severed, the false self unconcealed. Stricken with shame from the incursion of an infinite trace the dialogic movement in Leonard's verse is brought into sharper relief; *if thine is the Glory then mine must be the shame* (Levinas, p. 17; Cohen, 2016).

Prior to Levinas, Kierkegaard describes a type of singularity arising within Abraham from a paradoxical, irresolvable double bind forged in the reckoning of the Law's command and the Other's call (Taylor, 1987, p. 349). Kierkegaard (1983, p. 61) describes Abraham's faith without reservation, amidst feelings of dread, offence and terror, as a horror *religiosus*. Speech is reduced to silence in the face of such horror (Taylor, 1987, p. 347). The *Akedah* affects a breach induced by the Other, whose speech is foreign, absurd, one he is impotent to understand and cannot reveal. For Kierkegaard (1983, p. 55), reason and morality are universals that apply to everyone, but Abraham's paradox isolates him out as a single individual above the universal. His concealment and silence offend against the universal task to disclose the truth. Remaining silent, he resists the temptation to confess and restore himself to moral standing.

The archetypal 'tragic hero', on the other hand, makes his sacrifice public. Agamemnon, the general of the Greek forces readying to launch their fleet against Troy for Paris's theft of Helen, sacrifices his daughter Iphigenia to appease the wrath of the goddess Artemis, who had caused the winds to cease, forestalling their invasion (Euripides, 2020). (One of several stories justifying her hatred towards Agamemnon suggests he had killed her sacred stag, boasting he was a greater hunter than the goddess.) His story is part of the cultural myth, retold by Euripides as a king's sacrifice for the sake of his ambitions.

In Kierkegaard's view the particularity of the single individual, brought about by the paradox of faith, defies and suspends the *telos* (the final end or purpose) that universal laws, reason and morals cannot exceed. Assenting to the invisible command, Abraham's socially forbidden transgression of ethics and reason paradoxically "allude[s] to what remains of the sacred". They are mediated by what Blanchot (1973, p. 41) calls, the "power of exceeding" them through rupture or cutting the ties that bind.

In contrast to Agamemnon, Abraham is thwarted at the last moment by the mysterious hand of the one who had commanded his obedience. Juxtaposing Abraham's singularity, the universals of reason, law, ethics and morality become paradoxically entwined with a trace or remainder of the *Real*, whose absence effects a breach of the *symbolic order* from which singularity emerges. At the moment that Abraham raises his knife to kill Isaac, the *Law in the Name of the Father* is broken (*Thou Shalt Not Kill*). However, in a startling return to the ethical, the Law is obeyed through his obedience to the Divine command to lower the knife. Levinas clarifies in the next paragraph.

The Levinasian project recognizes ethics always as the *first* philosophy – a singular human act of responsibility to other – that calls into question Kierkegaard's 'ethics as a universal totality'. Rather, the apex of the drama comes, Levinas believes, when Abraham tends to the voice that forbids his act of sacrifice and leads him *back* to the ethical order. Levinas is astonished that he could even obey that first command, but the essential thing was that Abraham had gained enough differentiation from his blind obedience to hear the final call (Levinas, 1996, p. 74). When Abraham answers *Hineni!* to the angel's command to lower his hand, Abraham's gaze is *not* turned up towards the heavenly firmament but is cast squarely down at the *face* of his beloved child. Through faith and transgression, he has returned to his ethical responsibility that commands him not to kill. It is "written in the face of the other" (Severson, 2011, p. 171).

Levinas describes the moment of recognition when there is no refuge from the fundamental responsibility we assume for the anguish of the other in our midst. In the act of *hineni*, singularity is recognized in a *radical, lawless identity* that emerges in the subject that is forever answerable to the human other. This radical identity that is "older than every beginning" (Levinas, 2008, pp. 144–145) has sundered itself through an act of anarchy from the ego's performative role defined by laws, conventional ethics and reason that can reduce otherness to the same[2] (Bernasconi, 2002, pp. 241–242). For Levinas (2008, p. 242) the sovereign identity in egoistic service to itself has become, instead, an "identity of singularity" – the condition in which one might sacrifice and substitute oneself for *the other*.

Abraham, as a singular individual, leaves behind the moral and lawful domain of a person that "translates himself into the universal", reproducing that "faultless edition of himself, readable by all" (Kierkegaard, 1983, p. 76). From this moment on, Abraham's life is concealed. Does his silence come from a distaste for all worldly or heavenly glory, given his deep shame for the crime he had almost committed or the utter certainty that no one would believe the ravings of a madman? In any case, from his encounter with the wholly Other on the mountain, his life is no longer invested by the universal, socio-symbolic authority, but he has discovered instead a subjectivity that is and must remain singular.

Abraham has become an outlaw, a stranger, hidden from public view. The individual is propelled into exile with no escape or homecoming. He wanders into the desert utterly alone, an 'immigrant,' his life "like a book under divine confiscation [that] never becomes [public property]" (p. 77). Singularity can come with a radical price in the worldly sense.

Fate of a singular life: temporality in exile and disaster

Abraham of Genesis heeds the call of the Other *to come* to Mount Moriah, severing all family comfort and security in what is familiar. He embarks on a temporal journey through metaphorical desert spaces, like so many other storied individuals have done before him and since, without certainty or hope of arriving at a destination or a return home (Taylor, 1987, p. 303). History, myths and religions chronicle the solitary journeys of exiles, and the forced diasporas of displaced peoples between a homeland of no return and the uncertain future of a home to come – belonging to neither, moving upon a groundless ground. These images evoke the dialogic 'in-betweenness' of *temporal movement* and *spatialization*.[3]

From medieval alchemical sources the *Lapis Exilis Vilos* – 'the exiled and vile stone' – corresponds to the initial stages in the development of the Philosopher's stone, the fabled substance 'hidden in the dung heap' yet believed to be the agent for transformation of base metal into gold – representing instinctive nature being sublimated into forms of enlightenment through disciplined, dedicated work. From this perspective, the suffering of *exile becomes the most creative position.*

The story of Creation, as told through Kabbalist Isaac Luria's *theosophical tradition*,[4] begins prior to all existence, with only the 'Infinite God – the Absolute *All* and *Nothingness* without end' (*Ein Sof and Ein*). This is the original state of things, without form or direction. Wishing to gaze upon existence, the Infinite created the space of an empty void by withdrawing through divine contraction – *Tzimzum* (Halevi, 1980, p. 5). The Infinite *exiles* itself from the space and time of our finite universe through free will.

In the next phase, an influx of divine light fills the empty vault of our created world. At first it is contained in vessels on the Tree of Life (*Sefirot*), but these prove too fragile to hold the Infinite. They shatter, becoming shards of divine sparks that fall to earth and become encased in husks (*Klippot*) – a process called *Shevirat ha-kelim*. This likely reflects human fallibility in Creation. In the never-ending human labour of redemption and revelation, the sparks of light are freed from their captivity in the process of 'repairing the world', or *Tikkun ha-olam*. It reflects the emerging process of becoming in a world under constant chaos and revision.

Luria imagines the being of creation, born in the vacant blackness of a universe – an empty vault devoid of a God concealed from the human order of time through an act of exile and negation. Could God's withdrawal be necessary for the sake of human freedom or free will? This narrative deconstructs fundamental neo-platonic beliefs in which the manifest universe emanates from a perfect, *unchanging*, essential oneness and unity.[5] There is no pre-existing ideal of totality. On the contrary, as Luria sees it, our created world is brought into being by the contraction and withdrawal of an Infinite that cannot exist in our space and time because it is beyond being and presence.

In contemporary thought, the movement of *Tzimzum* in Luria's theosophy, fissuring the infinite nothing from the singular being of creation, is often considered as literary metaphor.

Isaac Luria's God, who withdraws and creates through self-exclusion, is drawn upon in the writing of Maurice Blanchot (1995, p. 13). He introduces *écriture* – language, writing and reading – as a force of 'disaster'. He writes, "I call disaster that which does not have the ultimate for a limit, but *bears the ultimate away in the disaster*" (1995, p. viii). That is, disaster is beyond ultimate being. The language of disaster *un-works* the paradigms of modernity and its fundamental positivism and rampaging technical, industrial and military advances. At its hands God and myth have died. Given the decaying state of our world now, modernity has come into question, with its massive storage of information and capacity for calculation – that is, its proneness to acquire *too much* 'light' which is slowly consuming us. Its own 'ultimate' totalities, unities and hierarchies have spatialized and frozen time's 'in-betweenness' and 'becoming' into a mass of frozen facts.

Like the shattering of vessels too weak to contain the infinite light in our world of being, the fractious and violent force of disaster implies the deep impact of an imploding star, which in the French is *désastre*, literally translated, "de-starification" (Vesco, 2018, p. 81). Blanchot clarifies. "The *disaster*: break with the star, break with every form of totality" (1973, p. 3).[6] This is like the disaster we face now in our ominous transition through the Anthropocene.[7]

The contraction of God from our world, contextualized in Blanchot's disaster writing, speaks to this time of the post-modern, when myths no longer renew and God as we know it is dead or absent. Yet, can we find the courage to empty ourselves out in a kind of *kenosis*, to wait for something without knowing or memory, from a future still to come, with empty hands expecting nothing (Giegerich, 2005, p. 231)?

'The presence of an absence': clinical and social revelations (Gerson, 2009, p. 1344)

In 1492 the horrors of the Spanish Inquisition culminated in the exile of its Jewish people. Arising from the ashes amidst great upheaval over two centuries, a new era of spiritual renewal began for Jewish communities throughout the world. Revelation born of suffering brought about an immediate, more human engagement with the Divine. The teachings of Rabbi Isaac Luria in the seventeenth century embodied this idea. He envisioned a created universe that had gone wrong, foretelling of continuing chaos and conflict in the world, but he also imagined humanity's capacity to heal its brokenness through 'good works'.

Luria's allegory of 'Husks' that conceal 'Blessed Sparks' that have fallen to earth from shattered vessels represents what Kabbalah calls our 'inclinations towards evil'. These have been signified throughout history as wars, persecution, exile, plagues and genocide. The goal of the unending process to relieve the world's suffering is the release of 'Sparks' revealing their light.[8] This is described by Martin Buber as "the ecstatic act of the individual as co-working with God to achieve redemption" (1956, p. 6).

Psychoanalytic and genocidal studies inform us about the question of concealment and revelation. In these accounts, survivors of genocide describe gaps in temporality that conceal traumatic experiences too annihilating for their minds to bear. This leaves behind a tormenting sense of absence because an *unconscious remainder* is left over – a presence of shades of memory that defy meaning.[9] Without warning, the disembodied past life in the camps may shock one's present state, un-concealing the former, 'bare, wretched life' that inhabits a psychic absence.

Resigned during internment to the inevitability of one's own or loved one's senseless murder, the inmates lived in terror and helplessness. Subjection to such horror and death, over months and years, can sear into one's innermost being, slowly eroding any spark of remembrance, recognition or substantiation of *simply being human*. Despite such degradation of body and mind, the survivors *survived* but often as tormented victims of *soul murder*. The Jewish poet and concentration camp survivor, Primo Levi, writes about a commonly shared dream of despair in the camps: *loved ones, who they had imagined would welcome them home, and with whom they would share their sufferings, do not believe them! Nor do they even listen. They merely turn away and leave in silence* (Levi, 1989, p. 12). The dreams of the prisoners depict a world that denies their truth, evoking the horror of a 'nameless dread' in an age reflecting the vast dehumanization of the human.

Samuel Gerson describes the Holocaust survivor who is haunted throughout life by the loss of a functioning, inner 'witness' – the lack of *a living third* that can inhabit psychic gaps, "absorbing absence, and transforming our relation to loss" (Gerson, 2009, p. 1342). They are left with a 'dead third' (p. 1343), an internal world of inner deadness. It is a nihilistic world without meaning, filled by emptiness and numbness, guarding against the unbearable, negating any feelings of what makes life worth living.[10]

Could the prisoners' shared dreams be an expression of their subjective need to eradicate the traumatic and unbearable presence of the absence? This internal state parallels the external one – a culture and government that turns its back to human rights, like a 'dead third' that is indifferent to the suffering of the other. Without a transitional, third space, there can be no possibility of mutuality, of singularity, only denial and hallucination. The abandonment and denial, anticipated in their commonly held dreams, mirrors the 'cultural amnesia' erected in response to catastrophic shame, where wretches are without witness to their suffering.

One must ask whether their dreams speak to the sheer impossibility of witnessing in the camps. Agamben writes how the survivors' testimony "contained at its core an essential lacuna. . . . The survivor's bore witness to something it is impossible to bear witness to . . . listening to something absent" (Agamben, 2018, back cover).

A clinical perspective

How do those of us who are psychotherapists respond to the disjunction between self and other in cases of complex trauma? Argentinian psychoanalyst Häydee Faimberg describes a moving clinical example that traces trauma retroactively in the psychic material of a descendent of Holocaust victims. Their work navigated temporal gaps and absences in the transference, revealing dissociated fragments of memory connected to inter-generational loss (Faimberg, 1988, pp. 99–117).

At a seminal time in the subject's young life, he was struck by a profound psychic rupture or explosion – like an 'imploding star' – that evoked defenses negating all meaning in his life. A grandson of Polish Jews lost in the Holocaust, his immigrant father had always denied his own horror at the loss of his parents, 'injecting' these gaps in memory and deadness into his son, leaving the boy with the sense of a terrifying, enduring presence of an absence (Gerson, 2009, p. 1344). Over time, this led to the son's hospitalization and psychoanalytic treatment. The patient had become an unwitting holder of his father's "seductions of blind denial" (ibid, p. 1341), enclosed in 'crystallized time'[11] (Faimberg, 1988, p. 99, 2005, p. 8). Such potent unknowns at the root of being exist out of reach of memory, hidden in the darkness of the mind's *husks* (see preceding sections).

At a critical moment in treatment, an event of *après coup* occurred,[12] triggered by a confluence of extreme losses: the economic collapse of his country, resulting in his financial ruin, along with the threatened loss of his analytic relationship because he could no longer pay. At this extremely stressful moment in the analysis, his analyst observed that he subtly and tenderly caressed his pant pocket, as if to make certain that something important was still there, like a precious thing of great value (ibid, p. 100).

The simple coins he held in his pocket, we come to learn, signify the presence of a kernel of memory, an unknowable remainder bringing the frozen past into the present, a work of *après coup* arising in the field between patient and analyst (Boothby, 2001, p. 162). At some point in the family tragedy, before the patient was born, the grandparents had stopped collecting money their son was sending to them during the war. The money had *no value* to the dead. At that point, their son, the patient's father, ceased to speak of his parents or their loss. He withdrew from the world after that and was never the same again. Revealed here in the fateful session is the preciousness of the patient's modest coins of little worldly value, for they contained an overfullness of a presence that was never gone – only hidden in the absence. They represented the grandson's unconscious identification to his lost grandparents and the key to the recovery of the families' memories of them. Through the 'revelation of the precious secret' in the transference, new meaning could arise from the secret fragment (the coins), bringing *retrospective* understanding to patient and analyst. Only then could the patient and his family begin to move into time through recognition of the past. The dead could then become substantiated, with the hope that the family 'ghosts' could live on as 'ancestors' in the patient's mind (Loewald, 1960, p. 249).

How do we, as psychotherapists, respond authentically to the other when the experience of deadness, of being 'stillborn' is their deepest truth? Should we, like Kierkegaard's Abraham, renounce our own 'heroic temptations' to hold onto each hopeful glimpse of rebirth and moment of optimism in the lives of our traumatized patients? Are they not simply a means of justifying our own *evasion* of the torturous paradox and responsibility, to relieve us of the pain and burden we are asked to share with the patient?

What is left then but an utter refusal to engage in any explanation or plan of action, only silence. We are powerless to alleviate the enormous suffering. Does our silence induce complicity that disregards the basic principle of 'do no harm'? Perhaps. However, recall in *Fear and Trembling* how Abraham was helplessly driven by faith in an unknown Other, towards an insane act of murder, that broke all reason and morality. Is his transgression in mind and heart of the law not to kill, not too dissimilar from our impotence to do or say anything to alleviate the misery of 'stillborn truth' that infects the one in our midst? Yet Abraham's strength was *in* his powerlessness to resist the Other's call (Kierkegaard, 1983, pp. 16–17, 53). In the paradox, singularity, born of shame for *our* part in 'killing the flame', breaks the boundaries of societal forms of morality and conscious reasoning (Cohen, 2018, p. 143; Taylor, 1987, p. 345). Levinas describes this lawless identity as an anarchy, there prior to all being and presence that inscribes the singular person with a fundamental *responsibility to the other*, an ethics before all things (Levinas, 2008, pp. 144–146). I can only describe this as a kind of faith in silence without knowing what is to come, where faith emerges, when thought ends (Kierkegaard, 1983, p. 53).

The profound question remains: does singularity reside in "courageously living with the enduring deadliness" in our traumatized patients, encountering the unseen phantoms that inhabit the psychic void (Gerson, 2009, p. 1351)? Can the temporal 'living third' sometimes emerge from the *presence of the absence* that we bear together (2009, p. 1354), opening possibilities for a humble, enduring and deeply felt life?

In their dialogic reasoning, Kabbalist masters considered the earthly husks as the evil inclination arising from *our* free will; the 'other side' from which light emerges to repair the world by acts of free will – darkness and light, one within the other, one in relation to the other. Therefore, they posed the question: If the husks contain the divine sparks then wouldn't they, too, hold sanctity in themselves? The material world, with all its pain and love, would then manifest these blessings in what is described as the revelation of the "presence of the sacred in the everyday world" (Buber, 1991, p. xi).

Afterthoughts

We end where we began with the question of what is *to come* in these ominous times. Taking a broad view, today like in the past, sovereign states seek systemic dominion and control over disenfranchised, fringe groups that society deems 'other' based on their differences from the dominant group. Over time scapegoats change in skin colour or ethnicity. Their *exclusion* from cultural, educational and economic opportunities to better their lives, and the *appropriation* of their labour force into menial, low-paying jobs, explode the gap of inequality and fix these 'lower-class' groups in systemic poverty.

The Third Reich awakened a revival of the *Völkisch* movement, the folk nationalism of Germany, invoking romantic ideals of the pure Aryan race reborn, bound to the ancient motherland through 'blood and soil'. Ultra-ethnic pride, formed like a patina over their abject humiliation and shame from their disgrace after World War I, galvanized xenophobic hatred towards history's scapegoat – the 'parasitic' Jewish *nomads* – usurping the place of 'true Germans'. Woody Guthrie – a nomadic troubadour from a folk movement of a different ilk – travelled America's vast highways, across river valleys, mountains and the Great Plains. He sang of the plight of the poor and disenfranchised during the depression era's Dust Bowl drought of the 1930s. His message was clear: This land was created for us all, equally – me *and* you (Guthrie, 1972).

Environmental disasters today, caused largely by global warming, are triggering worldwide Diasporas.[13] *Nomadism*, recognized in the immanent movement of migrant populations across borders, radically challenges and exceeds the *sedentary logic* of the subject, rooted for generations in one territory (Aldea, 2014). Their collision is re-igniting violence around the globe.

The European Union envisioned a borderless 'post-national project' attempting to challenge Europe's millennia-old history of imperialist domination over other peoples. Within that historical context, however, the response to immigration and its economic pressures on the European Union has brought about the rise of reactionary, white nationalism in nation-states and the upsurge of reactionary politics. These pressures pose the greatest threats to the EU's survival. Europe today is a tinderbox. They say that the United States of America is a land of immigrants. The Statue of Liberty with her raised torch welcomes the stranger. The myth we hold dear is one that defends the oppressed from tyrants, offers them refuge. These great ideals are at the heart of our fabric. Yet, we bear the stains of our genocide of Native Americans and appropriation of their lands. Further, things such as slavery and its lasting consequences, colonialism, and the atomic holocaust of Hiroshima provide grounds for doubting the 'goodness' of our treatment of 'the other'. The transparent racism in the call to 'Make America Great Again' should evoke profound shame upon any white citizen of the United States.

In the midst of our global Covid-19 pandemic ravaging the world, the Black Lives Matter protests have captured the soul of the world. People of all kinds are incensed by the violent acts of those we expect to be guardians and to serve. The problem is that it's not a question of some 'bad apples' but a systemic one. Police have been trained to uphold the law to protect and defend *ownership* and *private property – not people*, not the 'have-nots' who may threaten its destruction. The global economy's speed-of-light technologies that drive exponential profits, ensuring the security of the wealthiest and most powerful, is so embedded in our systems of government and culture that the privileging of basic human rights – the protection of life as sacred – is quickly eroding. Perhaps the relentless, monstrous bear inhabiting my dream is simply moving too fast for anything to stop it. Perhaps it is like the unconscious energies that threaten to spill forth in cultural as well as personal life. Aren't we implicated, both personally and collectively, in killing the light of the world? Don't we each carry within us the figure of Abraham? One Abraham is a solitary nomad who assents to an unforgiveable act, whereas the other Abraham, as a "true knight of faith, is a *witness*, never a teacher . . . for therein lies the profound humanity" (Kierkegaard, p. 80). There are no words left to say but *I am here. Hineni.*

Notes

1 The meaning of the *Real* has nothing to do with actual reality.
2 Sameness reifies the other by appropriating the other's difference and uniqueness by making it into the 'same'.
3 Spatialization of time, in this context, freezes temporal movement, forming discrete, permanent entities in space that are defined by history and memory (Sheer, 2012, p. 2).
4 Theosophical philosophy maintains that the *gnosis* (deep knowing) of the Divine is achieved through spiritual ecstasy, direct intuition or individual relations and is epitomized by the sixteenth-century Kabbalistic teachings of Isaac Luria.
5 Described in Plato's creation story, *Timaeus* (Plato, 2010, p. 1762), essentialism refers to fundamental, ideal forms originating from the creation of an ordered, perfect universe that brings 'the good' into being through reason. In the grand design, the universe emanates from the original perfection, and human souls are meant to restore the first unity by emulating the pre-arranged, unchanging ideals to reach a perfected completion.
6 Blanchot deconstructs formal language, writing and reading, employing dialogic, contradiction and paradox in his writing about the force of disaster. For instance, trust in language is a defiance of language but located in language. It is therefore the basis for its own critique. Thinking is required to decipher the words that engrave the meaning in their inscription. However, language conceals meaning in its 'crypticness', and the exposed secret deciphered by thought is not discoverable. His dialogic breaks all totalities (Blanchot, 1995, pp. vii–viii).
7 The Anthropocene is our current epoch in geological time representing humans' presence on earth and their dominant impact on climate and the environment.
8 To Kabbalistic mystics, evil, 'embodied' in the Husks, is considered in relative, dialogic terms to the 'Holy Sparks' they conceal. Both are needed to galvanize the free will of humanity in service to 'repair of the world' (*Tikkun*) by releasing the sparks from the nil of darkness.
9 Lacan designates similar trauma-induced and non-trauma-induced enigma as "das Ding" – *the Thing* in the Real, beyond symbolization, outside of language and the unconscious – "The Thing" always pursued, longed for or tormented by, but never possessed or realized.
10 In the context of this chapter the *living third,* whether mediating personal, relational or cultural spheres, dwells in relationship to the individual as a means of containing, providing continuity and making meaning to one's life. Faced with extreme, external trauma, we all are subject to sudden loss of this 'third-ness' in what is termed the *dead third.* The individual internalizes the inescapable sense of an absence of all meaning to life (Gerson, 2009, p. 1343).
11 'Crystallized time' refers to the crystallization in the patient's psyche, of the conviction that his father does not acknowledge his Polish parents' deaths. In his own psychic life, he endeavours to preserve the state of internal death in the effort to insulate his father's parents from the passage of time, linked to death (Faimberg, 2005, p. 88).
12 *Après coup* creates a reciprocal relationship between a crucial event from the past and its resignification afterwards in present time, where it acquires new psychic meaning. The past is never finished with us because the present is always being affected by it. New experiences can *retranslate* prior memories which then place our habitual thinking into question. Memories, at their core, initiate infinite translations that cannot be fixed or located in time (Hinton, 2015, pp. 367–369).
13 These nomadic peoples are driven by famine, drought, overpopulation, pandemics, tribal genocide and civil wars over dwindling natural resources.

References

Agamben, G. (2018). *Remnants of Auschwitz*. Trans. D. Heller-Roazen. New York: Zone Books.

Aldea, E. (2014). "Nomads and Migrants: Deleuze, Braidotti and the European Union in 2014." www.opendemocracy.net [Accessed February 2020].

Bahktin, M. M. (1984). *Rabelais and His World*. Trans. T. F. Rable. Bloomington, IN: Indiana University Press.

———. (2001). *The Dialogical Imagination*. Trans. C. Emerson. Ed. M. Holquist. Austin, TX: University of Texas Press.

Bernasconi, R. (2002). "What Is the Question to Which 'Substitution Is the Answer?" *The Cambridge Companion to Levinas*. Eds. S. Critchley & R. Bernasconi. Cambridge, UK: Cambridge University Press.

Blanchot, M. (1973). *Le Pas au-delà*. Trans. M. C. Taylor (unofficial). Paris: Gallimard.

———. (1995). *The Writing of the Disaster*. Trans. A. Smock. Lincoln & London: University of Nebraska Press.

Boothby, R. (2001). *Freud as Philosopher: Metapsychology After Lacan*. New York: Routledge.

Buber, M. (1956). *The Tales of Rabbi Nachman*. Trans. M. Friedman. New York: Horizon Press.

———. (1991). *Tales of the Hasidim: Book One: The Early Masters. Book Two: The Later Masters*. Foreword C. Potok. New York: Schocken Books.

Cohen, L. (1992). "Anthem [Song recorded by Leonard Cohen]." *On The Future*. Columbia.

———. (2016). "You Want It Darker [Song recorded by Leonard Cohen]." *On You Want It Darker*. Columbia.

———. (2018). *The Flame*. Eds. R. Fagen & A. Pleshoyano. Edinburgh: Canongate Books.

Dostoevsky, F. (1970). *The Brothers Karamazov*. Trans. A. R. MacAndrew. New York: Bantam.

Euripides. (2020). *Iphigenia in Aulis*. Trans. T. A. Buckley. Boylston, MA: Compass Circle.

Faimberg, H. (1988). "Telescoping of Generations: Geneology of Certain Identifications." *Contemporary Psychoanalysis*, 24, 99–117.

———. (2005). *Telescoping of Generations: Listening to the Narcissistic Links Between Generations*. London & New York: Routledge.

Garb, J. (2015). "Shame as an Existential Emotion in Modern Kabbalah." *Jewish Social Studies: History, Culture, Society*, 21, 1, Fall, 89–122. The Trustees of Indiana University. DOI:10.2979/jewisocistud.21.1.03.

Gerson, S. (2009). "When the Third Is Dead: Memory, Mourning, and Witnessing in the Aftermath of the Holocaust." *International Journal of Psychoanalysis*, 90, 1341–1357.

Giegerich, W. (2005). *The Neurosis of Psychology: Primary Papers Towards a Critical Psychology. Collected English Papers*, vol. 1. New Orleans: Spring Journal Books.

Guthrie, W. (1944/1972). *This Land Is Your Land* [Song recorded by Woody Guthrie]. New York: Woody Guthrie Publications, Inc. & TRO-Ludlow Music, Inc. (BMI).

Halevi, Z. B. S. (1980). *Kabbalah: Tradition of Hidden Knowledge*. New York: Thames and Hudson.

Hermans, H. J. M. (1996). "Voicing the Self: From Information Processing to Dialogical Interchange." *Psychological Bulletin*, 119, 31–50.

Hermans, H. J. M., Kempen, H. J. G. & Van Loon, R. J. P. (1992). "The Dialogical Self: Beyond Individualism and Rationalism." *American Psychologist*, 47, 23–33.

Hinton, L. (2015). "Temporality and the Torments of Time." *Journal of Analytical Psychology*, 60, 353–370. DOI:10.1111/1468-5922.12155. Dame Press.

The Jerusalem Bible. (1992). Trans. & Ed. H. Fisch. Jerusalem, Israel: Koren PublishersJerusalem.

Kierkegaard, S. (1983). *Fear and Trembling*. Ed. H. V. Hong. Trans. E. H. Hong. Princeton: Princeton University Press.

Levi, P. (1989). *The Drowned and the Saved*. Trans. R. Rosenthal. New York: Vintage International.

Levinas, E. (1996). *Proper Names*. Trans. M. B. Smith. Stanford: Stanford University Press.

———. (2008). *Otherwise Than Being: Or Beyond Essence*. Trans. A. Lingis. Pittsburgh, PA: Duquesne University Press.

Loewald, H. (1960). "On the Therapeutic Action of Psychoanalysis." In *Papers on Psychoanalysis*, pp. 221–256. New Haven, CT: Yale University Press, 1980.

Mills, J. (2014). *Underworlds: Philosophies of the Unconscious from Psychoanalysis to Metaphysics*. London & New York: Routledge.

Morgan, M. L. (2008). *On Shame*. New York: Routledge.

O'Donoghue, A. (2015). *Sovereign Exception: Notes on the Thought of Giorgio Agamben*. Critical Legal Thinking: Law and the Political. https://criticallegalthinking. com/2015/07/02/sovereign-exception-notes-on-the-thought-of-giorgio-agamben/ [Accessed August 2019].

Plato (2010). *Timaeus*. Trans. B. Jewett (Kindle Edition). London: Pantianos Classics [Accessed 3 January 2015].

Putnam, H. (2002). "Levinas and Judaism." In *The Cambridge Companion to Levinas*. Eds. S. Critchley & R. Bernasconi. Cambridge, UK: Cambridge University Press.

Rutti, M. (2010). "The Singularity of Being: Lacan and the Immortal Within." *Journal of the American Psychoanalytic Association*, 58, 1113–1138. DOI:10.1177/0003065110396083.

Severson, E. R. (2011). *Scandalous Obligation: Rethinking Christian Responsibility*. Kansas City: Beacon Hill Press Kansas City.

Sheer, E. (2012). "Introduction: The End of Spatiality or the Meaning of Duration." 17, 15, 1–3. DOI:10.1080/13528165.2012.728425.

Taylor, M. C. (1987). *Altarity*. Chicago: University of Chicago Press.

Vesco, S. (2018). "Redemptive Readings Between Maurice Blanchot and Franz Rosenzweig." In *Fault Lines of Modernity*. Eds. K. Millet & D. Figueira, pp. 79–93. New York: Bloomsbury Academic & Professional.

Chapter 9

What lies beneath

Shame, time and diachrony

Eric R. Severson

When the water of Black majority Flint, Michigan, ran red with poisonous levels of lead in 2014, the problem was not the result of singular moral failure but a repetition of failures reaching back centuries.[1] This does not mean that individual choices were not involved. A pivotal and singular decision was made, for instance, to change the source of water for Flint from the Detroit water system to the Flint River. Some effort has been made to blame the deadly results on the politicians who made that decision (Fleming, 2020). The supply change in April of 2014 seemed small at the time and went mostly unnoticed by the government officials. The residents, however, immediately reported problems. The water smelled foul, was clearly discoloured and tasted terrible. For eighteen months citizens complained and suffered a roster of immediate problems related to the water – itching skin, rashes, hair-loss and more. Deeper problems were happening to Flint residents. Lead poisoning is deadly but often not immediately so. Exposure to lead, in children, is "one of the most damning things you can do to a child in their entire life-course trajectory" (Cosier, 2016). In some neighbourhoods, the blood-lead levels in children have tripled since 2014. Yet it was not just lead that has sickened people in Flint. In 2016 there was a mysterious spike in the water-borne Legionnaires' disease, occurring also in the surrounding area, that resulted in more than a dozen fatalities. The outbreak began shortly after the change in water sources, and significant evidence points to a link between the Flint River and Legionella bacteria (Johnson, 2016). Still, the Michigan Department of Health and Human Services determined that the connection between the water and the water-borne disease was not "conclusive" (Johnson, 2016). As blame is shifted and fingers are pointed, the people of Flint continued to suffer the effects of this disaster years later, even after their water began passing safety tests and Obama drank a glass to prove it (Winowiecki, 2019).

The problem made national news in the United States in 2016 in the midst of the presidential campaign. Both candidates Hillary Clinton and Donald Trump called for the resignation of Michigan's governor, Rick Snyder. These two white politicians, Trump and Clinton, were vying for the nation's highest office and could agree on almost nothing. On Flint, though, their messaging was similar. Greedy Americans had cut corners, they both claimed, and led to a disaster. Neither of them mentioned *race* as a cause for the problems that emerged, although Clinton implied that if the problem "had happened" in a white community, the solution would have been rapid (Merica & Henderson, 2016). Trump's declaration sounded similar: "It's a shame what's happening in Flint, Michigan. A thing like that shouldn't happen" (Meckler & Nelson, 2016). Who could argue with that? And yet has anything meaningful taken place when Donald Trump, of all people, has cast the word shame into this situation? This common word and concept, shame, plays a powerful role in shaping public and personal discourse. Shame warrants ethical and psychological evaluation. Surely Flint's water crisis is *a time for shame*. What is shame? How is it useful or harmful in times of ominous transition?

The people of Flint may have been *far* less surprised than the rest of the country to discover that this problem manifested with the complex maze of public policy. The problem was difficult to resolve, in fact, because the waters that reached Flint homes were contaminated by multiple sources and for multiple reasons. The choice to utilize water from the Flint River brought corrosive water to ageing pipes with fittings that should have been replaced long ago. Corrosive river water accelerated the decay of lead-based plumbing. After ignoring complaints from Flint residents for years – 53% of Flint residents are African American with a poverty rate of 41% (Data USA, 2019) – officials finally switched the community back to the Detroit-based water supply. But they waited too long; clean source water now flowed through pipes that had corroded while the suffering of Flint residents was being ignored. Corrosion exposed decaying lead in the pipe system, which continued to leach into the clean water flowing from Detroit. Even with the old water source restored, lead levels in Flint water remained dangerously elevated. A horrified – but not particularly activated – nation looked on as trucks of bottled water rolled into the Michigan suburb. It became increasingly preposterous to suggest that this was a mere coincidence, that these events took place in a city with high poverty rates and a Black-majority population. The news out of Flint, though, was received differently along racial lines. Most white Americans failed to realize that what happened in Flint *could not have happened* in the places where the rich, powerful and privileged water their well-groomed lawns. Although Clinton was right in suggesting that the response was racialized, this too misses the point. The policy decisions that led to death in Flint, Michigan, were out in the open. Racism in America is not hidden but ignored by people in power – like a person suffering from cancer but ignoring or explaining away the symptoms.

The primary concern of this book is to trace *transitions*. In particular, our efforts throughout this volume point to the transitions that have lead the world into more perilous times. The switch to poisonous water in Flint *was* an ominous transition, and the people of Flint would have wisely raised concerns if they had been consulted. Clinton and Trump agreed that this was a bad choice, a wrong turn, and they both agreed that the decision was driven by the mismanagement of capital. Trump's invocation of "shame" suggests a posture, an attitude, toward the crisis.

Trump somehow managed to blame Mexico; Clinton blamed greedy politicians. The political scramble that followed was about manipulating the mechanism of shame so that it might fall squarely on faulty parties, some of which could potentially be held responsible for the death and disease that resulted from their decision. As of the summer of 2020, there have been no prosecutions. Shame, though, has emerged. Yet there is more than one kind of shame and a multitude of ways that shame can appear.

My purpose in this chapter is to provide a philosophical inquiry into the phenomenon of shame as it relates to contemporary racism. Shame, I will argue, is tangled up in the concept of time and particularly in the way that powerful people control the temporality of shame's operation. By investigating the relationship between time and shame, I hope to present multiple versions of shame – a beneficial shame and an oppressive version – exposing the way racism is enabled and protected by one form and pointing to alternatives available through other ways of conceiving time. The roots of racism, and the powerful force of shame in reinforcing racism, are deep taproots that run down through the history of European civilization. My efforts to reconsider shame, and point to a healthy version of shame, begin with Plato and Aristotle. After reviewing and critiquing their push for synchrony in their philosophies of time and shame, I turn back to contemporary manifestations of racism and white supremacy.

Ultimately, I hope some of these reflections can be useful to psychologists who help people saddled with unhealthy and crippling shame. People often turn to help from therapists to contend with shame but are frequently met with efforts to eliminate shame as a symptom – either through prescriptions or through practices meant to reduce shame. Psychological professions, I argue, would be wise to attend to the ethical, historical and philosophical significance of shame. The spectre of shame rises along with the awareness of the deep shame and denial that white people may experience in the face of the extreme suffering caused by chattel slavery, historic and recent lynchings, police brutality, educational inequality and the systemic degradation of Black Americans in particular. We are moving forward into an ominous future, and each move forward reveals deeper reasons for shame, uncovering that which has always been visible to *some* but easily ducked by many others. Whether or not this transition is ominous depends, in part, on the activation of a *positive* form of shame. The future need not be dreadful, but denying or avoiding the necessity of shame – carefully understood – will lead only to scapegoating, violence or a restoration of white supremacy under the guise of colourblind "normalcy."

Plato, Aristotle and *nun*

The pipes deep beneath the ground in Flint quietly disseminated poison into the bodies of its residents. As we dig into the history of Western thought, we find a similar leeching. Ideas, deep beneath the language and culture of the West, continue to poison the future before us.

In this section, I excavate the Greek philosophical idea of *time* as it relates to shame. One of the easiest ways to distinguish between guilt and shame is the way they relate to the passage of time. Guilt tends to refer to a passing emotion, or an infraction with a possible resolution, even if the road to restoration is difficult. Shame, on the other hand, points toward a more permanent state. Time and restitution can ameliorate the impact of guilt; shame defies the passage of time. The line between guilt and shame can be blurry, so these generalizations may have limited use. Still, the difference between guilt and shame matters philosophically. Guilt, for the most part, refers to redeemable infractions, sins and mistakes. In his essay on guilt and shame in Plato's work, philosopher Dan Lyons (2011, pp. 353–374) writes:

> In any culture, shame is more fearful than guilt, at least for energetic natural leaders. For instance, if you had to choose, would you rather be resented and hated, or despised and ridiculed? Guilt connotes punishment within the group; shame connotes abandonment, exclusion. Guilt can find excuses; shame is increased by any reference to weakness. Guilt can be forgiven; shame can be expunged only by some difficult change or triumph.

Shame aims, however, not at what a person has done but at who a person *is*; this means that in its purest form, shame is *timeless*. This already hints at both the value and the devastation of shame; this is a concept that requires delicate treatment if we are to retain the shame that heals and reject the shame that oppresses. This journey begins with an investigation of time.

Plato had some difficulty disentangling guilt from shame; the line between these two categories is often hard to draw. For simplicity's sake, consider an amusing example of guilt offered by Lyons, a letter to the Internal Revenue Service from a taxpayer: "Dear Sir: I cheated on my taxes last year; now I can't sleep. Here's a cheque for half the amount I stole. If I still can't sleep, I'll send the rest" (p. 354). Guilty persons find themselves with a road to at least some restoration, however difficult.[2] Guilt points to a restoration of balance. Shame, on the other hand, gets between a person and their image in the mirror; it is not alleviated by payment or punishment but cause for ostracization and utter exclusion. Shame is inflexible, permanent, unbending. People hiding "shameful" aspects of themselves are chiefly afraid of the abandonment associated with what is unforgivable.

If the ideas of guilt and shame are built on different approaches to time, then thinking carefully about time will be required to make progress. If "time" does not seem like a philosophically interesting subject matter, or doesn't seem to relate to shame at first glance, that might be a testament to the success of Plato and Aristotle in their work on time. They have, with help from many others, succeeded in shaping the way Western culture thinkers contemplate the passage of time. Time is a concept that is used to synchronize, to pull together the diverse experiences of our lives. It is with "time" that we set appointments, celebrate holidays, remember the passage of loved ones and coordinate our lives. This mechanism of time is *synchronizing*, for it pulls diverse lives into the same chronology. In his critique of Western thinking about time, philosopher Emmanuel Levinas compares this force to the written word. Whereas a spoken word reverberates with unknowable depth and history, a written word is ossified, present, possess-able, and at least pretends to offer itself to the internal field of knowledge. The other modality of time Levinas calls *diachrony*, and it refers to the time of the other person, from a time outside of the self. A spoken word – the Saying, as Levinas puts it – is encountered *outside* of data, knowledge, integration and totalization (2016, pp. 134–135). It summons not to knowledge, but to response, to action, to responsibility. Synchrony is necessary and important, for it allows us to coordinate our language, schedules and labours. But it is also a betrayal of other elements of our lives together; diachrony refers to the otherness of time, the more primal and human function of speech, gesture and care. Before expanding on Levinas's use of diachrony, and using it to point to *good* shame, I first need to further excavate the significant problems and benefits of synchronic time as we inherit it from the depths of Greek philosophy.

The concept of time, and the consequent assumptions about its primary meaning as synchronizing, are so thoroughly ingrained in modern life that rethinking them requires significant excavation. In one of Plato's later dialogues, *The Timaeus*, the ageing philosopher provides some of his most striking insights into his own metaphysical system.[3] The discussion in *Timaeus*, amongst Socrates and several friends, is sweeping and cosmological in nature. The conversation is posed as a response to comments Socrates had made the "previous day,"[4] perhaps challenging them to explore the mysterious origins of the tremendous beauty and order in the universe. Much of the heavy lifting in the dialogue is provided by the title character, Timaeus, who attempts to provide what he deems a likely account for the formation of the universe (cosmos; *κόσμος*). Timaeus suggests that some rational, consistent, mathematical and intentional handiwork must lay behind the world we perceive, a divine hand (demiurge; *δημιουργός*) that has crafted the material world. This divine craftsperson, according to Timaeus, is intentional and purposeful in this organization of the world, intending especially that an organized world would emerge from the labour. The hand that shapes the world does so all at once, seeing the whole view, shaping it is an outsider, the *other* to the chaotic world it shapes. And this God shapes and moves the world from a timeless, motionless, singular perch.

The merits or demerits of Plato's metaphysical cosmology and its theological implications – of much interest to early Christian theologians – have been the subject of much debate. Aristotle distances himself from his teacher in many ways, perhaps most acutely on the basis of *time*. By Aristotle's reckoning, Plato has too easily dispensed with the important function of time to bind and unite all motion and movement. The core of Aristotle's critique of his teacher, Plato, can be framed theologically: Plato's God is outside of time, creating time and pushing the created order from the outside. Aristotle does not deny the teleological movement of change, but he thinks the concept of time is nonsense, "unthinkable," if considered outside of the "now." Plato, sounding consistent with contemporary Big Bang theory, suggests that time originates "simultaneous with the world."[5] Aristotle is reluctant to think about time as anything other than a way to interpret change, an "affection of motion."[6] Aristotle, therefore, frames the meaning of time in terms of its relationship to change rather than the reverse (Coope, 2005, p. 31). Change is happening always; past nows looked different from this current now, and future nows will look different as well. But *time* for Aristotle is an endeavour to quantify or count the episodes of change. This makes time dependent upon the mind capable of counting.[7] Time, for Aristotle, is not something made by God but a by-product of the human experience of change. For God, all things are present and timeless. As Aristotle frames the discipline, a philosopher seeks this same positioning, posture and divine perspective. In this philosophy of *time* there is a surreptitious philosophy of power, and no wonder that both of these patriarchs dreamt of a world controlled by philosopher kings. These, the wisest and most civilized of *men*, gather time and history into their all-seeing purview and administer justice according to their nearly divine wisdom.

In both of these titans of Western thinking, Plato and Aristotle, the key to think about time is found in the synchronizing power of the "now." They diverge here, however. Plato's "now" is the time-of-the-present, with past and future moments representing aspects of the present. The only time, for Plato, is "now." In such a view of temporality, time is merely a condition of the world that is in becoming. There is no such thing as a past time or future time. There is only a "present" – moving along, always flanked by past "nows" and future "nows." Plato has Timaeus call the present the "moving image of eternity" (Plato, ca. 360 B.C.E./2000, p. 24). The medieval philosopher Boethius famously called this the "Eternal Now."[8] It falls to philosophy to create a broad and inclusive metaphysics of presence which explain all things past and future according to the powerful vision of what things *now* are.

Aristotle offers more nuance. He claims that "in time we can take nothing but nows," but by that he means that it is in the present that we contemplate the complexities of time. In fact, for Aristotle, the "now" is not *part of time at all*. He writes (2014, p. 420):

> If any composite thing is to be, it is necessary that while it is, all or some of its parts must be; but though time is composite, part of it has happened and part of it is going to be, while none of it is. The now is no part of it. For the part measures the whole, and the whole must be composed of the parts, but time does not seem to be composed of nows.

This does not mean, for Aristotle, that there is no existence of the "now," but he does want to emphasize that the now is the vantage point from which we perceive time, not part of it. This innovation allows Aristotle to take more seriously than Plato the complex role of causation in the way the present is shaped by time, by the layers of causation from the past that create possibilities for the future.

Despite some bickering among Western philosophers, the power of *now*, in Greek *nun* – the root of the English word *noon* – goes unchallenged. Both Aristotle and Plato privilege the "now" in their understanding of time. They agree that time is to be understood via the present as a by-product of our analysis of *nun*; most of Western philosophy has repeated and extended this insight. Time *seems* neutral and indifferent, but an unseen power lurks in the way time is gathered and organized into a synchrony. From the perch of their ivory towers, the philosopher kings establish linguistic, cultural, religious and academic *normalcy*. All things fall into the chronology of the powerful: holidays, festivals, work schedules, tax days, clothing, pronunciations, food, habits and ethnic practices. That which deviates from these temporally synchronized norms is a cause for shame, as we will explore in the next section. Whoever rules the interpretation of *nun* rules the world.

This excavation of the roots of thinking about time exposes a fundamental problem with the organizational forces of human society. In other words, this is how *power and truth* work, by way of the force of synchrony. Furthermore, these ways of thinking about time directly relate to the ethical dispositions created by these thinkers. The powerful – whether or not they realize it – make the clock, the calendar, determining the flow of resources and power. In Flint, this meant that the people in power synchronized – far beneath the earth and outside of Flint's borders – the flow of *water*. Those who flipped the switch, and ignored the steady complaints of residents, act without being acted upon. The waters of Flint *move*; white supremacy holds still.

In fact, this follows the model laid out by Plato in his dialogue *The Timeaus*, in which a blueprint for the world is laid out by the *demiurge*, the divine craftsperson who shapes chaos into order in the universe. At the pinnacle of Timaeus's speech he argues that humans devote themselves to cultivating their souls toward the original purposes of the demiurge. The process of being born confuses and disorients us, and it is through the restoration of a rational understanding of the universe that we are guided to realignment. Timaeus turns his metaphysical deliberations into ethical ones when he declares (Plato, ca. 360 B.C.E./2000, p. 86):

> We should redirect the revolutions in our heads that were thrown off course at our birth, by coming to learn the harmonies and revolutions of the universe, and so bring into conformity with its objects our faculty of understanding, as it was in the original condition. And when this conformity is complete, we shall have achieved our goal: that most excellent life offered to humankind by the gods, both now and forevermore.

For Timaeus, the moral person is the one whose vision for everyday decisions is determined by a grand metaphysical vision for synchronous order. The decisions made by people in power are guided by an *assimilating* vision.[9] Ethics that is formed from the leanings of Plato will lean toward assimilation to a common vision of behaviours that conform to a universal and rational vision of how chaos can be organized into harmony. This vision is essentially timeless, unchanging and fixed. One might detect something decidedly Platonic in ethical systems like the ones proposed by Immanuel Kant and John Rawls, who seek to apply over-arching visions and universal principles to everyday moral decisions. Time and ethics, here, run in parallel; both are best understood as that which organizes and synchronizes apparently divergent interpretations of the world and how we should live in it. Shame is a powerful tool of synchrony, deployed through overt and cov-ert means; shame provides powerful and mostly effective boundaries to enforce moral synchronization. This manifestation of shame I call "synchronic shame." This manifestation of shame is often a *good* phenomenon, particularly when laws and customs arise to protect the vulnerable, to synchronize the abolition of slav-ery, cruelty, exploitation, oppression and more. But synchrony is a dangerous ally; it quickly and easily turns poisonous. Persons and systems of power determine the structure of the world to which all things are pressured to conform. With the flick of a pen, thousands of dollars are 'saved' on water. Nobody, to date, has been prosecuted for the mayhem that ensued (Ahmad, 2020). The synchronizer is the centre that holds still.

Once the grand vision for the universe has been established, whether from Plato's "outside being" to Aristotle's analysis of being itself, the force of *nun* moves powerfully. Perhaps Plato offers us a road out of the trap of synchrony, albeit one that European philosophy has often failed to exercise. All of Plato's writings descend to us as dialogues and deliver their messages dialectically. Socrates himself seldom stakes a position that is not open to questioning. Hans-Georg Gadamer, a twentieth-century philosopher of history and herme-neutics, found in Plato the blueprint for a tireless dialectic that never allows itself to arrive at a perspective that is independent of the particular context of the viewer. Gadamer pointed out that no matter what philosophy seeks to con-template, we can never attain objectivity. Even the goal of seeing things objec-tively misleads philosophy. Human rationality, Gadamer teaches, is always situated and bound by context and perspective. These are not the enemy of philosophy but its context. Gadamer learned this restless dialectic from Plato.[10] Surely Plato, and Aristotle, would be chagrined that their deliberations on time hardened into tools of power and assimilation and pointed to new configura-tions of time.

What has been delivered by Western, European philosophy is a *colonial* philos-ophy of truth; the whole world has been asked to conform to the time of Europe. Things *other* than this experience of the "now" are to be conformed to that vision; otherness is subject to the logic of sameness. In the midst of this philosophy of time is an infrastructure of power; the persons, or system, that organize the *nun* arrange not just resources but time to their advantage. This is the political force of a metaphysics of presence, and it works as effectively without as it does with intentionality. Synchronic shame is a tool of control; those who are far from the centre, from the norm, are abnormal, untimely and shameful. Synchronic shame is sometimes helpful and sometimes devastating. Systemic racism, sexism, ableism and more are carried forward by a metaphysics of the *nun*, of presence. This is perhaps the primary movement of colonialism, constantly forcing the "norm" of the centre to everyone and everything on the periphery. To better understand the operation of shame, and before returning to the role of shame in American white supremacy, it is important to explore the role it was already playing in the philosophers of ancient Greece.

Aidôs in Plato and Aristotle

The place for *aidôs* (Greek for *shame*), for both Plato and Aristotle, is found in education. Children, after all, are in need of a great deal of help in discovering the boundaries of their world. The tool of shame, used amongst children and by adults to guide children, provides a powerful and pervasive force. Shame is efficient, for shamefulness is a perfect embodiment of Foucault's definition of power/knowledge. The power of an idea, such as "do not steal," functions best to shape moral development if it remains efficacious even when a child's behaviour is not monitored. Children should be *prone* to shame, Aristotle (ca. 340 B.C.E./1999, p. 79) teaches, because they are learning the boundaries outlined before them. This makes shame a quasi-virtue, "more like a passion than a state of character." In Book Four of his most famous work, *Nicomachean Ethics* (ca. 340 B.C.E./1999, p. 79), Aristotle writes:

> The passion is not becoming to every age, but only to youth. For we think young people should be prone to shame because they live by passion and therefore commit many errors, but are restrained by shame; and we praise young people who are prone to this passion, but an older person no one would praise for being prone to the sense of disgrace, since we think he should not do anything that need cause this sense.

Shame, at least in the *Nicomachean Ethics*, appears to be something that children, and society, should outgrow. In another of his books on ethics (usually thought to be written earlier), the *Eudemian Ethics* (2017, p. 64), Aristotle sings the praises of a proper shame, which stands as the virtuous state between shyness and shamelessness:

> Shame is a mean between shamelessness and shamed shyness. For he who cares not for any opinion is shameless; he who cares for every opinion equally is shamed shy; and he who cares for the opinion of the manifestly decent has shame.

The problem here parallels one traced previously regarding time: it is the powerful people who decide what seems decent. There are people with no shame, and people with too much shame, and in the middle there are people who feel just enough shame to keep them in the range determined to be "normal" by those in power.

In *Nicomachean Ethics*, though, Aristotle works on an alternative for shame, a better way to reside in the centre. For him, the solution *phronesis*, practical reason, acts as a replacement to shame. I take the warning from Aristotle seriously: when our social, political and ethical environments are shaped unreflectively by *aidôs*, we are ripe for a culture that oppresses and exploits. Shame, we will see, is more complex than Aristotle allows for in this passage, but he pointed in directions that are remarkably consistent with recent developments in our understanding of shame in the human mind and society. Neuropsychologist Allan Schore identifies a correlation between shame and the vagal nervous system. Shame activates parasympathetic, physiological responses that are associated with life-saving responses to trauma (Schore, 2008):

> In this passive hypometabolic state heart rate, blood pressure, and respiration are decreased, whereas pain-numbing and blunting endogenous opiates are elevated. It is this energy-conserving parasympathetic (vagal) mechanism that mediates the profound detachment of dissociation.

Silvan Tomkins traces the impact of shame on the modulation of emotions. In painful examples from childhood development, Tomkins depicts the impact of shaming on a child because parents utilize shame to prevent a child from *expressing* excitement, desire, disgust, fear and even shame itself.[11] Neurologically, psychologically and socially, the force of shame inhabits the space between emotion and expression, between experience and response. Shame is a mitigating force, but in the hands of power, it plays a mighty and terrifying role. It is vital that we understand the difference between the shame that gives life and the shame that supports oppression and abuse. In fact, good shame, which I am calling diachronic shame, points to the form of *aidôs* that arises out of *phronesis*, and not in opposition to it. Shame fits the Greek concept of *pharmakon*, which means it is both disease and cure. It takes work to divide the former from the latter.

Plato has Socrates make an attack on shame as well. *The Charmides* narrates an encounter between Socrates and Charmides, a promising young man looking to make his name in the world. Charmides settles in to listen and learn. The reasons for his willingness to attend to the teachings of Socrates have to do with his desire to please his mentor, Critias. In some ways, this makes Charmides a perfect student. But Socrates is annoyed by the way that *aidôs* motivates Charmides. Socrates quotes Homer's *Odyssey* (Plato, ca. 380 B.C.E. /1986, p. 27), where Telemachus scolds his father Odysseus for appearing in disguise: *aidôs*, he says, "is not good for a needy man." Shame is making Charmides hesitant, keeping him from bravely challenging Socrates and leading them both toward better thinking. *Aidôs* is now an obstacle that prevents the young man from challenging Socrates.

Shame, apparently, can get us only so far in thinking about virtue. Perhaps this is why, in his encounter with Meno, Socrates invited but did not *shame* the brazen young Meno to stay in Athens to get a proper education.

Shame is often devastating, precisely because it holds a person permanently to their exclusion and perpetual objectification. We should pay attention to the unified opinion of both Plato and Aristotle when it comes to the question of shame (*aidôs*). There is a positive use to the synchrony enacted by shame, they agreed, but it is a provisional and temporary one. Cultures the world over have utilized shame as a social tool for consolidating efforts and delineating social behaviour. Shame, perhaps more than any other tool, has been used to fortify and enforce the boundaries of morality. It is through shame that unseen power structures find their ways into the very bodies of the population. This makes philosophical reflections on shame crucial for contemporary moral questions. Those who exceed the bounds of norms are by definition *abnormal*. Oppression naturally results as people are marginalized – or much worse – for the sheer fact of their ab-normality, simply because their bodies or customs or language fail to conform. Both of these founders of Western philosophy are aware that synchronization of culture and society are life-saving, life-giving forces. Many modes of human survival and life require synchronization. They knew that shame would always play a role in the social and political arenas in which lives are pulled into conformity. In this space, shame is applied skin-deep (sometimes called "skin shame"). Yet it is the same mechanism that operates deep in the human psyche beneath social conventions and in the space of self-understanding. As such, "deep shame" relates to internalized values that are often too entangled with cognition to be recognized. Still, neither Plato nor Aristotle seem keen to think of shame (*aidôs*) as the best way to perform this synchronization, at least for adults.

The provisional usefulness of shame, for the patriarchs of Western philosophy, relates to the ability of shame to funnel divergent behaviour into a common and synchronized morality. Kids, not yet capable of proper *phronesis*, need the rough treatment of shame to fill in the obvious gaps they have in thinking. Shame should lift as reason settles into the growing mind. But what shame gives way to is another mode of synchrony and convergence: reason. Shame becomes useless, and perhaps a hindrance, when it prevents a genuine wrestling with ideas. For Socrates, dialectical conversation was crucial for arriving at yet-unseen answers to hard questions. Shame becomes counterproductive if it makes a person reluctant to challenge an interlocutor. But as much as Socrates prized disagreement, he did so for the sake of pursuing a more synchronous understanding of the truth. He was looking for the higher truth, ideas that any rational person could agree upon. *Aidôs* gives way to *phronesis*, but both aim for synchrony. In this sense, shame is for adults an unfortunate and immature tool for producing synchronized understanding and behaviour. Whatever the tool, shame or reason, Aristotle and his teacher seek the *nun*, the "eternal now" of perfect and comprehensive understanding. For Aristotle, as for Plato, shame declines as wisdom increases. Those who believe themselves to be ascendant, wise and powerful, in this tradition, are those for whom shame no longer plays a role. The ancient philosophers believed that shame would be replaced by a more exalted manifestation of wisdom and truth, a surer foundation for virtuous behaviour. What has come down to us throughout history is that with power comes *shamelessness*, either at the extremes we see in the tweeting of Donald Trump, or in the less visible shamelessness of controlling what is "normal." There is no use in the experience of shame for Trump for he imagines himself at the very centre of normalcy, as the definition of what is normal. When he calls the Flint water "a shame," he does so with no shame; he is disconnected and ascendant from the problem, not even remotely responsible for the suffering he claims to pity.

Shame and blame

The problems "beneath" Flint are found in the present. Every present moment is the accumulation of past moments, but the one who declares "shame" exerts a powerful grip on time. Shame, for better and for worse, frames and focuses time into the interpretive scope of those who are in power. In a previous volume, *Temporality and Shame* (2018), I explored the way shame operates in Nathaniel Hawthorne's *Scarlet Letter*. The townspeople of colonial Boston attempt to use shame to confine Hester Prynne to their judgement, not just for a lifetime but for eternity. Prynne escapes not by fleeing Boston but by converting their shame into defiance, independence and strength. The townspeople looked on Prynne's pregnancy the way Trump pointed at the rusty water of Flint. They bore no responsibility, and in the act of saying "shame," they separated themselves from the suffering they had created. Suffering framed by this type of shame, which I am calling *synchronic* shame, relieves any pressure on broken systems and exonerates everyone but the most obvious scapegoats. Synchronic shame has no connection to responsibility; it exonerates the shamer. It relieves the shamer of the need to move, to care, to be bound to the suffering it names. Those who say "what a shame" establish a platform from which to judge history, a neutrality high above complicity or responsibility. This place of neutrality is a *shameless* space, a white-washed and colourblind stronghold from which powerful people can look on suffering with indifference. This is, in fact, the clearest hallmark of privilege: those in power find gazing at suffering to be optional.

It is important to note the standard approach taken by people in power: blame the victim. When the state of Louisiana, mostly for financial reasons, ignored their ageing levies, they put their own city at great risk. In 2005, when Hurricane Katrina broke the levies and flooded massive portions of New Orleans, evacuations of the city left behind a disproportionate number of Black persons. In Orleans Parish, "the mortality rate among blacks was 1.7 to 4 times higher than that among whites" (Brunkard et al., 2008). Hundreds of residents, attempting to flee the city, found one of the primary escape routes out of town, the bridge to Gretna, blocked and barricaded and were forced to turn back to face the poisonous floodwaters in the city. The reasons? The white officials of majority-white Gretna, Louisiana, were afraid for their shops, stores and homes and wanted to be protected from the majority Black citizens fleeing the city. The blockade of the bridge to Gretna was followed by a barrage of blame placed on the victims of Katrina: why didn't they evacuate? This question places blame on the people who were subjected to a broad failure to challenge white supremacy. De'Ann Penner and Keith Ferdinand provide a collection of first-person stories told by Black survivors of Katrina in their book *Overcoming Katrina* (2016). In several stories, the soldiers deployed to rescue survivors treated them as dangerous enemy combatants. The fact that poor, elderly and racialized persons failed to file out of the city into safer suburbia was blamed not on the evacuation process but on the people left behind.

For Bush, the situation along the Gulf Coast was framed as an unpredictable disaster. The racialized response, the trapping of mostly Black persons in the drowning city, and inequality in the death toll were unpleasant surprises that *eventually* met with distant concern. This concern, though, did not place the structure of white supremacy at risk. The "present" is a hurricane problem, the failure of politics, blameworthy levy engineer, and most of all Black and elderly and poor people who "chose" not to leave the flooding city. This posture is established as the "now" from which this event is to be viewed, stripped of the oppression and disregard that made the disaster possible. And the powerful force that keeps this system in place? Shame.

Shame is, in fact, the forceful power that emanates from the one who controls time, the power or the present. Most of the people and institutions, stretching back decades and centuries, can easily find reasons that they are not "at fault" for the suffering they see. They can shake their head and say "what a shame," synchronizing a national or global response to the disaster. But synchronic shame trickles down and finds its way onto the bridge between New Orleans and Gretna. Synchronic shame is by nature *systemic*; it becomes endemic in a society and manifests itself in countless events. Synchronic shame flourishes where food is handed out to survivors, where charitable donations are collected, where children look down at their Black- or Brown-skinned fingers and realize their skin is the reason they find themselves empty handed. One survivor, Phillis Montana-LeBlanc, spoke of her experiences in line for food at the Louis Armstrong Airport, which was used for shelter in the days after the flooding. The unfeeling faces that handed out aid took the time to take special requests from white survivors but told Black recipients to take whatever they were given (Penner & Ferdinand, 2016, pp. 141–142). She was devastated by the inhumanity of the "rescuers," who seemed cruel and indifferent to Black residents.

> My emotions are starting to crumble. My mind is falling apart and I don't care anymore. This is wrong and it is driving me crazy. I can't hold it together anymore. "This is inhuman! We are human beings! Look at us, look at us!" They never budge. They never even look at me and I know they can hear me because I am standing right under them at the bottom of the escalators.
>
> (Harris-Perry, 2014, p. 140)

Montana-Leblanc felt ashamed that she was left in need of evacuation, ashamed of her body, her skin, her heritage, her situation, her hunger. These feelings of shame were created, exacerbated and reinforced by the way she was treated, the indifference of the people who came to offer help. These manifestations of shame appear from the ground up; they are the result of an endemic racism that places shame on Persons of Colour for merely being present in society. This shame is synchronic because it relates neither to Montana-Leblanc's behaviour nor to anything she could change about herself. She was misrecognized and ignored by people in authority in stark contrast to the treatment of white citizens in her same situation. And the result of these aggressions, small and large, is *shame*. As she put it, "I just take what is given to me and walk away, feeling somewhat shameful and honestly like a n*****, an animal" (Harris-Perry, 2014, p. 142). Many of the people giving out donations were volunteers, but their glances, faces and decisions reinforce the synchronic shame that emanated from the White House. In the high-noon of white supremacy, blame for the suffering of non-white Americans is foisted *with a smile* on those who suffer.

Here, it is worth noting the juxtaposition of two forms of shame. Herding human beings like "animals," and operating with indifference to their suffering, should be cause of shame, but Montana-LeBlanc and hundreds of others report facing a shameless racism in the "rescue" efforts. We will need a different way to talk about the good shame that should appear in moments like these. The shame that was missing in New Orleans is the kind that awakens us to the humanity of others. I am calling this type of shame *diachronic*. Levinas (2016, p. 168) suggests that the encounter with the other person offers a saving rupture of the insular, synchronizing, totalizing world of the self. There is no time in the synchronized present, only a world always "now" to *me*, and this is not freedom but bondage to the self. The face of suffering opens the totality of the ego. Time moves differently after synchrony, as diachronous. Instead of offering fragments of knowledge whereby I might better understand the now, the other person offers me responsibility, the urgent obligation to find my humanity in its porous relation to the suffering other.

Diachronic shame

Diachronic shame refers to the actions and choices that can never be undone, never overcome, never represented or "spun" to justify the suffering of others. The person who abuses a child, who commits murder, who participated in a lynching, is permanently altered by such an act. There is no future in which that deed can be wiped away, no conditions under which a person can become someone unsullied by these deeds. Trump uses the word "shame" in Michigan to mean something close to the opposite of diachronic shame; it is shame avoidance that he offers, the skin-'deep dismissal of a problem that he believes has no hold on him. What is at stake in the crisis of Flint's water is the truth: death, disease and a snail's-pace governmental response to the suffering in Flint are caused by white supremacy and capitalism. Blaming others, or pretending that this situation emerges randomly, are ways of avoiding diachronic shame.

Shame is a complex condition, a window into the space in which people understand themselves. In psychoanalysis, when a client identifies the experience of shame, it is frequently taken as a sign of progress, as a movement deeper into the space of self-understanding. In his two-volume work *Symbolic Misery* (2015), Bernard Stiegler suggests that we have a generalized, diffuse and unconscious shame that is borne by our society. This shame, which heavily influences politics and shapes our discourse, is powerful but without a definitive origin. The world is a mess, and although there are obvious culprits – advances in technology, capitalistic inequality, white supremacy and so on – even these are populated by moving targets. The efforts to avoid the impact of this shame, Stiegler indicates, drive it further underground. For Trump, blaming Mexicans for poisonous Michigan water is another way of avoiding the appalling and shameful inequalities and oppression of contemporary capitalism. White supremacy is a perpetual motion machine; shame does the work to keep the machine going.

What is missed when shame turns into *blame* is the opportunity for shame to be our teacher or to guide us beyond synchrony and into the unique, diachronic time of the other person. This, in fact, is psychoanalyst Ladson Hinton's suggestion in his article "Shame as a Teacher" (1999). He points out that shame, endured consciously, performs "a kind of *kenosis*-emptying," which leads to deeper openness and embodied living. "Shame can be trusted to keep us modest and low until . . . we can glean answers with integrity" (Hinton, 1999, p. 184). The suppression of shame, perhaps most obviously manifested in blaming and scapegoating victims, obliterates the register at which shame teaches. Jewish scholar Primo Levi, reflecting about experience in concentration camps, explores the importance of shame for survival. Captives had every reason to focus blame on the Nazi guards and to attempt to survive on the nourishment of hate. Ironically, though, Levi reports that his survival depended on resisting the powerful allure of hatred precisely because blame obliterates shame. Imre Kertész, another survivor of the Holocaust, spoke lucidly of the important role of shame. He wrote: "The secret of survival is collaboration, but by admitting this you come to face such a burden of shame which you prefer to reject rather than assume" (Kertész & Wilkinson, 2013). To collaborate, prisoners had to take responsibility for one another, be exposed to one another, but this meant relinquishing the modality of blame. The very humanity of the survivor depended on a porous posture of relatedness to others. The Nazis were abundantly worthy of blame for their suffering, but in the act of blaming others, the prisoners reported a removal of crucial and necessary components of their own humanity. To blame is to harden the exterior of the self against the alterity of the other. Blaming may be justified, but it abdicates power, autonomy and choice. In other words, psychologically and interpersonally, blaming is bad for the blamer and bad for the blamed.

In New Orleans, the suffering of Phillis Montana-LeBlanc, as she waits in line for her food ration in shame, does not need to be synchronized or understood in light of the big picture. She is a human being suffering racism, fear, hunger and humiliation; her face, her suffering, summon the people who see it toward their own humanity. Diachrony, as I understand it, pulls human beings out of the universal time and into particularized responsibility for the suffering other. The face of Montana-LeBlanc offered this opening to everyone she encountered. Her words, her eyes, her story is not the synchronic "shame" of an unfortunate hurricane but a long history of woundedness, racism and oppression. Her suffering *is* acute, but it is compounded by intersectional layers of racism, humiliation and oppression. Her situation is a *shame* but not of the sort that can be tisked at from a distance. This is diachronic shame, for it pulls us out of the neutral, philosophical, synchronic distance and into the urgency of Montana-LeBlanc's need. Synchronic shame blames Montana-LeBlanc for her suffering; diachronic shame is an invitation into participation in suffering. Synchronic shame serves to ignore and support racist policies and practices. Diachronic shame can only be antiracist, for it invites the one who encounters suffering into the active and urgent work of justice.

Flint presented a unique challenge for this usually effective strategy of blaming victims which utilizes time and shame to safeguard and consolidate power. How can the people of Flint be blamed for this moment when they had nothing to do with the choice to switch their water sources? How can time, history and the future be organized – and shame deployed – to protect the systems of power that produced this disaster? The answer is predictable, almost comical: *Mexicans*. Somehow, Trump would have us believe the people of Mexico are to blame for the thousands of children whose bodies today carry the poisonous lead sluffed from ageing pipes. Unable to blame Black persons for their own economic marginalization, Trump found another non-white ethnic group to demonize. But somehow, and all too predictably for people familiar with these dynamics of power, the shame that couldn't be placed on Flint was shifted to other Persons of Colour: Mexican auto workers.

Deep shame resides in between a person and their own skin, between a person and the mirror. It is as a second and devastating reality of trauma that it wounds at least twice. People are wounded by trauma once in the event of traumatization and again by the reshaping of self-understanding that is enacted by traumatic events. Diachronic shame is the presence of another person, the need of the other, in the very constitution of the self. This can be terrifying, particularly when it is used to manipulate and control. But diachronic shame can also be life-giving, open up the full humanity of those would embrace Kertész's "collaborative" survival, the need of the other embraced as my own, the suffering of the other my raw and fundamental responsibility.

Some concluding suggestions

My purpose in suggesting that we can trace this leaning to the early philosophical imaginations of Plato and Aristotle is not to blame them for these maladies;

neither am I interested in exonerating them. They should be read, in some ways, as visionaries and liberators writing in a time when their work helped overcome incredible, cruel and oppressive practices. At the same time, the philosophers of early Greece had a profound impact on the way we think today about time, about shame, about power and about politics. I reach back to these seminal philosophers to demonstrate the deep and pervasive architecture of oppression that troubles the world today. In 2020, the murder of George Floyd, on the heels of the killings of Ahmaud Arbery and Breonna Taylor, sparked global protests and energized the Black Lives Matter movement. The blood of these Black Americans, redder even than the waters of Flint, registered as a catastrophic problem to white Americans. Trump called the death of George Floyd a "disgrace," and the behaviour of people protesting this death a "shame." These are postures of synchrony, which is to say they deliver shame with indifference. The Flint Water Crisis, the racialized response to Hurricane Katrina, the deaths of Black persons at the hands of the police – these are perpetuated by the passive, motionless indifference of synchronic shame. Philosophy is complicit. I am complicit. There *are* other options, other ways to embrace shame. Diachronic shame undermines the powerful pedestal of indifference and opens us to a responsibility for others that is fundamental to our humanity.

Beneath psychology and philosophy, a common set of water lines carry ideas to the surface. The pipes are old, some of them crumbling and distributing ancient poison to the world today. As the groundswell of antiracist protests grew in the spring of 2020, comedian John Oliver challenged viewers to grab a shovel and start digging. The systems of white supremacy, he said, run deep and are "firmly entrenched."[12] My hope has been to overturn a few of the pipelines of ideas that continue to influence our discourse about race, bodies and shame. My investigations into time, as synchrony and diachrony, are efforts to uncover a major pipeline that quietly influences the way we think, the way we teach and the way we approach problems of suffering in the world. My nemesis in this endeavour is the backside of synchronic shame, which overplays the benefits of synchrony and weaponizes it to consolidate power. Plato and Aristotle believe shame is mostly useful for children, making them fear a lasting ridicule that would result from rebellion. They work toward a more mature motivation for human moral behaviour, one that is based on reason and not shame. Shame is left behind, therefore, as an instrument of self-reflection. This means that reasonable people disentangle, personally and emotionally, from the world upon which they live. This transition to *phronesis*, to practical wisdom, turns the child into an adult. The adult, in turn, administers shame to the youth or to those not wise or good enough to stand with the wise men atop the ivory tower of timeless wisdom. Unfortunately, this ancient philosophy of shame assumes that adults are channelling timeless wisdom into children; in practice, this is not about education but about *power*. The result is shameless leaders, who justify the pain and suffering inherent in the way they administer the worlds they control. Neither Plato nor Aristotle would have approved of this scenario, I think, and each would have suggested political structures that at least attempted to avoid such cruelty. Nonetheless, the pattern holds true: shameless leaders, the world over, use shame to support their power.

There are other options for the exercise of *phronesis*, however. Shame either interferes with a person's lived experience of the world, as it does with racism and sexism, or opens it more authentically and faithfully to that experience. Philosophy has contributed to these problems, but it also offers resources for rethinking what it means to be human. The solution I have offered here is a return to shame, to a diachronic shame that arises as an invitation to responsibility and action rather than control and justification. Beneath this claim is an anthropology of care, of connectivity, of responsibility, so that attunement to diachronic shame is principally a manner of preserving one's humanity. The shamelessness that arises from the neutral, colourblind, ascendant wisdom of the powerful is dehumanizing. When Montana-Leblanc cried out, "This is inhuman! We are human beings! Look at us!" (Harris-Perry, 2014, p. 140), she was offering soldiers and police officers an avenue to their own humanity, an opportunity to be freed from their dispassionate, uncaring, all-seeing view of the Katrina disaster. They declined not just the suffering of one person but access to their own full humanity. Responsibility, expressed as a response to diachronic shame, is liberation.

These claims open up avenues for psychologists. First, there is an avenue here for rethinking the power of "normalcy" as it relates to race, gender, culture, sexuality, dis/ability and more. Aristotle's *nun* is a machine without a conscience, subtly rendering shameful anything that does not conform to the normative. According to the logic of synchrony, there is a "proper" way to dress, to speak languages, to perform gender, to exist sexually and a "normal" body with full functionality. At best, such a philosophy embraces *tolerance* for those whose skin or bodies or habits deviate from the norm. But tolerance is fertile soil for oppression; racism, for instance, thrives where people merely tolerate one another. So, psychologists would be wise to help those experiencing shame to understand and deconstruct the great power of synchronic shame. Wherever the word "normal" is deployed, the great power of synchrony is at work, whatever the intentions of those who wield it. The Confederate States "vice president" Alexander Stephens claimed that the cornerstone of the Confederacy was the "normal" superiority of the white race. In what became known as the "Corner-stone Speech," he rested his rebel nation's ideology on "the great truth that the negro is not equal to the white man; that slavery subordination to the superior race is his natural and normal condition" (Kendi, 2017, p. 215). The incredible, devastating power of synchronic shame is found in its capacity to normalize inequality, to render some persons superior to others by nature. This work is done psychologically, and it is the responsibility of psychologists and philosophers to identify and disentangle from its devastating power. The battle against sexism, racism, classism, caste systems and other manifestations of bigotry runs directly against the synchronization of "normal." This battle is waged culturally, personally, philosophically, ethically and perhaps most importantly, *psychologically*.

The only thing more dangerous than shame is shamelessness, and this means that people who struggle with shame may need help understanding the complicated and precarious role shame plays in our lives. Synchronic shame makes a person feel contemptible, ridiculed and worthless, but to abandon shame is to develop a callousness that walls off the life-giving faces of other people. The road forward for people caught in shame is not to shamelessness but to *care* and to responsiveness. Diachronic shame is vulnerability and openness. This, too, is delicate work because wounded and shamed persons need safe, caring and supportive faces. The battle against synchronic shame is waged in the minutiae, in the way people look at others, in the gifts of time, care and resources that *humanize*. Endemic, racialized, synchronic shaming often appears in the so-called minutiae of life, in the details. It is a mistake to call these "micro-aggressions" when they together form a massive net of oppression and can lead at any moment to death.

Finally, this chapter was written in the midst of a tumultuous 2020. It is meant as an indictment of the Western philosophical tradition, a tradition upon which my training and career have been based. My work here is part of a broader commitment to excavate ideas that have led us to a world that remains devastated by division and inequality. By taking up the ideas of time and shame, and showing their relationship to power, we can get a glimpse at how we might think about our relations outside of the infrastructure that has created and reinforced white supremacy. This project – the interrogation of Western thinking in the interests of fighting the cancer of racism – is not a new one, and my contributions are modest and rooted in the work of philosophers like James Baldwin, Angela Davis and Charles Mills; theologians like James Cone and Delores Williams; and writers like Ibram X. Kendi, Toni Morrison and Ta-Nehisi Coates. However, I invite psychologists to grab a shovel and help with the digging. The history of psychology, like the history of philosophy, has been tangled up with the ideas of neutrality, normalcy and supposed objectivity. As in philosophy, the deconstruction of these tendencies is well underway among psychologists who are dedicated to thinking about psychology, communities and relationships after *nun*.

Notes

1 I extend thanks to my friend Ladson Hinton, whose conversations and insights have influenced almost every sentence in this chapter.
2 The following is a helpful phenomenological account of the experience of shame: "Guilt concerns a subject's action or omission of action and has a clear temporal unfolding entailing a moment in which the subject lives in a care-free way. Afterwards, this moment undergoes a reconstruction, in the moment of guilt, which constitutes the moment of negligence. The reconstruction is a comprehensive transformation of one's attitude with respect to one's ego; one's action; the object of guilt and the temporal-existential experience" (Karlsson & Sjöberg, 2009).
3 In his introduction to Plato's *Timaeus*, translator and commentator Donald Zeyl investigates the dating and sequence of Plato's dialogues, particularly the relationship between Plato's *Republic* as it relates to *Timaeus*. Zeyl concludes that however proximate or distant these two dialogues are dramatically and chronologically, the *Timaeus*

is meant to invoke the political and metaphysical theories of the earlier *Republic*. He writes: "We should probably conclude that Plato wants to remind his readers of the political theory of the *Republic*, or at least some aspects of it, without intending them to draw any conclusions about the chronology, or even dramatic, proximity of these works." Plato. (2000). "Introduction." In *Timaeus*. Trans. D. J. Zeyl. Indianapolis, IN: Hackett Publishing.

4 Ibid. The "previous day" comment may be a stylistic manner of pointing to the dialogue presented in Plato's *Republic*, whenever the discussions were deployed chronologically and dramatically.

5 Plato (2000).

6 Ibid, 420. See also: Telesio, B. (1976, pp. 187–188).

7 According to Coope: "[Aristotle] argues that the existence of this single order depends on the existence of beings, like us, who can count. It depends on the fact that we count *nows* in a certain way. To Count a now is to mark a dividing-point in all the changes that are going on at it. Our counting thus introduces a kind of uniformity into the world" (Ibid, p. 5).

8 Leftow (1990, pp. 123–142).

9 Zeyl writes: "It is not unreasonable to suppose that Plato thinks that some sort of assimilation is effected by this contact, resulting in conformity of the smaller to the larger. And once the motions of one's rational soul have been reconformed to those of the universal soul, one's soul has resumed the happy condition it was in prior to its incarnation and is thus fit to return eventually to its home star." Plato (2000). "Introduction." In *Timaeus*. Trans. D. J. Zeyl. Indianapolis, IN: Hackett Publishing.

10 See Gadamer (2001).

11 Alexander et al. (1995).

12 Nordyke (2020).

References

Ahmad, Z. (2020). "Flint Water Crisis Turns Six with No New Charges." *Michigan Live*, April 25. www.mlive.com/news/flint/2020/04/flint-water-crisis-turns-six-with-no-new-charges.html.

Alexander, I. E., Sedgwick, E. K. & Frank, A. (1995). "Shame in the Cybernetic Fold: Reading Silvan Tompkins." In *Shame and Its Sisters: A Silvan Tomkins Reader*, pp. 1–28. Durham, NC: Duke University Press.

Aristotle. (1999). *The Nicomachean Ethics*. Trans. D. Ross. Oxford: Oxford University Press.

———. (2014). *Complete Works of Aristotle, Volume 1: The Revised Oxford Translation*. Trans. J. Barnes. Princeton: Princeton University Press.

———. (2017). *The Eudemian Ethics of Aristotle*. Trans. P. L. Simpson. London: Routledge.

Brunkard, J., Namulanda, G. & Ratard, R. (2008). "Hurricane Katrina Deaths, Louisiana, 2005." *Disaster Medicine and Public Health Preparedness*, 2, 4, 215–223. https://doi.org/10.1097/dmp.0b013e31818aaf55

Coope, U. (2005). *Time for Aristotle*. Oxford: Oxford University Press.

Cosier, S. (2016). "Drinking in the Heavy Metal." *Natural Resources Defense Council*, February 7. www.nrdc.org/onearth/drinking-heavy-metal.

Data USA. (2019). "Flint, MI." April 23. https://datausa.io/profile/geo/flint-mi/.

Fleming, L. (2020). "Flint Prosecutors: Six-Year Anniversary Won't Stop Pursuit of Justice." *The Detroit News*, April 17.

Gadamer, H. (2001). *Beginning of Philosophy*. Trans. R. Coltman. London & New York: Continuum Books.

Harris-Perry, M. V. (2014). *Sister Citizen: Shame, Stereotypes, and Black Women in America*. New Haven, CT: Yale University Press.

Hinton, L. (1999). "Shame as a Teacher: 'Lowly Wisdom' at the Millenium." In *Florence 98: Destruction and Creation: Personal and Cultural Transformations*. Ed. M. A. Mattoon. Germany: Daimon Verlag.

Johnson, J. (2016). "Officials Confirm Legionella Bacteria Found in Flint's McLaren Hospital's Water Supply in 2014." *Michigan Live*, January 22. www.mlive.com/news/flint/2016/01/officials_confirm_legionella_f.html.

Karlsson, G. & Sjöberg, L. G. (2009). "The Experiences of Guilt and Shame: A Phenomenological – Psychological Study." *Human Studies*, 32, 3, 335–355. https://doi.org/10.1007/s10746-009-9123-3.

Kendi, I. X. (2017). *Stamped from the Beginning: The Definitive History of Racist Ideas in America*. New York, NY: Bold Type Books.

Kertész, I. & Wilkinson, T. (2013). *Dossier K.: A Memoir*. Scotland: Melville House.

Leftow, B. (1990). "Boethius on Eternity." *History of Philosophy Quarterly*, 7, 2, 123–142.

Levinas, E. (2016). *Otherwise Than Being or Beyond Essence*. Trans. A. Lingis. Pittsburg, PA: Duquesne University Press.

Lyons, D. (2011). "Plato's Attempt to Moralize Shame." *Philosophy*, 86, 3, 353–374. https://doi.org/10.1017/s0031819111000210

Meckler, L. & Nelson, C. M. (2016). "Trump, Rubio Try to Stay Clear of Flint Water Crisis." *Wall Street Journal*, January 19.

Merica, D. & Henderson, N. (2016). "Hillary Clinton Pledges to Stand with Flint Through Water Crisis." *CNN*, February 8. www.cnn.com/2016/02/07/politics/hillary-clinton-flint-michigan-water-2016-election/index.html.

Nordyke, K. (2020). "John Oliver Calls for Drastic Police Reform on 'Last Week Tonight'." *The Hollywood Reporter*, June 7.

Penner, D. R. & Ferdinand, K. C. (2016). *Overcoming Katrina: African American Voices from the Crescent City and Beyond*. London & New York: Palgrave Macmillan.

Plato. (1986). *Charmides*. Trans. T. G. West & G. S. West. Indianapolis, IN: Hackett Publishing.

———. (2000). *Timaeus*. Trans. D. J. Zeyl. Indianapolis, IN: Hackett Publishing.

Schore, A. N. (2008). "Right Brain Affect Regulation: An Essential Mechanism of Development, Trauma, Dissociation and Psychotherapy." PsycEXTRA Dataset, 112–144. https://doi.org/10.1037/e608922012-004

Severson, E. (2018). "A Time for Shame: Levinas, Diachrony and the Hope of Shame." In *Temporality and Shame: Perspectives From Psychoanalysis and Philosophy*. Eds. L. Hinton & H. Willemsen. London: Routledge.

Stiegler, B. (2015). *Symbolic Misery Volume 2: The Catastrophe of the Sensible*. Hoboken, NJ: Wiley.

Winowiecki, E. (2019). "Does Flint Have Clean Water? Yes, but It's Complicated." *Michigan Radio*, August 21. www.michiganradio.org/post/does-flint-have-clean-water-yes-it-s-complicated.

Index